Legal Aspects of Privately Financed Infrastructure Projects (PFIPs) in China

Shuang Liang

Legal Aspects of Privately Financed Infrastructure Projects (PFIPs) in China

The Case for International Standards

Springer

Shuang Liang
Southwest University of Political
Science and Law
Chongqing, China

ISBN 978-981-15-6802-2 ISBN 978-981-15-6803-9 (eBook)
https://doi.org/10.1007/978-981-15-6803-9

This Springer imprint is published by the registered company Springer Nature Singapore Pte Ltd.
The registered company address is: 152 Beach Road, #21-01/04 Gateway East, Singapore 189721, Singapore

Contents

Abbreviations

4P	The Public Private Partnership Programmer Ltd
AICT	African International Court and Tribunals
BITs	Bilateral investment treaties
BOLT	Build-Own-Lease-Transfer
BOO	Build-own-operate
BOOT	Build-Own-Operate-Transfer
BOT	Build-Operate-Transfer
BROT	Build-Rent-Operate-Transfer
BRT	Build-Rent-Transfer
BSAM	Beijing State-Owned Assets Management Co. Ltd
BT	Build and Transfer
BTO	Build-Transfer-Operate
CCJA	The Common Court of Justice and Arbitration
CCWater	Consumer Council for Water
CFA	The Commercial Finance Association
CISG	United Nations on Convention on Contracts for the international Sale of Goods
CITIC	China International Trust and Investment
DA	District Audit
DBFO	Design-build-finance-operate
EBRD	European Bank for Reconstruction and Development
ESCAP	Economic and Social Commission for Asia and the Pacific
FDI	Foreign Direct Investment
GATT	General Agreement on Tariffs and Trade
GDP	Gross Domestic Product
GP	Gateway Process
HM Treasury	Her Majesty's Treasury
ICSID	The International Centre for Settlement of Investment Disputes
INSOL	International Association of Restructuring, Insolvency & Bankruptcy Professionals

MAI	Multilateral Agreement on Investment
MO	Maintain and Operation
MOFCOM	Ministry of Commerce
MOHURD	The Ministry of Housing and Urban-Rural Development of the People's Republic of China
NAO	National Audit Office
NDRC	National Development and Reform Commission
NGOs	Non-governmental organizations
NPC	Standing Committee of the National People's Congress
OBR	Office for Budget Responsibility
OECD	Organisation for Economic Co-operation and Development
OGC	Office of Government
OHADA	The Organization for the Harmonization of Business Law in Africa
PCLG	Public Contracts in Legal Globalization
PFI	Private Finance Initiative
PFIPs	Privately Financed Infrastructure Projects
PPIAF	Public–Private Infrastructure Advisory Facility
PPP	Public–Private-Partnership
PRG	Project Review Group
PUK	Partnership UK
ROT	Refurbish, Operate, Transfer
SARS	Severe Acute Respiratory Syndrome
SMEs	Small and Medium-sized enterprises
SOEs	State-owned Enterprises
SoPC	Standardisation of PF2 Contracts
SPV	Special Purpose Vehicle
TAP	Treasury Approval Point
TRIMs	Trade Related Investment Measures
UN	United Nations
UNCITRAL	United Nations Commission on International Trade Law
UNCTAD	United Nations Conference on Trade and Development
UNDSD	United Nations Division of Sustainable Development
UNECE	United Nations Economic Commission for Europe
UNIDO	United Nations Industrial Development Organization
VFM	Value for money
WTO	World Trade Organization

List of Figures

Chapter 1
Introduction

1.1 The Aim and Objectives of the Book

The aim of this book is to research how the Chinese laws on PFIPs might be improved so as to reach international standards and so that Privately Financed Infrastructure Projects (PFIPs) can be developed in China under the protection of relevant Chinese laws.

Current Chinese laws on PFIPs have many defects. Only if the laws on PFIPs are improved and reformed, can the model of PFIPs develop sustainably in China. This book aims to find the most appropriate way to improve and reform the Chinese laws on PFIPs, based on the research and analysis of three issues:

- The international guidance on PFIPs made by international organizations—this book follows the Legislative Guide and the Model Provisions made by UNCITRAL as a guideline.
- The successful legislative experience on PFIPs made by other countries will provide supplementary references.
- The specific background of legislation on PFIPs in China.

In this book, the Legislative Guide on Privately Financed Infrastructure Projects (2001) (hereafter refers to "Legislative Guide") and Model Legislative Provisions on Privately Financed Infrastructure Projects (2003) (hereafter refers to "Model Provisions"), made by the United Nations Commission on International Trade Law (hereafter refers to "UNCITRAL"), are used as the international standard in the improvement and reform of Chinese laws on PFIPs, and provide guidance for the development of a legal model for PFIPs. However, international guidance has its own shortcomings. Legislation made by certain countries such as Britain may offer better guidance. Even if the international guidance by UNCITRAL and the samples of legislation on PFIPs by other countries offer examples of the legal model of PFIPs, the most important element in the legislative reform in China is the specific Chinese context. Therefore, the reform of legislation on PFIPs in China should consider all

S. Liang, *Legal Aspects of Privately Financed Infrastructure Projects (PFIPs) in China*,
https://doi.org/10.1007/978-981-15-6803-9_1

three aspects to eliminate undesirable restrictions on Private Sector participation in infrastructure development and make laws more able to facilitate PFIPs.

In order to achieve the aim proposed above, the objectives of this book are to solve the following six research questions:

- Prove that the PFIP model can benefit China, but that the current Chinese laws on PFIPs hinder its development and may bring adverse effects to China.
- Prove the Legislative Guide and the Model Provisions made by UNCTRAL are the best international standard for Chinese legislative reform on PFIPs, while drawing on the progressiveness of laws on PFIPs in countries such as Britain as supplemental references.
- Analyse the guidelines of the Legislative Guide and the Model Provisions, the supplemental references from other countries and the specific Chinese context, to work out the defects in current Chinese laws on the general legislative and institutional frameworks of PFIPs and discuss how to improve and reform the laws.
- Analyse the guidelines of the Legislative Guide and the Model Provisions, the supplemental references from other countries and the specific Chinese context, to work out the defects in current Chinese laws on the concessioner selection procedure of PFIPs and discuss how to improve and reform the laws.
- Analyse the guidelines of the Legislative Guide and the Model Provisions, the supplemental references from other countries and the specific Chinese context, to work out the defects of relevant laws in China on the agreements involved in PFIPs and discuss how to improve and reform the laws.
- Analyse the guidelines of the Legislative Guide and the Model Provisions, the supplemental references from other countries and the specific Chinese context, to work out the defects in current Chinese laws on the dispute settlement of PFIPs and discuss how to improve and reform the laws.

1.2 The Background

1.2.1 The Background of PFIPs

Traditionally, offering and developing public infrastructure and services, such as public transportation and public health, is the responsibility of Public Sector. This responsibility is not only the fundamental function of the Public Sector, but is also confirmed by the laws in various countries and by certain international agreements. For example, in UK, the Infrastructure Planning Commission was established under the Planning Act 2008[1] which made provision about the authorisation of projects for the development of nationally significant infrastructure. The government has

[1]Planning Act 2008 (c. 29) Introductory Text.

increased this responsibility by issuing further official documents. The first infrastructure plan for the UK was the National Infrastructure Plan of 2010,[2] which was published by the Government in October 2010 and which outlines the scale of the challenge UK infrastructure faces and the investment needed to ensure sustainable growth. In China, the Constitution of The People's Republic of China clearly states that the Public Sector are responsible for the development of education and health services.[3] The United Nations core publication, Agenda 21, declares that all countries should promote and support the investment and infrastructure required for sustainable economic growth and diversification on an environmentally sound and sustainable basis.[4]

However, as the need for public infrastructure increases, Public Sector are also feeling increasing pressure on budgets, and are finding it difficult to afford these high costs, especially during the post-September 2008 recession. For example, in the UK, the high investment in public infrastructure combined with the national deficit has led to insufficient delivery of services by public infrastructure. At the end of December 2012, the UK government debt was £1,387.4 billion, equivalent to 90.0% of the GDP.[5] In China, there is serious conflict between a huge population and a lack of infrastructure. Some poor areas in China still lack essential infrastructure such as transportation links, energy supplies and clean water. In the international situation, the ESCAP (Economic and Social Commission for Asia and the Pacific) has estimated that approximately $600 billion per annum is required in infrastructure investment in Asia-Pacific region, but that there is a $200 billion funding gap per year.[6]

It is noteworthy that some critics doubt that China is rich enough to afford the cost of its infrastructure development because it is investing enormously in US treasury securities. These critics point out that, as China has the capacity to buy so many US treasury securities, Chinese financial resources should be adequate. As of 18th April 2017, China, as the largest creditor of US treasury securities, already held

[2]HM Treasury, *'National Infrastructure Plan 2010'* (25 October 2010), <https://webarchive.nationalarchives.gov.uk/20130129110721/http://www.hm-treasury.gov.uk/ppp_national_infrastructure_plan.htm> accessed on 13th July 2020.

[3]The Constitution of the People's Republic of China, adopted on March 14, 2004:

Article 19: The state develops socialist educational undertakings and works to raise the scientific and cultural level of the whole nation. The state runs schools of various types, makes primary education compulsory and universal, develops secondary, vocational and higher education and promotes pre-school education…

Article 21: The state develops medical and health services,…, encourages and supports the setting up of various medical and health facilities by….

[4]UNDSD *'Agenda 21'* (1992) 2.37 (d) A/CONF.151/26/REV.1 (VOL.I).

[5]Office for National Statistics, *'Government Deficit and Debt Under the Maastricht Treaty, Calendar Year 2012'*, <http://www.ons.gov.uk/ons/rel/psa/eu-government-debt-and-deficit-returns/march-2013/stb---march-2013.html> accessed on 28th June 2019.

[6]UN news, *'ESCAP is looking for the solution to the Asia-Pacific region lack the infrastructure'*, <http://www.un.org/chinese/News/fullstorynews.asp?newsID=7458> accessed on 12th July 2019.

$1.0597 Trillion in US treasury securities.[7] However, China's huge investment in US treasuries is due to many other reasons rather than its budget surplus.

Firstly, the foreign-exchange reserves,[8] rather than the government revenue, are the main means by which China buys US treasury securities. China has kept increasing foreign-exchange reserves for certain inevitable reasons.[9] However, foreign-exchange reserves cannot be used directly to develop domestic infrastructure.[10] At the same time, with the exception of the US treasury securities, the Chinese foreign-exchange reserves are not appropriate for investment in other international hard currency or gold or petrol.[11]

Secondly, the Chinese government buys US government bonds because China hopes to stabilize the exchange rate of Chinese Yuan to US dollar, in case of shrinkage of Chinese foreign exchange reserves. It is not to earn the interest on the investment. When China reduces its holding of US treasury securities, United States will have to print more currency notes to bailout its market, which would result in a risk of

---

[7]China Daily news, 'China raises its US treasuries holding in February', <http://www.chinadaily.com.cn/interface/zaker/1143603/2017-04-18/cd_28972922.html> accessed on 3rd, July 2019.

[8]Foreign-exchange reserves comprise the foreign currency held by a government or central bank. Not all currency could be foreign-exchange reserves; most reserves are made up of United States dollars, and to a lesser extent the euro, the United Kingdom pound sterling, and the Japanese yen.

[9]Firstly, China foreign trade has huge trade surplus in the past decades, i.e. Chinese export is much more than its import. Therefore, Chinese central bank has been increasing foreign currency reserves. Secondly, since 1994 China implements mandatory foreign exchange system. Under mandatory foreign exchange system, except the specific foreign exchange accounts allowed by state, either the enterprises or the individuals must sell the foreign exchange to the authorized business banks. And then the authorized business banks must sell the position which is higher than the limitation by State Administration of Foreign Exchange to central bank. In this mandatory system, the central bank is the largest disk access and forms the state's foreign change reserves. Though this mandatory restriction was relaxed after 2008 through amending the Foreign Exchange Law, the huge foreign exchange reserve has already formed. Song Guo-you, *"China's Purchase of American Treasury Securities: Source, Prof it and Impact"* (Fudan Journal (Social Sciences Edition), 2008, No. 4) P31–38.

[10]There are two reasons why Foreign-exchange reserves could not be directly used to develop domestic infrastructure: firstly, in the central bank's balance sheet, foreign currency reserve assets are consistence with the equal liabilities on RMB. If the foreign currency reserve assets are used to build infrastructure rather than return the liabilities, it would result the central bank insolvency to bankruptcy. Secondly, it may cause inflation or other serious consequences because of abusing RMB. When these foreign currencies are sold to foreign banks, equal amount of RMB is issued. If these foreign currencies are sold in the foreign exchange market to exchange RMB to build infrastructure, it will be eventually purchased by central bank by RMB and form a secondary issue and the RMB in the market will more than needed. Tian Jun-rong, *"whose foreign exchange reserves?"* (Newspaper People's Daily, 17th, October 2011) 017, <http://finance.people.com.cn/GB/15911496.html> accessed on 5th, July 2019.

[11]Compared with American dollar, the other international hard currency such as euro, the United Kingdom pound sterling, and the Japanese yen are more unstable because of economic crisis. The gold and petrol has no such huge supply in the market to satisfy with Chinese demand. Yuan Dong-mei,& Liu Jian-jiang, *"The reasons why China hold so much US treasury securities"* (Contemporary Economic Research, 2012, No 12) P28–32.

devaluation for the US dollar. The devaluation of the US dollar would shrink the value of the Chinese foreign exchange reserves.[12]

Thirdly, China aims to protect the Chinese export industry with its large holding of US treasury securities. Since US is the largest market importing Chinese products, any American recession would negatively impact the Chinese export industry. Meanwhile, if American dollar were to devalue, the Chinese export industry would suffer higher costs and lower profits.[13]

Finally, the reason why the Chinese government buys US government bonds includes an underlying political purpose: China offers the US economic funding in exchange for the US' support of its policy making or diplomacy.[14]

Therefore, there is no conflict between the seemingly generous investment in US treasury securities by China and its lack of funding for developing infrastructure within China. As a matter of fact, most countries in the world are facing similar funding shortages.

In this case, private finance is enormously in demand in the Public Sector for the development of infrastructure.

1.2.2 The Definition of PFIPs

PFIPs, in this book, stands for Privately Financed Infrastructure Projects, which are public infrastructure projects (the physical facilities that provide essential services to the general public) financed by Private Sector.

A Private Sector partner establishing a Special Purpose Vehicle (SPV)[15] has the financial responsibility, and undertakes physical construction, repair or expansion works of infrastructure for the Public authority under the Project Agreement. The Private Sector is authorized to operate the infrastructure and charge a price to the facility users (the public or public authorities) to enable it to recover both its investment and operating expenses as well as a reasonable rate of return.[16]

Therefore, a complete PFIP involves at least four relationships (see Fig. 1.1).

---

[12]Jiang li-li, *'Analysis the inevitability and appropriate radio of China holding US Treasury securities'* (Special Zone Economy, 2010, No 12) P90–92.

[13]Jiang li-li, *"Analysis the inevitability and appropriate radio of China holding US Treasury securities"* (Special Zone Economy, 2010, No 12) P90–92.

[14]Tao jie-yun, *"The advantages and disadvantages of China holding of US treasury securities"*(Commercial Times, 2010, No 12) P42.

[15]SPV (special purpose vehicle): a special purpose entity is a legal entity (usually a limited company of some type or, sometimes, a limited partnership) created to fulfil narrow, specific or temporary objectives, e.g. a specific project. The Project Company as an SPV cannot carry out any other business that is not part of the specific project. E. R. Yescombe, *'Public-Private Partnerships: Principles of Policy and Finance'* (ELSEVIER 2007) P109.

[16]*'Legislative Guide on Privately Financed Infrastructure Project'* (2001) UNCITRAL (A/CN.9/SER.B/4), Introduction and Background information on PFIPs, paras 8; E. R. Yescombe, *'Public-Private Partnerships: Principles of Policy and Finance'* (ELSEVIER 2007) P2–3.

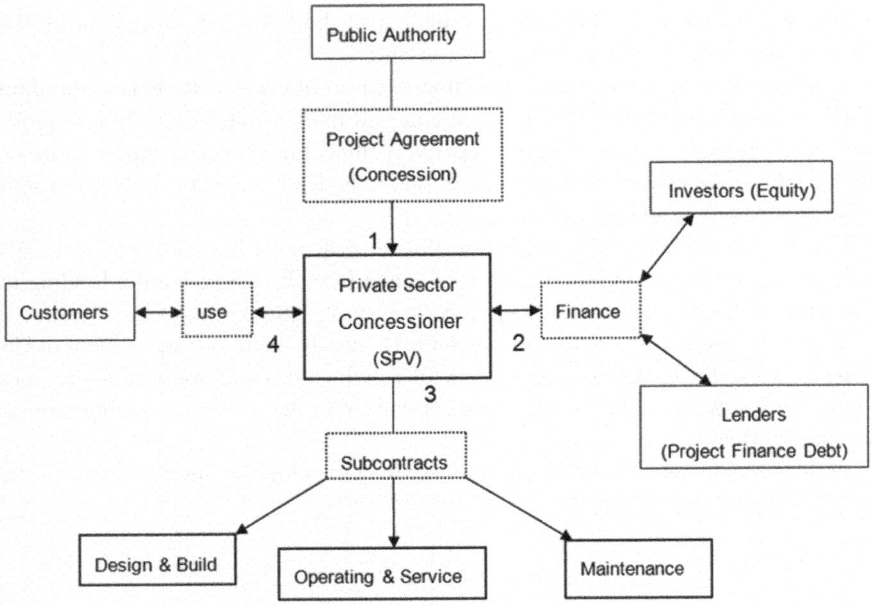

Fig. 1.1 The structure of general PFIPs

The first relationship is between the Public Authority and the Private Sector. A concession is allowed by the Public Authority in the form of Project Agreement, while the SPV established by the Private Sector plays a role as a concessioner.

The second relationship is between the Private Sector and the Financier, who may be Investors such as shareholders or lenders such as banks. The SPV established by the Private Sector is obliged to finance the projects.

The third relationship is between the Private Sector and the Subcontractors who may be constructors, operators or maintainers. The SPV who obtains the concession from the Public Authority may be a single entity composed of constructors, operators and maintainers or it needs to subcontract with other entities after acquiring the concession. The SPV established by the Private Sector is obliged to construct, operate and maintain the project infrastructure.

The fourth relationship is between the Private Sector and the Customers. The SPV operates the projects to pay back its investment on the project, service debt and operating costs, and to raise reasonable profits during the concession period. The SPV established by the Private Sector has the right to charge the facility users.

1.2.2.1 Replacing "BOT" with "PFIPs"

It is worthy to explain where the word "PFIPs" is from.

"BOT"[17] was originally used to describe infrastructure financed by private investors. Before long, however, "PFIPs" was considered to describe such projects more exactly and replaced the outdated "BOT".

The first time UNCITRAL paid attention to the area of Privately Financed Infrastructure Projects (PFIPs) was at the congress on International Trade Law—"Uniform commercial law in the 21st century"—held in May 1992 in New York as part of the 25th session of the Commission. However, as the term "PFIPs" had not been developed at that time, "BOT" was used. The Build-Operate-Transfer ("BOT") project is a project in which a government grants a concessioner a period of time to develop a project; the private concessioner builds, operates and manages the project for a number of years; the concessioner is permitted to refund their construction costs and derive reasonable profits from the operation and commercial exploitation of the project; and at the end of the concession period, the project's infrastructure ownership is transferred to the government without charge.[18] During the Congress in 1992, it was proposed that the Commission consider undertaking work in the field of BOT project financing.[19]

As a consequence of that proposal, the following Commission sessions paid attention to BOT. At the 26th session in 1993, the Secretariat informed the Commission that it was monitoring the work by the United Nations Industrial Development Organization (UNIDO) on the preparation of "Guidelines for the Development, Negotiating and Contracting of BOT Projects".[20] At the 27th session in 1994, the Commission emphasized the relevance of BOT and requested the Secretariat to prepare a note on possible future work on the subject of BOT projects.[21] At the 28th session in 1995, the Commission discussed the requested note.[22] At the 29th session in 1996, the Commission decided to prepare a legislative guide on BOT and related types of projects.[23]

The word "BOT" was officially replaced by "PFIPs" at the 30th session in Vienna in 1997:

> The Commission may wish henceforth to use the words 'privately-financed infrastructure projects' to refer to its work in this field, rather than the words 'build-operate-transfer' (BOT), which had so far been used.[24]

---

[17] BOT is the fundamental and typical selection. The government grants a Private Sector a concession to build an infrastructure, and operate it during the concession period to cover the cost and reasonable profit, and then to transfer the infrastructure back at the end of the concession period without charge.

[18] UNCITRAL, 27th Session, A/CN.9/399-*Build-operate-transfer projects*, P2.

[19] Ibid., P1.

[20] UNCITRAL, 26th Session, A/CN.9/378-*Possible future work: proposals for possible future work made at the UNCITRAL Congress: note/by the Secretariat*, P5.

[21] UNCITRAL, 27th Session, A/CN.9/399-*Build-operate-transfer projects*, P1–3.

[22] UNCITRAL, 28th Session, A/CN.9/414-*Possible future work: Build-Operate-Transfer projects.*

[23] UNCITRAL, 29th Session, A/CN.9/424-*Possible Future Work: Build-Operate-Transfer projects*, P21, para 89.

[24] UNCITRAL, 30th Session, A/CN.9/438-Privately-Financed Infrastructure Projects: Draft Chapters of a legislative guide on privately-financed infrastructure projects, P1 footnote.

The precise use of the word "BOT" refers to only one particular type of infrastructure project with private funding, i.e., Build-Operate-Transfer. However, as the BOT model evolved in practice, various other types were formed, which do not follow a pure "BOT" model, such as "build-own-operate" (BOO),[25] "build-own-operate-transfer" (BOOT),[26] "build-own-lease-transfer" (BOLT) or "build-rent-transfer" (BRT). Therefore, the word "BOT" is not appropriate as a generic expression for the different forms of private financing of public infrastructure projects. However, the Commission's work in this field expected to cover all types of public infrastructure projects involving private financing, including, but not limited to, BOT models and its evolved types.[27] Therefore, the term "Privately Financed Infrastructure Projects" (PFIPs) was developed to replace "BOT" as a generic term. It is worth noting that, in China, BOT (and its types) is accepted and used widely. This means that the word "BOT" (and its types) is popular in Chinese academic discourse, while the more precise "PFIPs" is still strange to Chinese scholars.

1.2.2.2 Other Two Similar Concepts

It is to be noted that features of PFIPs distinguish it from other two similar concepts (Public Procurement and Public-Private Partnerships) as follows:

PFIPs Vesus Public Procurement

PFIPs financed by the Private Sector are different from infrastructure projects purchased by conventional public procurement.

The primary difference between PFIPs and Public Procurement is the source of finance. Infrastructure projects purchased in conventional public procurement are financed by Public Sector funding, using tax revenues or public borrowing, whereas PFIPs are financed by private investors. In conventional procurement, the Public Sector funds the whole infrastructure project: it provides the initial capital of the project, manages the operation and maintenance costs and covers any cost overrides. In PFIPs, once the project is handed to the Private Sector, the Private Sector covers the costs of the project. The SPV (special purpose vehicle) takes all the responsibility of the debt of the project. It is no longer the financial responsibility of the Public Sector. Therefore, PFIPs allow the government to meet public infrastructure delivery, but do not have to pay for the construction, operation and maintenance of that infrastructure.

[25] BOO is similar as the BOT, but the Private Sector owns the facility permanently and is not under an obligation to transfer it back to the contracting authority.

[26] BOOT is similar as the BOT that the government grants a Private Sector a concession to finance and build an infrastructure, and operate it during the concession period to cover the cost and reasonable profit, and then to transfer the infrastructure back at the end of the concession period without charge. However, under this arrangement the Private Sector owns the infrastructure facility and its assets until it is transferred to the contracting authority.

[27] (n 24).

Additionally, in PFIPs, the risks of infrastructure projects are partly or wholly transferred from the Public Sector to the Private Sector. In conventional procurement, although the Public Sector rarely designs or builds large public assets like power stations, roads, rail systems and buildings alone (they contract with relevant specialists to provide such services), the Public Sector, which funds these projects, has to cover unforeseen costs, by way of example those due to time delays. The private investor is only a supplier who offers products to government, and the relationship is terminated once the purchase is complete. The risks of the project remain with the Public Sector, and therefore the taxpayers. However, in PFIPs, the SPV receives payments ('service fees') for the project in a pre-agreement, which are intended to repay the financing costs and give returns to investors. The service fees are subject to deductions for any failure to meet output specifications, and there is generally no allowance for cost overruns which occur during construction or operation of the facility.[28] In some cases, the Private Sector takes responsibility for both the construction of the asset and the provision of related services, such as the maintenance of the road, etc.[29] Moreover, even if the project turns out to be less profitable than originally envisaged because of a breach of duty by government or force majeure, the SPV has to bear the loss first and only then has recourse against the government rather than the government bearing the risks directly.

PFIPs Versus PPP

Though the PFIPs and Public-Private-Partnership (PPP)[30] overlap in their scopes and structures, and are often used synonymously, their foci partially differ.

PFIPs and PPP can be shown in similar structures, as in the following: BOT (Build, Operate, Transfer)[31]; BTO (Build, Transfer, Operate)[32]; ROT (Refurbish, Operate, Transfer)[33]; BOOT (Build, Own, Operate, Transfer)[34]; BROT (Build, Rent,

[28] Yescombe E. R., *'Public-Private Partnerships: Principles of Policy and Finance'* (ELSEVIER 2007) P4; Peter Trepte, *'Regulating procurement'* (Oxford University Press, 2004) p28.

[29] Hartley Keith, *'problems of using partnering and similar private sector practice in the Public Sector environment: the example of PPPs/PFI'* in Arrowswith Sue and Trybus Martin (eds), *Public procurement: the continuing revolution* (Kluwer law international 2003) p191.

[30] PPP is a partnership between the Private Sector and the Public Sector, which covers a number of arrangements in which Private Sector have a role in projects to develop Public Sector infrastructure.

[31] (n 17).

[32] BTO emphasize that the infrastructure is transferred to the contracting authority immediately upon its completion, and then the concessioner is awarded the right to operate the facility for a certain period.

[33] ROT means the Private Sector needs not to build a new infrastructure. The existing infrastructure facilities are turned over to Private Sector to refurbish, while the Private Sector is authorised to operate for a given period of time. At the end the infrastructure is transferred back to the public authority after the concession period without charge.

[34] (n 26).

Operate, Transfer)[35]; PFI (Private Finance Initiative)[36]; MO (Maintain and Operation)[37]; DBFO (Design, build, finance, operate)[38]; BOO (Build, own, operate)[39] and so on.[40] However, the structures of PPP are not limited to the above structures, which are based on infrastructure projects, but also include all partnerships between the public and Private Sector, such as programme cooperation with government or licensing for the exploitation of natural resources or the privatization of government property. By contrast, PFIPs just refer to partnerships in infrastructure project.[41] Therefore, the scope of PFIPs is not as wide as the scope of PPP.

Even when both PPP and PFIPs refer to infrastructure projects, their emphases are different. PPP does not consider the extent of private finance or participation in the infrastructure project. Any joint venture between the private and Public Sector may be called a PPP. PFIPs not only emphasise the sourcing of finance from the Private Sector but also requires a certain level of participation by the Private Sector in the infrastructure project, i.e. it pays attention to the operation and organisation of a project financed by the Private Sector with the aim being the successful completion of these projects.

1.2.3 The Feasibility of the PFIPs

This book focuses on PFIPs. However, this does not mean that the PFIP model solves all infrastructure problems. Developing countries such as some countries in Africa without experience in PFIPs do not want to bear high administrative costs so they often apply for loans with low interest or no interest from their domestic banks or World Bank. Although the PFIP model is not a perfect solution, it has a number of

[35]BROT, in addition to the obligations and other terms usual to BOT projects, the concessioner rents the physical assets on which the facility is located for the duration of the agreement.

[36]PFI, a Public Sector body contracts with a Private Sector provider to purchase services it requires on a long-term basis. Typically this will involve the provider in the design, construction, financing and operation of a new capital asset (e.g. a road). On completion of the project, the Public Sector buys the services, but not the capital asset itself.

[37]M&O (or O&M Maintain and Operation) means the Private Sector finances on the maintenance of the existing infrastructure and then operates the facility to return its cost and reasonable profits during the allowed period.

[38]DBFO is used to emphasize the Private Sector additional responsibility for designing the facility and financing its construction.

[39](n 25).

[40]'Legislative Guide on Privately Financed Infrastructure Project' (2001)UNCITRAL (A/CN.9/SER.B/4) p 5–6.

[41]The Legislative Guide, Introduction and Background information on PFIPs, paras 8; E. R. Yescombe, *'Public-Private Partnerships: Principles of Policy and Finance'* (ELSEVIER 2007) P2–3.

advantages which prove its feasibility under the proper circumstances, and can be considered as a solution for countries such as China.

Fiscal expenditure reduced

The fundamental advantage of PFIPs is that they reduce fiscal expenditure. The investment in a PFIPs falls outside the public budget and is offered by private investors. From the Public Sector's perspective, the PFIPs provide "off-balance sheet" finance for public service assets. This means that any borrowing from the private investor incurred by the SPV implementing PFIPs is not considered to be public borrowing, but the debt of the SPV.[42] Although in countries such as China, it is not difficult for the Public Sector to borrow money from banks or other financial institutions, the risks to national debt and deficit increase at the same time. For example, access to capital at low interest rates after adopting the Euro may have played a role in Greece's debt crisis in 2010, in addition to domestic factors. Perceptions of stability conferred by their Euro membership allowed Greece to borrow at a more favourable interest rate than would likely have been the case had they remained outside the Euro zone. However, access to artificially cheap credit allowed Greece to accumulate high levels of debt and postpone debt maturity. When the national debt crisis began, this debt became difficult to control.[43]

It is noteworthy that recently the UK Treasury Committee have criticised the off-balance sheet and outside department budget treatment of the PFI[44] debt in UK and the fact that such debt is recorded outside departmental budgets. The report argues that it is unreasonable to put PFI debt outside the national deficit statistics and budget, because it will contribute to misuse of PFI and encourage poor investment decisions in the long term.[45]

Although the UK government agreed with these arguments in the case of PFI in the UK and has tried to add the PFI debt into its balance sheet and department budget,[46] these arguments cannot deny the positive impact of the PFIPs model into fiscal expenditure.

Firstly, PFI is only one type of PFIP. The PFI model is criticised because the current fiscal account just shows that there is no immediate high-level payment so that the departments might be under their budget limitation. It cannot show that the total of the instalment may be higher than the once-off payment, which may increase

[42]Vinter Graham D., *'Project finance'* (3rd ed, Sweet & Maxwell, London 2006) p422.

[43]Nelson Rebecca M. and others, *'Greece's Debt Crisis: Overview, Policy Responses, and Implications'* (Congressional Research Service, 14, May, 2010) P6.

[44](n 36).

[45]House of Common Treasury Committee, *'Private Finance Initiative'* 17th Report of session 2010–12 (House of Commons, 18th July 2011), Chapter 2. Accounting and budgetary incentives, http://www.publications.parliament.uk/pa/cm201012/cmselect/cmtreasy/1146/1146.pdf Accessed on 10th July 2019.

[46]House of Common Treasury Committee, *'Private Finance Initiative: Government, OBR and NAO Responses to the Seventeenth Report from the Committee'* 25th Report of session 2012–12 (House of Commons, 19th December 2011), Appendix 1: Government Response, P8–9 http://www.publications.parliament.uk/pa/cm201012/cmselect/cmtreasy/1725/1725.pdf Accessed on 10th July 2019.

the real fiscal debt.[47] However, in other types of PFIPs such as BOT, the Private Sector charges the public user rather than the Public Sector, which means there is no fiscal expenditure of government in the past or future (there may be some subsidy under contract) and so no increase in fiscal debt. Therefore, the criticisms of PFI for accounting and budgetary reasons cannot apply to all the PFIPs because the other types of PFIPs effectively reduce fiscal expenditure.

Secondly, even in the case of PFI in the UK, the PFI model avoids increasing national debt, eases fiscal pressure and reduces fiscal expenditure. At the beginning, there is not too much fiscal expenditure on public infrastructure because the Public Sector spends comparatively less on payments for service due to it does not have to make a huge investment in the construction and operation. The UK budget is not large enough to support the demand for infrastructure and the government cannot accept more Public Sector borrowing.[48] In the case of budgetary limitations, borrowing limitations and an increase in demand for infrastructure, the PFI was adopted even if the total cost was higher. The UK government has tried to add the PFI debt to its balance sheet and department budget, but this would not change the choice of using PFI.

Value for money[49]

Firstly, infrastructure and services traditionally constructed and delivered by the Public Sector may be more efficiently constructed and delivered by the Private Sector. Mr Philip Green has a view that the Public Sector may not be making efficient use of government finance. The prices in the market are not compared in advance and management in the Public Sector does not spend public money as wisely as it would its own.[50] However, in PFIPs, the Public Sector only decides upon the facilities and services it needs and then seeks a private investor to complete the project. Since a competitive selection process, such as contract bidding, is offered by the Public Sector, private investors, competing for the contract bidding, try to find the "best" value for money (hereafter refer to VFM) solution that meets the requirements of the Public Sector.[51] The cost of administrative monitoring by the Public Sector is high at

---

[47]In PFI model, the government need purchase the public service from Private Sector at the end though the government does not afford the cost of construction and operation at the beginning, which means the once payment becomes to the instalment. House of Common Treasury Committee, *'Private Finance Initiative'* 17th Report of session 2010–12 (House of Commons, 18th July 2011), Chapter 1 Introduction, para 2:

'The return on both equity and debt capital is sourced from the periodic "unitary charge", which is paid by the public authority from the point at which the contracted facility is available for use.'.

[48]House of Common Treasury Committee, *'Private Finance Initiative: Government, OBR and NAO Responses to the Seventeenth Report from the Committee'* 25th Report of session 2012–12 (House of Commons, 19th December 2011), Appendix 1: Government Response, P11.

[49]The UK National Audit Office (NAO) defines Value for Money as being 'the optimal use of resources to achieve intended outcomes'.

[50]Green Philip, *'Efficiency review by Sir Philip Green: key findings and recommendations'*, 11 October 2010. P20.

[51]Vinter Graham D., *'Project finance'* (3rd ed, Sweet & Maxwell, London 2006) p 422.

the outset for certain developing countries without experience in using PFIPs, but this cost will decrease once the necessary procedures, systems and laws are established.

It is noteworthy that a recent report made by critics of the Treasury Committee suggests that PFIs in the UK do not approach the best VFM. It points out that, as private finance costs are higher than public finance costs (since government has always been able to obtain cheaper funding than private providers of project finance), PFI will only provide VFM if this difference in cost is outweighed by the savings and efficiencies during the life of a PFI project.[52] However, the data and cases show that the quantity, quality, price, inflexibility and the level of risk transfer of these projects are no better than those agreed upon by conventional procurement methods; or they may be worse.[53] In PFIs, the Public Sector gives the Private Sector a payment which includes service costs and reasonable profits, so it seems the Public Sector pays more money in exchange for the same or less service offered by conventional procurement methods. The difference between direct government funding and the cost of this finance has increased significantly since the financial crisis.[54]

As discussed before, PFI is only one type of PFIP. In the other types of PFIPs such as BOT, the Public Sector just covers the cost of project monitoring or management, or certain subsidies thereof. The Public Sector need not permit to purchase the services produced by the infrastructure financed by Private Sector. Meanwhile, under the government administration, the Private Sector is not easy to over-charge for using the public service. Therefore, the only way the Private Sector can secure higher profits is to look for more efficient and quality outputs, which fits the theory of VFM.

Although the UK government agrees that certain improvements could be made so that the VFM assessment process of PFI is more robust, the government considers the PFI projects in the UK to have already followed the VFM Principle. The government response is that VFM is a relative concept, which requires the comparison of the potential or actual outcomes of alternative delivery and financing options. Long-term forecasting requires assumptions to be made about the future. The outputs should not be considered in isolation as standalone cases for, or against, the use of private finance. A sensitivity analysis of the output should be considered alongside qualitative factors including the viability, achievability and desirability of using private finance. This analysis informs the final assessment of whether the project represents value for money.[55] It is inappropriate that the critics only compare the financial costs and the outputs of the PFI projects. Moreover, the transfer of risk to the Private Sector has worked as anticipated. The Public Sector has been protected when projects have gone wrong, with losses being borne by the Private Sector.[56]

---

[52]House of Common Treasury Committee, *'Private Finance Initiative'* 17th Report of session 2010–12 (House of Commons, 18th July 2011), P56, para 8.

[53]Ibid., Chapter 3 Value for money.

[54]Ibid., P3, para 2.

[55]House of Common Treasury Committee, *'Private Finance Initiative: Government, OBR and NAO Responses to the Seventeenth Report from the Committee'* 25th Report of session 2012–12 (House of Commons, 19th December 2011), Appendix 1: Government Response, P9–10.

[56]Ibid., P11.

New Technology and advanced management skill transferred

As far as developing countries are concerned, in addition to attracting foreign private finance for developing their domestic infrastructure, using PFIPs has a fringe benefit—the import of new technology from other countries.[57] The foreign private investors may use new technologies or advanced management techniques in the construction and operation of their PFIPs. Although these new technologies or advanced management techniques may be acquired by normal bid or purchase, the real cost of the project may be higher in the latter case.

Critics may argue that new technology and advanced management might not be applied in PFIPs. The concessioners in PFIPs are usually consortia, which often include a construction company and an operation company. Another construction company or operation company may have the better technologies or skills, but, unless these technologies and skills are part of the chosen consortium's bid, they will not be used.[58]

However, this criticism is not an argument against PFIPs. It simply raises the problem of market competition. Under efficient marketization, in order to win in the competition or obtain more profits, the private investor has the incentive to pursue better technologies and skills.

Market competition increased

By contrast with conventional procurement, when private finance is brought into the infrastructure market, it increases market competition.

A potential criticism is that the long, complex and costly process may limit the number of participants to bid for projects. This would mean that only companies who can afford to lose millions of pounds in failed bids can be involved, which would result in an uncompetitive market. The competition is likely to be less intense, when compared to conventional procurements.[59] However, this criticism conflates two different kinds of competition. The competition under conventional procurement is actually the competition for the public capital of infrastructure investments. No matter the result of the competition, the Public Sector covers the gain and loss of the infrastructure projects. By contrast, the competition under PFIPs creates real competition in infrastructure market because the private investor, rather than the public investor, covers the gain or loss of the project. In China, for example, if the government finances infrastructure projects, whether or not the concession is awarded through competitive bid, state-owned enterprises find it easier to win the project concession.[60]

---

[57]Holloway Julian, *'Infrastructure projects in mainland China'* (Const. L.J. 2004, 20(5), 278–279) P279.

[58]House of Common Treasury Committee, *'Private Finance Initiative'* 17th Report of session 2010–12 (House of Commons, 18th July 2011), P57, para 15.

[59]Ibid.

[60]Cao Fuguo, *'Regulating procurement of privately financed infrastructure in China: a review of the recent legislative initiatives and the emerging regulatory framework'* (2007), Public Procurement law review (P.P.L.R.2007, 3, 147–173), P147.

In summary, PFIPs can enlarge the source of capital to build infrastructure. The arguments against PFIPs for reasons of VFM assessment, transfer of risk, transfer of new technology, market competition and so on, can be solved through proper management, adequate systems and laws, to achieve a balance satisfactory to all participants in PFIPs.

1.2.4 The Worldwide Legislation on PFIPs

The number of PFIPs is gradually increasing in China, including infrastructure projects financed by foreign private investment, which play an important role in Chinese economic development. However, current Chinese regulations are hindering the development of PFIPs in China.[61] Although in the past few years Chinese regulations on PFIPs have improved, they are not yet adequate for the full development of PFIPs. In order to make the legislation consistent with the development of PFIPs, it is necessary for China to reform its current regulations on PFIPs. The new legislation should aim to achieve a balance between the desire to facilitate and encourage of private participation in PFIPs, and the various public interests and concerns of the host country.

As a matter of fact,PFIPs have been applied worldwide since in the early 1980s and have benefitted the host countries.[62] Those countries have drafted various regulations or laws on PFIPs in order to protect and facilitate the development of PFIPs. Japan has passed a specific law on PFIPs to regulate their use. *The law relating to the Promotion of the Realization of Public Facilities by Using Private Funds* was legislated in Japan in 1999.[63] Britain does not have a specific law on PFIPs, but the regulations on PFIPs are presented in a number of relevant policies and guidelines. For example, the first policy on PFI presented by the British government was *PFI: Meeting the Investment Challenge* in 2003. *PFI: Strengthening Long-term Partnerships*, which confirms the importance of PFIs, was published in 2006. *The Infrastructure Procurement: Delivering Long-term Value*, which states the necessity of PFIs, was published in 2008. *The Standardisation of PF2 Contracts (SoPC)*, which was issued in December 2012, is the latest version of the standard wording and guidance to be used by Public Sector bodies and their advisors when drafting PF2 contracts.[64] This shows that

[61] Ibid., P148–149.

[62] Smith A.J., *'Privatized Infrastructure: the role of government'* (1999) Thomas Telford, P234–235.

[63] Wang Tie Shan, *'Comparative research on PFI project between Britain and Japan'* (2008) IEC, No1: 49.

[64] HM Treasure, *'Standardisation of PF2 Contracts'* (December 2012), <https://assets.publishing.service.gov.uk/government/uploads/system/uploads/attachment_data/file/221556/infrastructure_standardisation_of_contracts_051212.pdf> accessed on 13th July, 2020; Infrastructure UK, *'PF2: A User Guide'* (December 2012), <https://assets.publishing.service.gov.uk/government/uploads/system/uploads/attachment_data/file/207382/pf2_userguide.pdf> accessed on 26th July, 2013; The National Archive, <http://webarchive.nationalarchives.gov.uk/20130129110402/http://www.hm-treasury.gov.uk/infrastructure_ppp_contractual.htm> accessed on 26th July, 2019.

countries are trying to improve their regulations on PFIPs in a variety of forms so that investments can be properly regulated under law.

In this context, the United Nations Commission on International Trade Law (UNCITRAL)[65] issued the Legislative Guide on PFIPs (2001)[66] (the Legislative Guide) and its supplement Model Legislative Provisions on PFIPs (2003)[67] (Model Provisions), to assist the establishment of legal frameworks favourable to PFIPs. Although the Legislative Guide and Model Provisions do not provide a single set of model solutions, a country can use them to evaluate different approaches and then choose the most suitable for its own national or local context. To some extent, the Legislative Guide and Model Provisions are beneficial to a worldwide harmonization[68] of the treatment and promotion of PFIPs for (foreign) private investment in public infrastructure.

1.3 Research Questions

This book intends to solve six research questions:

1.3.1 Research Question 1

With the development of PFIPs in China, has it become necessary to reform Chinese laws on PFIPs to match up with and facilitate the development of PFIPs?

- What benefits has the PFIP model brought to China? Only if PFIPs have brought benefits to China would it be significant to improve the laws protecting and facilitating the PFIP model.
- Do current Chinese laws on PFIPs match up with the development of PFIPs in China? If not, it is necessary to research how to improve the laws.
- What are the shortcomings of the current Chinese laws on PFIPs and do these shortcomings result in adverse effects? Only by finding out the defects of the current Chinese laws on PFIPs can one know which points to improve and reform.

---

65 The United Nations Commission on International Trade Law (UNCITRAL) was established by the General Assembly in 1966 (Resolution 2205(XXI) of 17 December 1966). It is the core legal body of the United Nations system in the field of international trade law. UNCITRAL's business is the modernization and harmonization of rules on international business.

66 '*Legislative Guide on Privately Financed Infrastructure Project*' (2001)UNCITRAL (A/CN.9/SER.B/4) (hereafter referred to as the Legislative Guide).

67 '*Model Legislative Provisions on Privately Financed Infrastructure Projects*' (2004) UNCITRAL (A/58/17), paras 12–171 (hereafter referred to as the Model Provisions).

68 Mistelis L., '*Is Harmonisation a Necessary Evil? The Future of Harmonisation and New Sources of International Trade Law*' in I Fletcher, L Mistelis and M Cremona eds *Foundations of International Trade Law* (London, Sweet & Maxwell, 2001).

- Whether or not conditions in China are amenable to accepting law reforms on PFIPs?
- What is the aim of the reform of Chinese laws on PFIPs? This book will propose aims for law reform to achieve so that new laws on PFIPs facilitate the development of PFIPs, rather than hinder it.

1.3.2 Research Question 2

Why adopt the Legislative Guide and Model Provisions[69] made by UNCITRAL as guidelines for improving the Chinese laws on PFIPs? Why use other countries' laws on PFIPs as supplementary references?

- Why prefer the Legislative Guide and Model Provisions made by UNCITRAL to other international agreements or treaties about PFIPs as the guidelines for improving the Chinese laws on PFIPs? What are the advantages of the Legislative Guide and Model Provisions? What are the disadvantages of these other agreements and treaties?
- Why consider other countries' laws[70] for supplementary references? Why can they not be the sole guideline for China?

1.3.3 Research Question 3

With reference to the guidelines of the Legislative Guide and Model Provisions[71] and to supplementary references from other countries,[72] how can the general legislative and institutional framework on PFIPs in China be improved?

- What recommendations are given by the Legislative Guide and Model Provisions to establish general legislative and institutional framework in favour of developing PFIPs? What is the background of the recommendations and its meaning in detail?
- With regard to the principle of transparency, how do the recommendations offered by the Legislative Guide and Model Provisions compare with current Chinese laws on PFIPs and should any issues be addressed?
- With regard to the principle of fairness, how do the recommendations offered by the Legislative Guide and Model Provisions compare with current Chinese laws on PFIPs and should any issues be addressed?

---

[69]The Legislative Guide, Introduction and Background information on PFIPs; and the Model Provisions, Chap. I on General provisions.

[70]Such as British law, EU law and so on.

[71]The Legislative Guide, Recommendation 1–11, Chap. I on general legislative and institutional framework; the Model Provisions, Chap. I on General provisions, Model Provision 1–4.

[72]The British regulations about the regulatory institutions; The British special regulations about the customer protection by Consumer Council for Water (CCWater).

- With regard to the principle of long-term sustainability, how do the recommendations offered by the Legislative Guide and Model Provisions compare with current Chinese laws on PFIPs and should any issues be addressed? Could any other country's laws on PFIPs offer supplementary reference?
- With regard to the principle of eliminating undesirable restrictions, how do the recommendations offered by the Legislative Guide and Model Provisions compare with current Chinese laws on PFIPs and should any issues be addressed?

1.3.4 Research Question 4

With reference to the guidelines of the Legislative Guide and Model Provisions[73] and to supplementary references from other countries,[74] how may the selection procedures of the concessioner of PFIPs be improved to make the process more fair and transparent in China?

- To ensure the process is fair and transparent in the Pre-selection stage, what recommendations are offered by the Legislative Guide and Model Provisions? What are the current Chinese laws about this stage? Are there any issues should be addressed?
- To ensure the process is fair and transparent during selection, should competitive selection procedures be used in PFIPs? Compared with the selection procedures in general bids and procurement, what are the special requirements of selection procedures for PFIPs? What recommendations are offered by the Legislative Guide and Model Provisions? What are the current Chinese laws on selection? Are there any issues that should be addressed?
- To ensure the process is fair and transparent in its post-selection stage, what recommendations are offered by the Legislative Guide and Model Provisions if the unsuccessful bidders wish to question the result? What are the current Chinese laws on this stage? Are there any issues that should be addressed?
- To ensure the process is fair and transparent to unsolicited proposals, what recommendations are offered by the Legislative Guide and Model Provisions? Given that China has neither research nor practice in unsolicited proposals; would it be worthwhile to introduce this selection model in China?

---

[73]The Legislative Guide, Recommendation 14–39, Chap. III on Selection of the concessioner; and the Model Provisions accompanied therein, Chap. II on Selection of the concessioner, Model Provision 5–27.

[74]EU regulations on market access are used as supplemental reference.

1.3.5 Research Question 5

With reference to the guidelines of the Legislative Guide and Model Provisions[75] and to supplementary references from other countries, how should China reform the laws relating to the agreements involved in PFIPs?

- What kinds of agreements may be included in PFIPs? What are the relationships between them?
- To what extent should the law regulates Project Agreements but avoids jeopardising the necessary flexibility? In light of the recommendations from the Legislative Guide and Model Provisions, what items could be involved in the project agreement? Considering China's specific situation, what mandatory requirements may be added to these items?
- In respect of the finance agreement, what recommendations are offered by the Legislative Guide and the Model Provisions to the financial agreement? May these be used in Chinese law reform?
- In respect of the subcontracting agreement, what recommendations are offered by the Legislative Guide and the Model Provisions to the subcontracting agreement? May these be used in Chinese law reform?
- In respect of the user agreement, what recommendations are offered by the Legislative Guide and the Model Provisions to the user agreement? May these be used in Chinese law reform?

1.3.6 Research Question 6

With reference to the guidelines of the Legislative Guide and Model Provisions[76] and to supplementary references from other countries,[77] how should the laws of dispute settlement in PFIPs be reformed in China?

- In light of the Legislative Guide and Model Provisions, what channels could be offered to settle disputes between the contracting authority and the concessioner? Could the concessioner of PFIPs in China use these channels? Are there any undesirable restrictions in current Chinese laws?
- In light of the Legislative Guide and Model Provisions, could the disputes between the concessioner and its contractors, lenders and suppliers be solved through the

[75]The Legislative Guide, Chap. IV on Construction and Operation of infrastructure: Legislative framework and Project agreement, Chap. V on Duration, Extension and Termination of the Project Agreement; and the Model Provisions accompanied therein, Chap. III on Contents and Implementation of the Concession contract, Chap. IV on Duration, Extension and Termination of the Concession Contract.

[76]The Legislative Guide, Chap. VI on Settlement of Disputes; and the Model Provisions accompanied therein, Chap. V on Settlement of Disputes.

[77]The definition of public contract in Britain is broad.

freedom to choose litigation or arbitration? Are there any undesirable restrictions in current Chinese laws?
- In light of the Legislative Guide and Model Provisions, what channels could be offered to settle the disputes involving customers or terminal users? How would this reform current Chinese legislation?

1.4 The Contribution of This Research

1.4.1 Research Gap Filled

This book fills the research gap with respect to the legal aspects of Chinese PFIPs.

The current literature on the legal aspects of Chinese PFIPs is limited. The reasons why previous research is insufficient are as follows:

Firstly, the legal aspects of Chinese PFIPs have not been paid enough attention. Recently, however, the development of emerging PFIPs has achieved a certain level and the market of private investment has become mature.

Secondly, there is little literature researching the legal aspects of Chinese PFIPs with most research focusing on the economic, financial or management aspects.

Thirdly, even those research papers that study the legislative aspect of Chinese PFIPs are restricted by region or limited to specific types of PFIPs or sections of procedure. Therefore, this literatures presents research only on specific provinces, specific types of PFIPs such as BOT or specific sections of PFIP procedures such as concession bids.

It is noteworthy that this book systematically analyses and discusses Chinese PFIPs, with particular emphasis on legal aspects. Considering the development trend of the legislation pertaining to Chinese PFIPs, this book analyses the legal aspects of Chinese PFIPs across China. This book suggests a comprehensive legal framework which meets the international standards.

Most importantly, this book makes the claim that the current Chinese laws on PFIPs need improvement and reform. Moreover, it offers reform recommendations and discusses their applicability to each specific phase of a PFIP.

1.4.2 UNCITRAL Guidance Transferred

This book makes some progress in looking into the applicability of the Legislative Guide and Model Provisions in China.

Little work has considered the combination of Chinese regulations on PFIPs and the Legislative Guide and Model Provision on PFIPs. The literature usually analyses either the Chinese regulations or the Legislative Guide and Model Provisions, rather than analysing both in combination them together.

Thus far, the only article to combine the Chinese regulations on PFIPs and the Legislative Guide and Model Provisions by UNCITRAL is "*Regulating Procurement of Privately Financed Infrastructure in China: a Review of the Recent Legislative Initiative and the Emerging Regulatory Framework*"[78] by Professor Fuguo Cao. This book here expands upon Cao's ideas and brings them into line with more contemporary findings.

Firstly, Cao's article, which was written in 2007, is outdated to some extent. In the five years after *the State Council Opinions on Encouraging, Supporting and Guiding the Development of the Non-state Sector Economy*, issued by the Chinese State Council in 2005, many provincial regulations on PFIPs were issued in various Chinese provinces. The State Council also issued *Several Opinions of the State Council on Further Doing a Good Job in the Utilization of Foreign Investment* in 2010, which encourages foreign private investment through the use of PFIPs.

Secondly, although Cao compares Chinese laws on PFIPs and the Legislative Guide and Model Provisions made by UNCITRAL, he does not thoroughly discuss the applicability of the Legislative Guide and Model Provisions for use in China. His article intends to review three current Chinese provincial laws on PFIPs and address their defects, but it does not discuss how the recommendations made by the Legislative Guide and Model Provisions could be applied to reform Chinese law on PFIPs.

The contribution of this book is that it systematically analyses both current Chinese laws on PFIPs and the Legislative Guide and Model Provisions made by UNCITRAL, and discusses the applicability of the Legislative Guide and Model Provisions for use in China to suggest reforms to the Chinese legislation on PFIPs, so that this might be promoted to an international standard, which would facilitate foreign private investment in China's public infrastructure. Meanwhile, building on Cao's arguments, this book updates information about laws on PFIPs in China.

1.4.3 Global Harmonization Contributed

This book is important for global legal harmonization because it looks at the extent to which UNCITRAL instruments can be transplanted into domestic laws.

UNCITRAL, as a core legal body of the United Nations system in the field of international trade law that specializes in commercial law reform worldwide, was established to modernize and harmonize the rules on international business.[79] Only when the countries accept and apply the legislative guides and model provisions formulated by UNCITRAL can the aims of modernization and harmonization be

---

[78]Cao Fuguo, '*Regulating procurement of privately financed infrastructure in China: a review of the recent legislative initiatives and the emerging regulatory framework*' (2007), Public Procurement law review (P.P.L.R.2007, 3, 147–173).

[79]Official Records of the General Assembly, 21st Session, Resolution 2205 (XXI), A/RES/2205(XXI), 17 December 1966, <http://www.uncitral.org/uncitral/en/about/origin.html> accessed on 15th July, 2019.

achieved. As a matter of fact, UNCITRAL has not only issued the Legislative Guide and Model Provisions on PFIPs, it has also issued many other instruments in other areas of international business. Whether global legal harmonization in these areas can be achieved depends on the extent to which countries accept and apply these instruments.[80]

This book, taking the Legislative Guide and Model Provisions on PFIPs made by UNCITRAL as an example, analyses and discusses how the UNCITRAL instruments could be transplanted into Chinese laws. It therefore provides a good case example for China's receptivity to future transplants of other guides and model provisions made by UNCITRAL.

1.5 Methodology

Three kinds of methodology are used during the research to complete this book.

1.5.1 The Doctrinal Approach

The doctrinal approach will involve an examination of the existing regulations, recommendations and statutes on PFIPs. The main focus will be the Legislative Guide and Model Provisions on PFIPs made by UNCITRAL and the current Chinese laws on PFIPs. At certain points, the book will also reference conventions made by other international organizations and the law in other countries. The purpose of this approach is to establish defects in current Chinese laws on PFIPs and consider whether the recommendations in the Legislative Guide and Model Provisions provide the best way to solve these defects. If certain aspects remain problematic, the book explores whether they could be supplemented by the laws of other countries, for example Britain.

1.5.2 The Theoretical Approach

The theoretical approach will consider principles of international investment law such as harmonization, fairness, transparency and efficiency, etc.[81] The use of this

[80] McCormack Gerard, *'Secured credit and the harmonisation of law, the UNCITRAL Experience'* (Edward Elgar, USA 2011) P2–6, P15–20.

[81] Qureshi Asif H, and Ziegler Andreas R., *'International Economic Law'* (2nd edn Thomson: sweet & maxwell 2007) P399–437; Subedi Surya P, *'International Investment Law'* (2nd edition, Oxford and Portland, Oregon 2012), P8–11, P189–192.

approach is to demonstrate what international standards the Chinese law reform on PFIPs should aim to achieve.

1.5.3 The Comparative Approach

The comparative approach is the primary methodology used in this book. It includes the comparison between the Legislative Guide and Model Provisions made by UNCITRAL and other international agreements to indicate why the Legislative Guide and Model Provisions provide most appropriate guide to Chinese law reform on PFIPs; the comparison between the draft and final versions of the Legislative Guide and Model Provisions to explain the background and the meaning of the recommendations; the comparison between British laws and other countries' laws on PFIPs to explain why British law is chosen as a supplement; the comparison between the recommendations in the Legislative Guide and Model Provisions and current Chinese laws on PFIPs to establish the defects in Chinese laws. This approach best establishes the most suitable provisions for the reform of Chinese legislation on PFIPs.

The cases from both China and other countries are compared as well. The data and cases pertaining to Chinese PFIPs will be sourced from the database established by the China Construction Department, which is open to public. Some additional data will be taken from the websites of the companies acting as concessioners in PFIPs. The comparison of the successful cases and failed cases can establish the defects of Chinese laws on PFIPs. The data and cases pertaining to PFIPs in other countries will be sourced from the databases established by the World Bank,[82] which always plays a lender role in PFIPs or Public-Private Infrastructure Advisory Facility (PPIAF)[83] which has sponsored and assisted the organization of UNCITRAL Colloquia on PFIPs.[84] It will compare the impact of the various regulations in other countries by referencing particular cases.

---

[82]The World Bank is a vital source of financial and technical assistance to developing countries around the world. It provide low-interest loans, interest-free credits and grants to developing countries for a wide array of purposes that include investments in education, health, public administration, infrastructure, financial and Private Sector development, agriculture and environmental and natural resource management.

[83]The Public-Private Infrastructure Advisory Facility (PPIAF) was created in 1999 to act as a catalyst to increase Private Sector participation in emerging markets. It provides technical assistance to governments to support the creation of a sound enabling environment for private service provision.

[84]UNCITRAL Colloquia on Privately Financed Infrastructure: Legal Framework and Technical Assistance, 2–4 July 2001, Vienna.

1.6 Outline of the Book

This book considers how to reform current Chinese laws on PFIPs to facilitate their development in China, by transplanting the Legislative Guide and Model Provisions made by UNCITRAL into Chinese legislation.

This book consists of eight chapters. Following this chapter as an introduction, Chap. 2 demonstrates that current Chinese legislation is not consistent with the development of PFIPs in China and a reform is needed. Chapter 3 demonstrates that the Legislative Guide and Model Provisions made by UNCITRAL is the best international regulation to guide the reform of Chinese legislation on PFIPs. Chapter 4 discusses how to reform Chinese legislation on PFIPs in terms of general legislative and institutional framework. Chapter 5 discusses how to reform Chinese legislation on PFIPs in terms of concessioner selection. Chapter 6 discusses how to reform Chinese legislation on PFIPs in terms of the project agreements involve in PFIPs. Chapter 7 discusses how to reform Chinese legislation on PFIPs in terms of the settlement of disputes. Chapter 8 will conclude this book.

1.6.1 Chapter 1 Outline

This chapter is gives the aim and objectives of the book at the beginning. After illustrating the definition and analysing the feasibility of the PFIPs, the research questions which will be answered in the book are listed in this chapter and given detailed explanation. Contributions of the book are displayed to show the significance and importance of the research. This chapter also refers to the methodologies used and outlines how the book will proceed at the end.

1.6.2 Chapter 2 Outline

Chapter 2 focuses on China. This chapter includes four issues:

- It examines whether the PFIP model benefits the development of China.
- It considers whether current Chinese laws on PFIPs are appropriate to protect PFIPs from standard risks.
- It examines whether Chinese politics, judiciary and market are mature enough to accept law reforms on PFIPs.
- It considers the aims of Chinese law reform on PFIPs are expected.

1.6.3 Chapter 3 Outline

Chapter 3 focuses on UNCITRAL. This chapter includes three issues:

- It analyses and discusses the international agreements made by other international organizations (WTO, OECD, World Bank) and the treaties between China and other countries, to point out why they could not provide the guidelines for Chinese law reform on PFIPs.
- It gives the background of UNCITRAL and its Legislative Guide and Model Provisions. Moreover, it explains why this book chooses the Legislative Guide and Model Provisions[85] made by UNCITRAL to provide the guidelines for Chinese law reform on PFIPs.
- It analyses and discusses the reasons why the other countries' laws[86] are used as a supplementary reference, and the reasons why they are just used as a supplementary reference, rather than as the guidelines for Chinese law reform.

1.6.4 Chapter 4 Outline

Chapter 4 discusses how the general legislative and institutional frameworks on PFIPs should be reformed in China, with reference to the Legislative Guide and Model Provisions made by UNCITRAL[87] and supplemented by reference to laws in other countries.[88] This includes six recommended changes to current frameworks.

- The flexibility principle and concise principle: there should be optional use of the recommendations in the Legislative Guide and Model Provisions, rather than their wholesale adoption into Chinese law reform on PFIPs.
- The structure of the Legislative Guide and Model Provisions could also be applied to new Chinese legislation.
- Transparency. On the one hand, it requires that laws and administrative procedures should offer clear and readily accessible laws and efficient procedures. On the other hand, it requires that laws and administrative procedures should force the Public Sector to publish information on decisions. The Beijing Regulations[89] in

[85]The Legislative Guide, Introduction and Background information on PFIPs, paras 1–76; UNCITRAL Commission 34th Session: 25 June–13 July 2001, Vienna, A/CN.9/488—Possible work on privately financed infrastructure projects: show the source and aim of Model Provisions.

[86]Such as British laws, EU laws and so on.

[87]The Legislative Guide, recommendation 1–11 and chap. I, General Legislative and Institutional Framework; Model Provisions, Chap. I on General Provisions, Model provision 1–4 on Preamble.

[88]The British regulations about the regulatory institutions; The British special regulations about the customer protection by Consumer Council for Water (CCWater).

[89]Beijing Regulation is the most typical provincial regulation on PFIPs in China. At the moment, most provincial regulations on PFIPs in China are established following its framework. Therefore, it is chosen as the template in this book. The Urban Infrastructure Concession Regulation of Beijing

China is used as an example to show the defects in transparency in current Chinese law.

- Fairness. It requires a balance between public interest, private interest and customer interest. China has an unreasonable "public interest precedence principle" and has no concern for customer interest.
- Long-term sustainability. On the one hand, it requires the legislation to ensure that the host country has the institutional capacity to undertake the various tasks entrusted to public authorities involved in infrastructure projects throughout their phases of implementation. On the other hand, it requires the legislation to ensure marketization to achieve a correct balance between competitive and monopolistic provision of public services. The model provisions about regulatory institutions are not sufficient in the Model Provisions.[90] Therefore, the Chinese reform on the regulatory institution should make reference to the model in Britain.[91]
- Eliminating undesirable restriction. This requires the elimination of undesirable restrictions on Private Sector participation in infrastructure development and operation. The chapter therefore discusses three Chinese laws on PFIPs which make undesirable restrictions—the Constitution, the Land Law and the Foreign Exchange Law.

1.6.5 Chapter 5 Outline

Chapter 5 discusses how the concessioner selection procedures of PFIPs should be reformed in China, with reference to the Legislative Guide and Model Provisions made by UNCITRAL[92] and supplementary reference to other countries.[93]

- The pre-selection stage should be fair and transparent. There are two matters at stake: One is whether an infrastructure project is needed. The other is whether a private investor should be allowed to access the infrastructure projects. The Legislative Guide and the Model Provisions[94] do not consider how the law authorizes private investors to access the host countries' markets, so EU regulations are consulted here to discuss the best way to reform Chinese law.

Municipality, passed on Dec. 1, 2005 by the People's Congress of Beijing Municipality, effective on March 1, 2006. Hereafter referred to as "the Beijing Regulation".

[90]The Legislative Guide, recommendation 7–11 and Chap. I, General Legislative and Institutional Framework, E on Authority to regulate infrastructure service paras 30–53. But the regulatory institution is not referred in the Model Provisions at all.

[91]The British regulatory institutions on PFIPs include: OGC(Office of Government Commerce) issue the regulation and policies on PFIPs; PUK (Partnership UK) and PRG (Project Review Group) give supporting on finance; GP (Gateway Process), DA (District Audit) and 4P(The Public Private Partnership Programmer Ltd.) regulate PFIPs.

[92]Model Provisions, chap. II on Selection of the concessioner, Model provision 5–27; the Legislative Guide, recommendation 14–39 and chap. III on Selection of the concessioner.

[93]EU regulations on market access are used as supplemental reference.

[94]Neither the Legislative Guide nor the Model Provisions refer to the pre-selection stage.

- The private concessioner selection procedure should be based on fair and transparent competition. PFIPs require not only fairness and transparency, but also economy and efficiency. Concomitantly, the laws should provide suitable regulations on its competitive selection procedure. There is no specific selection procedure for the concessioner of PFIPs in China, but the general selection procedures in bidding[95] and procurement[96] are used. However, in certain circumstances, concessions may be awarded without competitive procedure. The law should clarify these exceptional circumstances to ensure the fairness and transparency of the procedure.
- After a concessioner is selected, disputes on the selection result or procedure should be settled properly. In order to safeguard proper adherence to the rules governing the selection procedure, bidders should have the right to seek a review of the actions by the contracting authority that are in violation of those rules, or of the rights of bidders.
- As an exception from the general concessioner selection procedure, there is a special selection procedure, i.e. unsolicited proposal. In China, there is no procedure whereby unsolicited proposals may be acknowledged and accepted. It is worth considering the applicability of unsolicited proposal, and this book offers a hypothesis of the role of this for the future in Chinese Law.

1.6.6 Chapter 6 Outline

Chapter 6 discusses how the relevant laws on the agreements involved in PFIPs should be reformed in China, with reference to the Legislative Guide and Model Provisions.[97]

- The legal framework for PFIPs includes four kinds of agreements. The project agreement is the core agreement and may restrict the other three kinds of agreements—finance agreement, user agreement and subcontracting agreement. At the same time, the other three kinds of agreements may also affect each other.
- The Legislative Guide and the Model Provisions consider that the content of project agreement should be flexible enough to negotiate, but that there may be some mandatory orders to limit the flexibility in drafting the project agreement. Six issues in project agreement are discussed: Organization of the project company;

[95]The Bidding Law of the People's Republic of China, adopted by the Standing Committee of the Ninth National People's Congress at the 11th Session on 30th August, 1999 and effective date at 1st January, 2000.

[96]Government Procurement Law of the People's Republic of China, adopted by the Standing Committee of the Ninth National People's Congress at the 28th Session on 29th June, 2002 and effective date at 1st January, 2003.

[97]The Model Provisions, Model provision 28–48; the Legislative Guide, recommendation 40–68, Chap. IV on Construction and operation of infrastructure: legislative framework and project agreement and Chap. V on Duration, extension and termination of the project agreement.

Real estate (project assets, land, easements); Security interests; Performance guarantee; Protection of customers; Duration, extension and termination.
- The Legislative Guide and Model Provisions suggest that the finance agreement should consider the step-in right of lenders to take over the concession when the previous concessioner cannot continue the project. This suggestion should be considered for Chinese law reform.
- The Legislative Guide and Model Provisions suggest that the subcontracting agreement should consider a possible conflict of interest in the project company when its investor is also the subcontractor. This suggestion should be considered for Chinese law reform.
- The Legislative Guide and Model Provisions suggest that the user agreement should consider extra protection for special customers using the public service. This suggestion should be considered for Chinese law reform.

1.6.7 Chapter 7 Outline

Chapter 7 discusses how the regulations on the dispute settlement of PFIPs should be reformed in China, with reference to the Legislative Guide and Model Provisions[98] and with supplementary reference to other countries.[99]

- The disputes between the contracting authority and the concessioner.[100] It is difficult to define whether the nature of the project agreement in PFIPs is "public" or "private". The Legislative Guide and the Model Provisions recommend a series of methods that range from conciliatory methods to antagonistic methods. However, in practice in China, the public authority often intervenes in this kind of agreement and a lot of disputes are solved by administrative act or Administrative Law.
- The disputes between the concessioner and other participants in PFIPs.[101] The Legislative Guide and the Model Provisions recommend that the settlement of these disputes should be open to agreement by the parties. The current Chinese laws are consistent with the recommendations from the Legislative Guide and the Model Provisions.

---

[98] The Legislative Guide, Chap. VI on Settlement of Disputes; and the Model Provisions accompanied therein, Chap. V on Settlement of Disputes.

[99] The definition of public contract in Britain is broad.

[100] Model Provisions, Chap. V on Settlement of disputes, Model provision 49; the Legislative Guide, recommendation 69 and Chap. VI on Settlement of disputes, paras 3–41
Administrative Reconsideration Law of The People's Republic of China, adopted at the Ninth Meeting of the Standing Committee of the Ninth National People's Congress on 29th April, 1999; amended in accordance with the Decision Amendment Parts of Laws as adopted at the tenth Session of the Standing Committee of the Eleventh National Congress on August 27, 2009.

[101] Model Provisions, Chap. V on Settlement of disputes, Model provision 51; the Legislative Guide, recommendation 70 and Chap. VI on Settlement of disputes, paras 42
Contract Law of the People's Republic of China, adopted at the Ninth National People's Congress 2nd Session on 15th March, 1999, executive at 1st October, 1999: Chapter 7 on Liabilities for Breach of Contracts; Chapter 8 on Other Provisions.

- The disputes involving customers or terminal users.[102] The Legislative Guide and the Model Provisions recommend that, in addition to litigation and arbitration, the host countries should establish special mechanisms for handling claims brought by their customers. China already has the relevant mechanisms.
- This book hypothesises that the parties in PFIPs could establish complete consistency in the arbitration provisions for the various contracts, but that this would be difficult to achieve.

1.6.8 Chapter 8 Outline

Building upon the above analysis and discussion, the last chapter, Chapter 8, will conclude the main findings of the research as regards Chinese legislation on PFIPs. By reconnecting arguments from previous chapters, the conclusion will clearly indicate that: it is the time to reform Chinese legislation on PFIPs; the Legislative Guide and Model Provisions made by UNCITRAL could guide this reform of Chinese legislation on PFIPs; the Chinese legislation reformed with reference to the Legislative Guide and Model Provisions made by UNCITRAL could be improved to facilitate PFIPs in China.

[102] Model Provisions, Chap. V on Settlement of disputes, Model provision 50; the Legislative Guide, recommendation 71 and Chap. VI on Settlement of disputes, paras 43–45
Consumer protection Law of the People's Republic of China, adopted at the Standing Committee of the Eighth National People's Congress at 4th Session on 31st October, 1993 and executive at 1st January, 1994.

Chapter 2
The Necessity of Reforming Chinese Legislation on PFIPs

2.1 Introduction

PFIPs have brought many benefits since they began to be used in China in the 1980s.[1] During this development period, however, some of the challenges facing PFIPs have also become apparent. Many of these challenges could be avoided or remedied through the reformation or improvement of laws. Therefore, it is necessary to reform the Chinese laws on PFIPs. Chinese policies and the Chinese market have also developed and matured. Therefore, it is the proper time to reform and improve the Chinese laws on PFIPs to catch up with international developments in the use of PFIPs and facilitate their use in China.

The aim of this Chapter is to prove that legislative reform on PFIPs in China is necessary and possible, and new laws would facilitate the development of PFIPs in China.

This chapter has four objectives. The first objective is to prove that the private finance of public infrastructure is feasible in China and has brought many benefits to China through reviewing the history of development of PFIPs in China. The second objective is to demonstrate that China needs to reform its current laws on PFIPs by highlighting the shortcomings of the current Chinese laws on PFIPs, which are not strong enough to face the challenges to Chinese PFIPs. The third objective is to examine whether the financial conditions in China are mature enough to start this process of legislative reform. The final objective is to forecast what may be reasonably expected from the new laws. The guidelines to be followed will be analysed in Chap. 3 and the reform necessary to achieve the aims expected will be discussed in detail in Chap. 4 through Chap. 7.

[1] Shen Jiyong, Wang ShouQing, Qiang Maoshan, *'The Political Risks in China's BOT/PPP Project: a case study'*, Chinese Businessmen Investment and Finance, pp 50–56, No. 1, 2005.

S. Liang, *Legal Aspects of Privately Financed Infrastructure Projects (PFIPs) in China*,
https://doi.org/10.1007/978-981-15-6803-9_2

This Chapter consists of four sections. Section 2.2 describes the developing history of PFIPs in China and the benefits brought to China by PFIPs. Section 2.3 states the risks facing PFIPs in China and the shortcomings of current laws on PFIPs, which cannot address these risks. Section 2.4 presents the current conditions in China (politics, judiciary, market), which show that the situation is mature enough to achieve legislative reform. Section 2.5 indicates the aims that the new laws should achieve through the reform, so that the new laws can cope with the development of PFIPs and facilitate them in China.

This chapter answers the first research question—whether China needs to reform its laws on PFIPs to facilitate PFIPs in China. The chapter concludes that it does.

2.2 The Impact of PFIPs in China

Ever since the planned economy in China has begun to transfer to a market economy, most markets in China have allowed private finance sector to enter. With the exception of national defence and some special industries related to the lifelines of the national economy, the infrastructure market has opened up to private finance. The PFIPs model has been developing in China for more than twenty years and been used in various projects.[2] Most PFIPs have been a remarkable success and brought many benefits to China.[3]

2.2.1 The Developing History of PFIPs in China

The following are five examples of typical PFIPs used for various different kinds of infrastructure in different periods. They show that, in China, PFIPs have begun to be used in more and more important large-scale projects and applied to a wider scope of projects. Meanwhile, the legal structures of PFIPs have become more complicated.

---

[2]Qi Xia, Ke Yongjiang,Wang ShouQing, '*Analysis of Critical Risk Factors Causing the Failures of China's PPP Projects*' (2009), China soft science, pp 107–113, (5), 2009.

[3]Chan A.P.C., Chan D.W.M., Yeung J.F.Y., Xu Y.L, Wang S.Q. and Ke Y.J. '*Critical Risk Factors Affecting the Success of PPP Projects in China: A Delphi Study*', Journal of Management in Engineering, ASCE, 2010, 136(5): 484–494.

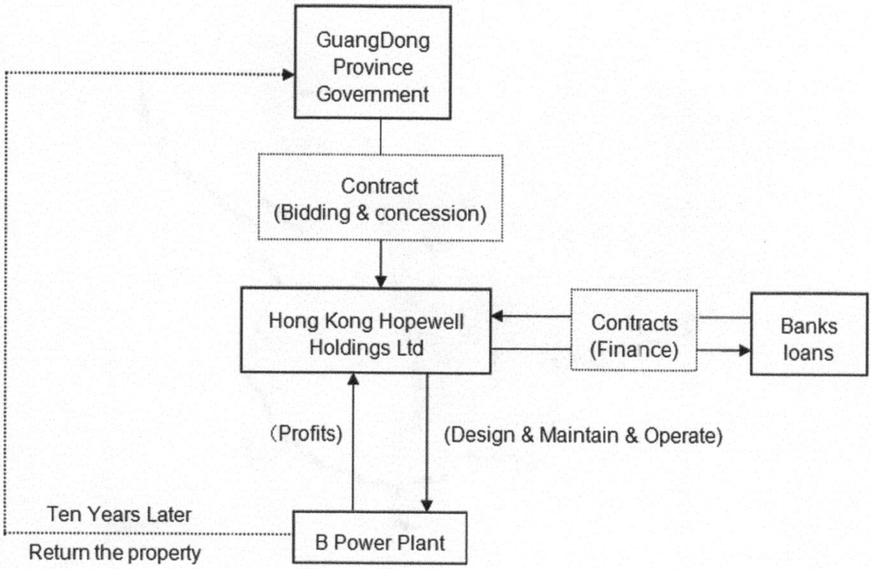

Fig. 2.1 PFIP Legal structure in B Power Plant

2.2.1.1 First PFIP in China: Shajiao B Power Plant

In China, the first infrastructure project to use private investment was the B Power Plant in Shajiao, Guangdong Province, in 1984.[4] This project adopted a BOT structure in which Hong Kong Hopewell Holdings Ltd. financed and constructed the whole project in exchange for the concession to operate the Power Plant for ten years, after which it returned the Plant to the GuangDong Provincial Government in good condition. The legal structure (see Fig. 2.1) in this first Chinese PFIP was based on simple contracts and there was no management or control by relevant regulations or laws on PFIPs. The Fig. 2.1 illustrates that Hong Kong Hopewell Holdings Ltd. was at the core of the project. It made financial contracts with banks to obtain the loan to invest in the B Power Plant. It also made a concession contract with GuangDong Provincial Government to entitle it to design, maintain and operate the B Power Plan and make returns on the profits. Ownership of the B Power Plan passed to the GuangDong Provincial Government after the concession, as per agreement in the concession contract.

[4] Wang Ren Nong, *'Practice and Legal perfection of BOT investment in China'* (2005) Journal of Jinling institute of technology (vol.19 No.4, 2005) 42.

Fig. 2.2 The provinces involved in China's Western Development. *Source:* The website of China Western Development, http://www.chinawest.org.cn/news/show-4328.html accessed on 9th March 2020

2.2.1.2 PFIPs Used in China's Western Development

PFIPs have been widely applied in China's Western Development[5] in the past ten years. At the beginning of this period, the density of rail and road per square kilometre in China's Western Regions was only 1/3rd of the national average. In the Western Regions (see Fig. 2.2), not only was the level of transport infrastructure lower than the national average, but other forms of infrastructure were also backward.[6] Therefore, infrastructure had to be greatly improved before the Western Regions could be

[5]In January 2000, a Leadership Group for China's Western Development was created by the State Council, which marked the start of deploying Chinese western region. The Chinese economy is unbalanced seriously between eastern and western regions. China's western regions includes 6 provinces (Gansu, Guizhou, Qinghai, Shaanxi, Sichuan, and Yunnan), 5 autonomous regions (Guangxi, Inner Mongolia, Ningxia, Tibet, and Xinjiang), and 1 municipality (Chongqing). These regions occupy 71.4% of mainland China's area, which own 82.5% of the nation's total water resource, 36% of the nation's coal reserves, 53% of its natural gas reserves. However, the western regions only have 28.8% of national population in 2002, and only produce 16.8% of national GDP in 2003. GDP per capita in Chinese western regions is only about 2/3 of the national average, even less than 40% of the average of eastern regions. The aim of China's Western Development is to facilitate the development of western economy so that the gap between rich eastern and poor western could be narrowed. Therefore, in this case, enormous infrastructure is demanded in Chinese western region. *'Western development strategy'*, China daily Newspaper (22nd December, 2009) <http://www.chinadaily.com.cn/china/westdevelopment/200‘2/22/content_9215054.htm> accessed on 22nd July, 2019; *'Economy improving in China's west region'*, China daily Newspaper (22nd July, 2013) <http://english.peopledaily.com.cn/90778/8335126.html> accessed on 23rd July, 2019.

[6]Xia Aiping, Li Jianzhong, *'Innovation in infrastructure financing in western area: a PPP pattern'* (2004), Journal of ChongQing Technology and Business University(West Economic Forum), Feb. 2004, pp 75–78.

further developed.[7] As a part of China's Western Development, both domestic private investment and foreign private investment have financed public infrastructure such as roads, rail and hydraulic projects in the Western Regions.[8] It is notable that PFIPs have been successful even in least developed rural areas of the Western Regions, although they were only applied in some small projects.[9] For example, PFIPs were applied in all small-scale irrigation construction in the least developed city—Yan'an. The total investments of approximately 3 million US dollars only involved 1 million US dollars of government finance; the rest came from private finance. The assets belonged to Public Sector in the end, while the concessioners took the right to charge the users and the responsibility to manage, operate and maintain the facilities.[10]

2.2.1.3 PFIP Used in Beijing Olympic Stadium

The most famous PFIP in China is the Olympic stadium, constructed in 2006.[11] It was co-owned by the Beijing State-Owned Assets Management Co. Ltd (BSAM), which represented the Beijing local government and owned 58% of the total assets, and the China International Trust and Investment (CITIC) Consortium, which held the rest of the assets. Composed of BSAM and CITIC, the Special Purpose Vehicle (SPV)[12] in this instance was called the National Stadium Co Ltd. and was responsible for financing, construction, operation and management of the project. CITIC had a post-games concession to operate the stadium for 30 years. It is notable that this PFIP involved a foreign element—the Golden State Holding Group Corporation, which owned 2.1% of the shares in CITIC.[13] The legal structure (see Fig. 2.3) of this PFIP is much more complicated than that of the Shajiao B Power Plant. Firstly, with regard to financial source, the Beijing Olympic Stadium project financed by more than one private investor and they put in their own money as well as bank loans. In this case,

---

[7] Wang Zhou Xi & Zhang Yong, *'Feasibility Analysis of PPP Financing Pattern on Infrastructure Construction in the West Part of China'* (2003) Journal of Northwest Sci-Tech University of Agriculture and Forestry (Social Science Edition).

[8] Ibid.

[9] Guo Rui Ping & Guo Juan-Juan, *'The application and perfection of the PPP Mode in China's western rural infrastructure supply'* (2009), Research on Western Development, May, 2009, pp 19–23.

[10] Guo Rui Ping & Guo Juan-Juan, *'PPP model for the supply of China's western rural infrastructure'* (2009), Journal of Chang'an University (Social Science Edition) (Vol 11 No. 3, Sept 2009).

[11] Beijing National Stadium, <http://www.chinauniquetour.com/arts.asp?place=4&id=5223> accessed on 23rd February, 2020.

[12] SPV (special purpose vehicle): a special purpose entity is a legal entity (usually a limited company of some type or, sometimes, a limited partnership) created to fulfil narrow, specific or temporary objectives. The Project Company as an SPV cannot carry out any other business that is not part of the project. E. R. Yescombe, 'Public-Private Partnerships: Principles of Policy and Finance' (ELSEVIER 2007) P109.

[13] The website of Golden State Holding Group Corporation, <http://www.goldenstate.com.cn/index2.html> accessed on 23rd February, 2020.

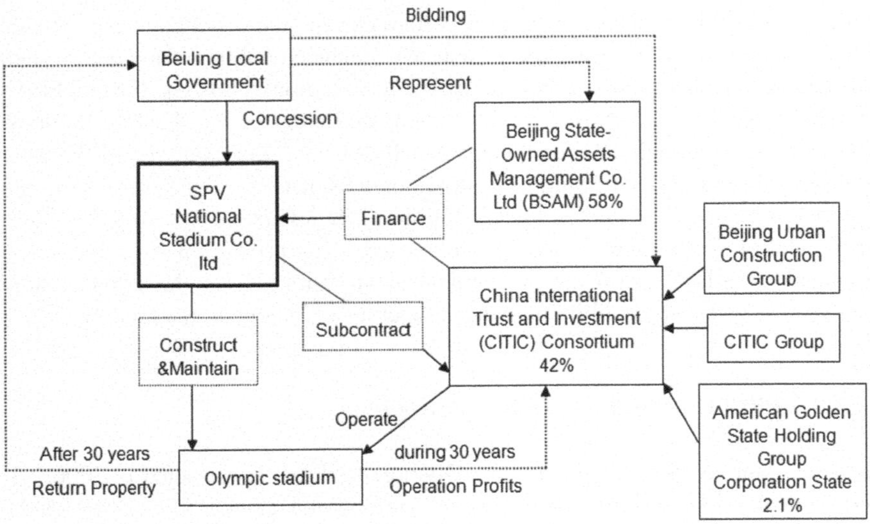

Fig. 2.3 PFIP Legal structure in Olympic stadium

the Beijing Olympic Stadium project had various investors involved. Figure 2.3 illustrates how the National Stadium Co Ltd. was the core in the project. It was financed by BSAM which represented the Beijing local government and CITIC which included many finance sources, such as the CITIC Group itself, the Beijing Urban Construction Group and the American Golden State Holding Group. 42% of the investment was derived from private investors. Secondly, with regard to profit disposition, a number of shareholders were entitled to share profits in Beijing Olympic Stadium project. The National Stadium Co Ltd. obtained concession from the Beijing local government and took the responsibility to construct, maintain and operate the Olympic stadium. Its profits from this project would be shared with its investors in CITIC. The BSAM, which represented the Beijing local government, gave up its share in the profits because the Olympic stadium property would be owned by the Beijing local government after a 30 year concession. Thirdly, with regard to project performance, the National Stadium Co Ltd. did not take all the responsibilities of design, maintenance and operation nor did it assign the responsibilities to other companies. The National Stadium Co Ltd. made a subcontract with CITIC, in which CITIC took responsibility for the operation and got a corresponding payment from the National Stadium Co Ltd. The fact that CITIC obtained the payment from National Stadium Co Ltd. may result in a conflict of interest because CITIC is also one of the investors in National Stadium Co Ltd. This kind of subcontract makes the legal relationships more complicated in this PFIP project and a proper legal framework needs to be in operation to monitor the relationships involved.

2.2.1.4 PFIPs Used in Low-Rent Housing

PFIPs are also used in the emerging Low-rent Housing Plan[14] in China. Private investment finances low-rent housing in various forms. For example, some private investors cover all costs in house construction, own the property and then operate them as low-rent housing (BOO)[15]; some private investors pay all costs for the house construction and operation, but the low-rent housing is returned to the government at the end of the concession (BOT)[16]; some private investors only pay for the operation and maintenance costs of existing state-owned low-rent housing (O&M)[17]; other private investors are initiatives to finance and offer services under relevant regulations and laws (PFI).[18] Although private investors in Low-rent Housing PFIPs may not have large profits, they garner other social benefits such as a reputation for enterprise and the public trust. Figure 2.4 illustrates the various private investment contributions to building public infrastructure in Low-rent Housing Projects by model. Private investors can invest in existing houses, build new houses or re-build or renovate existing houses through various models, such as Service, O&M, BOT, BOO or PFI. Since there is a variable legal structure in Low-rent Housing PFIPs, the Public-Private relationships are different in the infrastructure projects. The Service model, in which the private investor just offers a direct service, involves the lowest level of private investment into public infrastructure buildings. In ascending levels of private investment are the O&M, BOT and BOO models. The PFI model involves the highest level of private finance.

[14]Chinese government offers the minimum living standard houses with very little Charge or without charge to its citizens who are too poor to afford normal rent. It is alike the social housing in Britain, which were built and operated by local councils to supply uncrowded, well-built homes on secure tenancies at reasonable rents to people who cannot afford buying a house. Paul Reeves, *'An Introduction to Social Housing'* (2nd ed, Elsevier Butterworth-Heinemann 2005), P1–3, P245–248.

[15]BOO is similar as the BOT, but the Private Sector owns the facility permanently and is not under an obligation to transfer it back to the contracting authority.

[16]BOT is the fundamental and typical selection. The government grants a Private Sector a concession to build an infrastructure, and operate it during the concession period to cover the cost and reasonable profit, and then to transfer the infrastructure back at the end of the concession period without charge.

[17]O&M (or M&O Maintain and Operation) means the Private Sector finances on the maintenance of the existing infrastructure and then operates the facility to return its cost and reasonable profits during the allowed period.

[18]PFI, a Public Sector body contracts with a Private Sector provider to purchase services it requires on a long-term basis. Typically this will involve the provider in the design, construction, financing and operation of a new capital asset (e.g. a road). On completion of the project, the Public Sector buys the services, but not the capital asset itself.

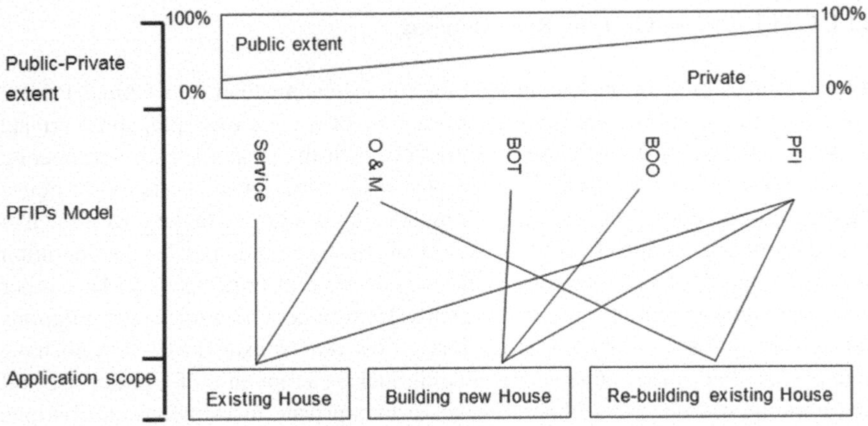

Fig. 2.4 PFIPs Legal structure in Low-rent housing. *Source:* Wang Qian Kun & Wang Shu Qiang, '*Application of PPP pattern in low-rent housing*' (2007), Construction Economy (Vol. 10, No 300, 2007) P27

2.2.1.5 PFIPs Used in Railway Network Plan

According to the requirements in the "Long-term Railway Network Plan",[19] China's railway infrastructure is scheduled to rise from 73,000 km of track at the end of 2003 to 10 million km by 2020. Most of the railway projects have been, and will continue to be, implemented as PFIPs.

To sum up, despite a slowdown after 2008 economic crisis, the PFIP model is continues to be widely applied in China, as illustrated in the following bar chart (Fig. 2.5). As the following pie chart (Fig. 2.6) illustrates, the PFIP model is broadly applied in various infrastructure sectors.

2.2.2 The Benefits Brought to China by PFIPs

With the development of PFIPs in China, the benefits brought to China by PFIPs have risen gradually.

Firstly, PFIPs solve the shortage of government funding for public infrastructure. Private finance played an important role in China's Western Development. Between 2003 and 2008, the investment capital for infrastructure in Western China was 1.2 trillion Yuan (approximately £120 billion), which included capital 61.6% from national finance, 4.6% from foreign investors and 7% from domestic private investors.[20] According to the budget drawn up by the People's Bank of China, the

[19]January 2004, the State Council Standing Committee discussed and adopted the "long-term railway network plan", which is the first industry plan approved by the State Council and is also the railway construction blueprint until 2020.

[20]National Bureau of Statistics of China, '*Basic industries and infrastructure building have brilliant achievements*', published on 15th September, 2009 <http://www.stats.gov.cn/tjfx/ztfx/qzxzgcl60zn/t20090915_402587081.htm> accessed on 24th July, 2013.

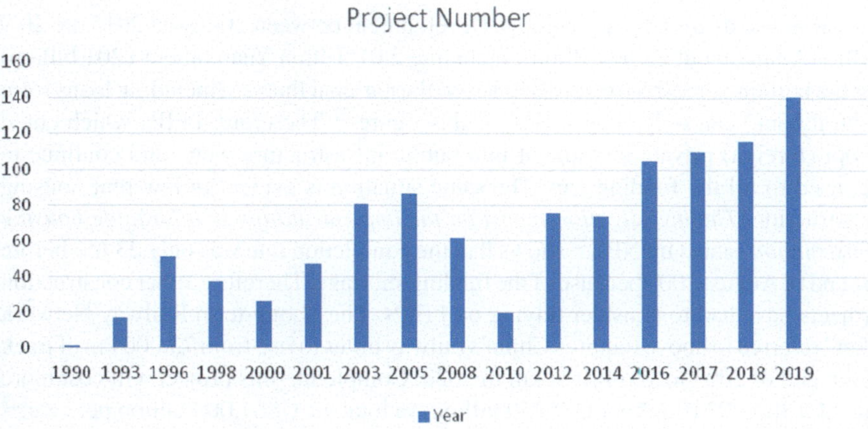

Fig. 2.5 Private Investments in the Chinese Infrastructure Development. *Source:* World Bank (2009), *'Country Snapshots: China. Private Participation in Infrastructure Database'*, http://ppi.worldbank.org/en/snapshots/country/china accessed on 6th March 2020. The data are shown in a table in the website of World Bank and I reform them into a bar chart which is clearer

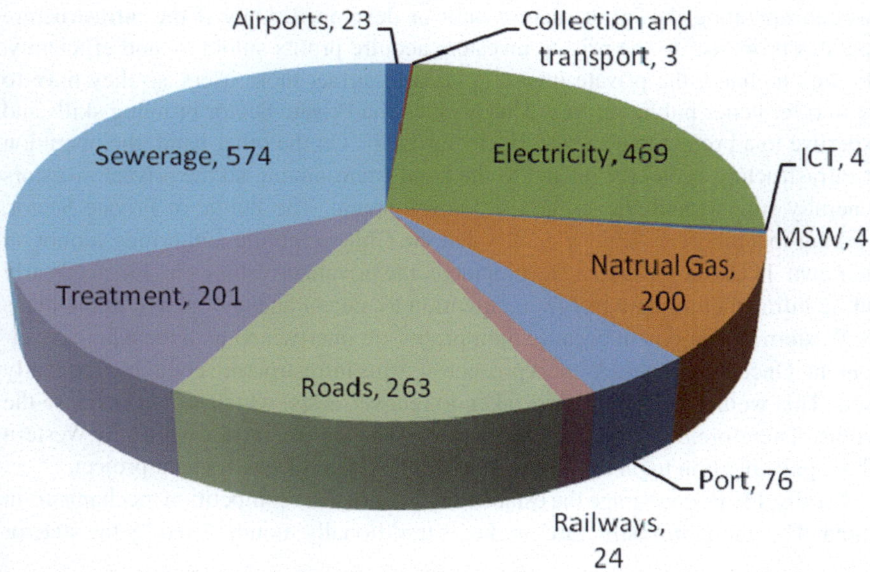

Fig. 2.6 Private Investments in the Chinese various infrastructure sectors until 2019 (project number). *Source:* The data are shown in a bar chart in the website of World Bank and I reform them into a pie chart which is clearer

capital demands for China's Western Development between 2006 and 2015 are 20.9 trillion Yuan (about £2.09 trillion), including 2.01 trillion Yuan (about £201 billion) for the building of infrastructure. However, the national finance (including loans from central bank) can only supply 70% of this figure.[21] Therefore, PFIPs which could adopt (foreign) private investment into public infrastructure were, and continue to be, used to fill the funding gap. The same situation is evident in low-rent housing construction. *The investigation report on the implementation of affordable housing construction* issued by NPC[22] shows that the completion rate was only 23.6% before the end of August 2009 because of the funding shortage. Therefore, other construction projects have had to consider relying on PFIPs. The "Long-term Railway Network Plan" referred to above requires China's railway miles to rise from 73,000 km of track at the end of 2003 to 10 million km in 2020. Completing this project will cost more than 2 trillion RMB (about US$250 billion) in total, or US$1,000 billion per year.[23] Government would find it impossible to fund this huge investment fully. Therefore, PFIPs which can raise private investment are an appropriate way to solve the twin dilemmas of the railway development and funding shortages.

Secondly, PFIPs promote the initiative of private investors in assisting the further development of Chinese public service. Generally, the PFIPs involve a long-term agreement, which allows the private investors to return their costs and get profits through operating the infrastructure built or developed. Only if the infrastructure operates properly, do the private investors acquire profits smoothly and efficiently. On the one hand, the private investors need to attract more users, so they have to try to offer better public service. This leads to the Private Sector bringing skills and expertise to a project that the Public Sector lacks. On the other hand, the operation of infrastructure is closely related to the local environment, so the private investors generally support and encourage local development. The Public or Private Sector, working together, can achieve results that the Chinese public authorities cannot on their own. In China's Western Development, the private investors who financed early public infrastructure may pay more attention to, encourage and adhere to the plans for Western Development because their profits are intertwined with the whole development. Once the Chinese West is prosperous, this infrastructure could be frequently used. This would reduce the time taken to recover costs, which would increase the profits. Therefore, the private investors who finance the infrastructure in Western China pay attention to, and support, the whole Western Development project.

Thirdly, PFIPs encourage the establishment of market competition mechanisms in China. The public infrastructure market is traditionally monopolised by the state or

---

[21] The People's bank of China, *'China's Western Development finance reform survey'* (19th December, 2005), <http://finance.people.com.cn/GB/1037/3952777.html> accessed on 24th July, 2019.

[22] NPC stand for Standing committee of the national people's congress.

[23] January 2004, the State Council Standing Committee discussed and adopted the "long-term railway network plan", which is the first industry plan approved by the State Council and is also the railway construction blueprint until 2020.

SOEs.[24] In PFIPs, there is competition between private investors to win the concession, and public infrastructure projects are implemented by the concessioner who is considered to be the most suitable.[25]

Fourthly, PFIPs promote efficiency and reduce costs. The B Power Plant in Shajiao, Guangdong Province provides a convincing example. This project was completed a year ahead of schedule—in only 22 months—because the private investor, who wanted to be repaid as soon as possible, was efficient in constructing the plant.[26] More importantly, the operation cost of the project was lower than that of the Guangdong State-owned Electricity Grid. There are doubts as to whether the returns for the private investor were too large, but, after an investigation, the Guangdong Provincial Economic Commission concluded that the rate of return was reasonable.[27] First, the private investor used excellent management and operational skills to promote efficiency and reduce costs. Secondly, the risks the concessioner took were equal to the rate of return, since a one year extension of the project would have reduced the rate of return.[28] Examples such as these have led to the recognition of PFIPs by all levels of government.[29]

Finally, PFIPs can assist in fighting corruption on major infrastructure projects, especially in China. In traditional government procurement, the Chinese government itself finances the projects. Even if the concession of designs, constructions and operations may be awarded to private companies or SOE, it is hard to say whether all funds are used on the project. The statistics of the Supreme People's Procuratorate of the People's Republic of China show that, from September 2009 to March 2011, the amount of money related to corruption in infrastructure projects is 2.99 billion Yuan (about £299 million).[30] However, in the case of PFIPs the Chinese government only monitors and regulates the project construction and operation of private investors, rather than controlling the funding of the infrastructure project. Though the PFIPs model may not prevent bribes or other actions lacking in integrity during the concessioner selection processes or the administration of the contract, at the very least government officials cannot misappropriate public funds which were distributed for these projects. Therefore, the PFIPs model prevents a degree of governmental corruption in infrastructure projects. Additionally, even if the private investor bribes

---

[24]SOEs stand for State-owned Enterprises which is a legal entity created by a government to undertake commercial activities on behalf of an owner government.

[25]Cao Fuguo, 'Regulating procurement of privately financed infrastructure in China: a review of the recent legislative initiatives and the emerging regulatory framework' (2007), Public Procurement law review (P.P.L.R. 2007, 3, 147–173).

[26]The website of Shenzhen Government, <http://www1.szzx.gov.cn/content/2013-04/23/content_8987013_5.htm> accessed on 23rd February, 2020.

[27]Ibid.

[28]Ke Y.J., Wang S.Q. and Chan A.P.C. *'Risk Allocation in Public-Private Partnership Infrastructure Projects: Comparative Study'*, Journal of Infrastructure Systems, 16(4): 343–351.

[29]Ibid.

[30]The Supreme People's Procuratorate of the People's Republic of China, *'Report on 20 typical corruption cases on infrastructure projects'* (18th May, 2011), <http://news.xinhuanet.com/politics/2011-05/17/c_121426712.htmaccessed> on 25th July, 2019.

the government officials or the private investors suffer from the extortion of bribes during the selection processes or the administration of the contract, it may be easier for the Anti-Corruption Department to cooperate with the private investors in PFIPs, who wish to protect their capital and their long-term interests, than the SOE,[31] who may be inclined to conspire with government officers.[32]

2.3 The Shortcomings of China's Current Laws on PFIPs

In China, not all PFIPs have achieved the successes of the cases detailed in Sect. 2.1. As PFIPs have developed and become longer, larger and more complicated, some PFIPs have failed because of the various risks facing them, causing losses to both the Public and Private Sector. However, some of these risks are caused by the shortcomings of the current Chinese laws on PFIPs. Some of these risks could be reduced or avoided by improving the laws, and others could be remedied afterwards by enhancing provisions in existing laws. In other words, the current Chinese laws are insufficient to protect PFIPs from these risks, so it is necessary to reform Chinese laws on PFIPs.

2.3.1 Chinese Laws on PFIPs

Although China's current laws on PFIPs are not perfect, the relevant regulations and laws have been improving.

The first Chinese PFIP—B Power Plant in Shajiao, Guangdong Province in 1984—was based on simple contracts. The modern Contract Law of the People's Republic of China had not been issued at that point. Therefore, it seems that the contracts in the first Chinese PFIP were regulated under the People's Republic of China on Economic Contract Involving Foreign Interest and the Economic Contract Law of the People's Republic of China.[33] However, neither statute could properly regulate the contracts in the project. The former one only regulates economic enterprises rather than Public Sector.[34] The latter only regulates contracts without foreign elements. As a matter of fact, there was no law or regulation to monitor or manage the first PFIP.

[31] In China, the government senior officers are usually appointed to the senior executives in State-owned Enterprises to ensure the SOE under control of government. Therefore, the government and the SOEs have interest binding more or less.

[32] Avina Jeffrey, *'Public-Private Partnerships in the fight against crime: an emerging frontier in corporate social responsibility'* (Journal of Financial Crime 2011)P282.

[33] Both of them were repealed in 1999 and replaced by Contract Law of the People's Republic of China.

[34] The People's Republic of China on Economic Contract Involving Foreign Interest 1985, expired in 1999:

A number of laws and regulations relevant PFIP were issued in the decade following that of the first PFIP case. Relevant laws included:

Guarantee Law issued on 30th June 1995[35]
Contract Law issued on 15th March 1999[36]
Bidding Law issued on 30th August 1999[37]

Relevant legal documents included[38]:

Circular Concerning the Issues of Absorbing Foreign Investment through BOT issued in 1995[39]
Circular Concerning the Issues of the Approval and Administration of Experimental Foreign-invested Concession Projects issued in 1995.
Temporary Provisions of the Ministry of Construction on Utilizing Foreign Capital in Municipality Public Utilities issued in 2000.

Over this period, PFIPs could be regulated by general laws but there were still no specific provisions for PFIPs. Although the first legal document on PFIPs—Circular Concerning the Issues of Absorbing Foreign Investment through BOT—was issued in 1995, it was only a principle to attract foreign investment and had no specific legal provisions.

Article 2: This Law shall apply to economic contracts concluded between enterprises or other economic organizations of the People's Republic of China and foreign enterprises, other economic organizations or individuals.......

[35]The Guarantee Law of the People's Republic of China, adopted at the 14th Meeting of the Standing Committee of the Eighth National People's Congress of the People's Republic of China on June 30, 1995, and shall enter into force as of October 1st, 1995:
Article 2: This Law is enacted with a view to promoting the accommodation of funds and the circulation of commodities, ensuring the enforcement of creditor's rights and developing the socialist market economy.

[36]The Contract Law of the People's Republic of China, adopted and Promulgated by the Second Session of the Ninth National People's Congress on March 15th, 1999:
Article 3 Contract parties enjoy equal legal standing and neither party may impose its will on the other party.
Article 8 A lawfully formed contract is legally binding on the parties. The parties shall perform their respective obligations in accordance with the contract, and neither party may arbitrarily amend or terminate the contract. A lawfully formed contract is protected by law.

[37]The Bidding Law of the People's Republic of China, adopted by the Standing Committee of the Ninth National People's Congress at the 11th Session on August 30, 1999, and shall enter into force as of January 1st, 2000:
Article 3 Bidding shall be carried out for the following construction projects, including the survey, design, construction, supervision of the project, and the procurement of the important equipment, materials relevant to the construction of the project: (1) large projects of infrastructure facility or public utility that have a bearing on the social public interest and the safety of the general public.......

[38]Ke Yongjian, Wang Shouqing & Chan Albert PC, *'Public-private partnerships in China's infrastructure development: lessons learnt'* <http://www.changingroles09.nl/uploads/File/Final.Ke-Wang-Chan.pdf> accessed on 25th July, 2019.

[39]It is the first Chinese legal document specific on PFIPs.

When the Chinese Western Development started in 2000, more legal documents facilitating PFIPs were issued, adding to the above laws and legal documents, and some of them even focused on the Western Development.

Relevant legal documents included[40]:

2001 Several Opinions of the State Development Planning Commission concerning the Promotion and Guidance of Private Investment

2002 Notice of the General Office of the State Council on the Relevant Issues concerning the Appropriate Handling of the Existing Projects Guaranteeing the Fixed Return from Investments by Foreign Parties
2002 Opinions of the Ministry of Construction on Accelerating the Marketization of Urban Utilities
2004 Administrative Measures on the Concession of Municipal Public Utilities
2004 Decision of the State Council on Reforming the Investment System

Some legal documents on PFIPs focused on Western Development:

2008 The notice on the technology policy and technical guidelines on the environmental infrastructure in small towns in Western China[41]
2010 Central and western regions of infrastructure project loan interest subsidy management[42]

In this period, Chinese legislation started to confirm the position of private investment in infrastructure projects. However, even if some legal documents were issued for PFIPs in China's Western Development, PFIPs in general have not received any specific legislation yet.

When the Olympic stadium was built in 2006, the PFIPs were supported by further legal documents and many provincial regulations on PFIPs were passed.

Relevant legal documents included[43]:

2005 Several Opinions of the State Council on Encouraging, Supporting and Guiding the Development of Individual and Private Economy and Other Non-Public Sector of the Economy

Provincial regulation on PFIPs[44]:

2005 Local administrative measures on the concession of municipal public utilities in Hu'nan, Shanxi, Hefei, Wuhan, Shenzhen, Beijing,[45] etc.

---

[40](n 38).

[41]The notice on the technology policy and technical guidelines on the environmental infrastructure in small town of Chinese western, issued by the Ministry of Housing and Urban-Rural Development of the People's Republic of China (MOHURD) on 13th November, 2008.

[42]Central and western regions of infrastructure project loan interest subsidy management, issued by the Ministry of Finance of the People's Republic of China on 15th March, 2010.

[43](n 38).

[44](n 38).

[45]Beijing Urban Infrastructure Concession Regulation 2005.

During this period, provincial regulations on PFIPs were passed in some provinces. However, there was no national legislation on PFIPs.

The Chinese laws and regulations on PFIPs have kept improving.

2008 Research Reports of PPP Legislation in Infrastructure Development
2010 Several Opinions of the State Council on Further Doing a Good Job in the Utilization of Foreign Investment[46]
2010 The opinions on encouraging and guiding the healthy development of private investment[47]
2012 The opinion on encouraging and guiding private capital investment into railways[48]
2012 The notice on encouraging and guiding the healthy development of private investment management issues relating to foreign exchange[49]
2012 The notice on encouraging private capital to participate in the construction of low-rent housing projects[50]
2017 The notice of the Ministry of Finance, the Ministry of Housing and Urban-Rural Development, the Ministry of Agriculture, and the Ministry of Environmental Protection on Comprehensive Implementation of Public-Private Partnership in Sewage and Waste Treatment Projects Participated in by the Government
2019 The notice of the National Development and Reform Commission on Legally Strengthening the Administration of Investments in and Construction of PPP Projects

In this period, Chinese legislation made further efforts to encourage private investment into public infrastructure but most of them were issued by departments of government rather than national legislation.

[46]Several Opinions of the State Council on Further Doing a Good Job in the Utilization of Foreign Investment, issued by the State Administration for Industry & Commerce of the People's Republic of China on 7th May, 2010.

[47]The opinions on encourage and guide the healthy development of private investment, issued by State Council on 7th May, 2010.

[48]The opinion on encourage and guide private capital investment in railway, issued by the Ministry of Railways on 16th May, 2012.

[49]The notice of encourage and guide the healthy development of private investment management issues relating to foreign exchange, issued by State Administration of Foreign Exchange on 11th June, 2012.

[50]The notice of encourage private capital to participate in the construction of low-rent housing projects, issued by Ministry of Housing and Urban-Rural Development of the People's Republic of China (MOHURD) on 20th June, 2012.

2.3.2 *The Shortcomings*

In China, there is still no national or sectoral legislation governing the awarding of concessions or the supervision of the operation in PFIPs.[51] In certain provinces, there may be provincial regulations on PFIPs, but they are only valid in corresponding provinces, i.e. the regulation is only applied and valid to the PFIPs in the province where the local government made it.[52] Some negative consequences have arisen due to there being only provincial regulations to regulate the behaviour of PFIPs in China.

2.3.2.1 Instability

The current Chinese laws on PFIPs are unstable.

Provincial regulation is much easier to change than national legislation. In China, national legislation must be approved by more than half of the members of the National People's Congress (NPC),[53] whereas provincial regulation is issued and altered by the provincial government. Sometimes provincial regulations are changed, following a decision by central government or a change in national law.[54] This means the regulations issued by provincial governments may be unreliable, and the subsequent change in regulations may result in the failure of PFIPs. Long-term PFIPs are particularly prone to risk from changes in the laws. The adoption, issuance and modification of laws may happen after the signature date of the project agreement, which may suspend or terminate the projects. For example, since "Notice of the General Office of the State Council on the Relevant Issues concerning the Appropriate Handling of the Existing Projects Guaranteeing the Fixed Return from Investments by Foreign Parties" was issued in September 2002, those existing projects with a promised fixed rate of return from local government were forced into "modification", "purchase", "transfer" or "cancellation" on the basis of the particulars of the concerned project.[55]

---

[51] Cao Fuguo, 'Regulating procurement of privately financed infrastructure in China: a review of the recent legislative initiatives and the emerging regulatory framework' (2007), Public Procurement law review (P.P.L.R. 2007, 3, 147–173).

[52] e.g. Urban Public Utilities Concession Regulation, issued by the province Shenzhen of China in 2004; Urban Infrastructure Concession Regulation, issued by the province Beijing of China in 2005; Public Utilities Concession Regulation, issued by the province Xinjiang of China in 2005.

[53] The Constitution of the People's Republic of China, adopted on March 14, 2004

Article 64: …Statutes and resolutions are adopted by a majority vote of more than one half of all the deputies to the National People s Congress….

[54] If the provincial government amend the provincial regulations, it should be approved by a majority vote of more than on half of all the deputies to the Provincial people's Congress. However, the provincial regulation have to be repealed immediately once it contradict with national legislation.

[55] Wang S.Q. (2006), *"Lessons learnt from the PPP practices in China (keynote speech)"*, Asian Infrastructure Congress 2006, organized by Terrapinn and sponsored by IAPF, Hong Kong, 29–30th Nov, 2006.

2.3.2.2 Contradiction

The current Chinese laws on PFIPs are contradictory at times.

Different provincial regulations on PFIPs may result in different laws being applied to the same project in different provinces. Infrastructure such as road and rail is often constructed a part of cross-provincial projects, which means they may be under the jurisdictions of different provinces. The cross-provincial PFIPs may fail because of the divergence between local regulations.[56] For example, the opening of toll gates that interlink provinces should be decided by negotiation between the related provincial governments. However, the negotiations may fail. Although the Transportation Department under the State Council could mediate between the provinces and make a final decision, this would still delay the project.[57] It is difficult and unnecessary to judge which provincial regulation is right and it is unreasonable to use different regulations in different parts of the same project. This means the private company who is the concessioner has to follow different regulations and pay higher costs.

2.3.2.3 Ambiguity

The provincial regulations on PFIPs in China are not comprehensive and not specific about all aspects of PFIPs.

The procedure on PFIPs is not clear, and the rights and responsibilities of the parties in PFIPs are not clear either. To take the Urban Infrastructure Concession Regulation (Beijing) of 2005 as an example[58] (hereafter referred to as "Beijing Regulation"), the provincial regulations are often general and ignore many matters pertaining to PFIPs.

Firstly, although some provisions refer to the selection procedure of the concessioner, the selection procedure is vague and requires the consultation of other laws. Article 11 of the Beijing Regulation provides that concessioner shall be selected by such competitive procedures as bidding.[59] This indicates that a bidding procedure may be preferred, in which case the Chinese Bidding Law will automatically apply.

---

[56] Cao Fuguo, 'Regulating procurement of privately financed infrastructure in China: a review of the recent legislative initiatives and the emerging regulatory framework' (2007), Public Procurement law review (P.P.L.R. 2007, 3, 147–173).

[57] Highway Law of the People's Republic of China 1998, Article 64.

[58] Beijing Regulation is the most typical provincial regulation on PFIPs in China. At the moment, most provincial regulations on PFIPs in China are established following its framework. Therefore, it is chosen as the template in this book. The Urban Infrastructure Concession Regulation of Beijing Municipality, passed on Dec. 1, 2005 by the People's Congress of Beijing Municipality, effective on March 1, 2006.

[59] Article 11 of the Beijing Regulation.

However, "other" procedures may also be employed, provided they are "competitive", such as Government Procurement Law.[60] The Beijing Regulation does not provide further details for the "other" competitive procedures, so the procedure may be competitive negotiation. Since the Beijing Regulation simply says nothing on this point, it leaves too much scope for the details to be ascertained. The long selection procedure may result in the failure of PFIPs.[61] Even if the relevant laws could be ascertained, the general competitive procedures may not be appropriate rules of selection, given the features of specific PFIP concessioners.

Secondly, although the regulations have provided mandatory provisions on the obligations and rights of the Public and Private Sector, they are a very general legal framework and some specific aspects on PFIPs have not been considered or considered in detail. The Beijing Regulation has no provision regulating subcontracting, which is common in PFIPs. Additionally, government is required to compensate for the losses suffered by the concessioner if the interest of legitimate expectation of the concessioner is prejudiced due to a change in government policy,[62] but this method of compensation has not been regulated.

2.3.2.4 Poor Protection on Private Investors

The private investors in PFIPs do not have adequate legal protection in China.

The private investors may lose their reasonable interests because of political risks: These risks may include poor political decision-making processes, public/political opposition, government unreliability and corruption.[63] For example, in the Qingdao VEOLIA Wastewater project, the negotiation took a long time because Qingdao local government frequently changed their minds. The government agreed at first to quite a high off-take price[64] but later wished to re-negotiate this with Veolia.[65] Another example is the Beijing No. 10 Water Plan Project. The reasonable proposal of raising Beijing water prices was rejected by local government because of social stability and

---

[60] The Bidding Law of China does not provide for procedures other than the formal bidding procedures, and while in contrast the Chinese Government Procurement Law does provide more procurement procedures such as competitive negotiation, among others, it only governs project procurement which is financed by state budget.

[61] Cao Fuguo, *'The emerging legal framework for private finance in infrastructure in China: a preliminary review of the Beijing Concession Regulation'* (2006), (P.P.L.R. 62).

[62] Article 30 of the Beijing Regulation.

[63] Ke Yong Jian, Wang Shouqing & Chan Albert PC, *'Public-Private Partnership in China's Infrastructure Development: Lessons Learnt'*, in H. Wamelink, M. Prins & R Geraedlts (eds), Proc. of Int'l Conf. on Changing Roles: New Roles and New Challenges (TU Delft, Faculty of AREH, The Netherlands, Oct 5–9, 2009, pp 177–188).

[64] The price promised to pay for the service produced by the infrastructure.

[65] Asian Development Bank, *'Some important issues and recommendations on marketization (PPP) of China urban water industry'*, under Policy Reform Support project-4095, <http://www.adb.org/projects/30436-012/detailsaccessed> on 25th July, 2019; translate into Chinese on <http://doc.mbalib.com/view/4dfef56bab2c24464666a13add686f50.html> accessed on 25th July, 2019.

public interest considerations. British Anglian Water Corporation, one of the private investors in this project, had to withdraw their investment from this project.[66]

Current Chinese law is weak in relation to protecting private investors from political risks. Current Chinese Contract Law only covers normal civil rights.[67] When the government acts as a negotiating party in PFIPs, Contract Law cannot be applied properly to control the government's behaviour. Once the government delays negotiation on the basis of the public interest, the private investor will be faced with high costs. In order to enhance the investor's confidence, there should be laws to restrict unnecessary delays by the government, or to provide appropriate compensation for the investor's loss. China has no relevant laws or regulations at all in this regard. The Administrative Reconsideration Law[68] and Administrative Procedure Law[69] provide that private investors may require administrative reconsideration of a specific administrative act, but this process causes delay to the project. The loss caused by delay in these cases cannot be calculated or compensated according to current State Compensation Law in China.

Private investors may also lose their profits through economic factors. The risks involve financing risks, insufficient income, competition and market demand. For example, the Beijing Jingtong Expressway could not derive sufficient profits at the start of the project because of adjacent toll-free roads competing and this resulted in an insufficient vehicle flow rate.

Although there is Anti-Unfair Competition Law, its scope does not cover the above situation in relation to PFIPs.[70] To some extent, this state of affairs arises due

[66]Ibid.; Ke yong-jian, Wang Shou-qing, etc., *'Changes of Political Risks in China's PPP Projects'* (The 6th National Civil Engineering Forum for Graduate Students, Tsinghua University2008), <http://myweb.polyu.edu.hk/~bsachan/NSFC/private/documents/publications/2008-PoliticalRisks.pdf> accessed on 25th July, 2019.

[67]The Contract Law of the People's Republic of China, adopted and Promulgated by the Second Session of the Ninth National People's Congress on March 15th, 1999:

Article 2 Definition of Contract; Exclusions

For purposes of this Law, a contract is an agreement between natural persons, legal persons or other organizations with equal standing, for the purpose of establishing, altering, or discharging a relationship of civil rights and obligations.

[68]The Administrative Reconsideration Law of the People's Republic of China 2009;

Article 2 This Law is applicable to a citizen, legal person or any other organization who considers that his or its lawful rights and interests have been infringed upon by a specific administrative act, and applies for administrative reconsideration to an administrative organ which accepts the application for administrative reconsideration, and makes a decision of administrative reconsideration.

[69]The Administrative Procedure Law of the People's Republic of China. adopted at the Second Session of the Seventh National People's Congress on April 4, 1989, promulgated by Order No. 16 of the President of the People's Republic of China on April 4, 1989, and effective as of October 1, 1990

Article 2 If a citizen, a legal person or any other organization considers that his or its lawful rights and interests have been infringed upon by a specific administrative act of an administrative organ or its personnel, he or it shall have the right to bring a suit before a people's court in accordance with this Law.

[70]The Anti-Unfair Competition Law of the People's Republic of China, Adopted by the Third Session of the Standing Committee of the Eighth National People's Congress On September 2nd, 1993

to government awarding extra concessions to other road operators. However, there are currently no the relevant laws to control the government's behaviour in China.

The private investors may also lose their reasonable interests because of *force majeure. Force Majeure* is a circumstance beyond the control of the project developer or government, such as a natural disaster or an accident. For example, the contract negotiation in the Jiangsu Sewage Treatment Plant was forced to be suspended because of the SARS Epidemic in 2003.[71]

The State Compensation Law in China does not mention any compensation provisions under *force majeure.* However, making provision for compensation could enhance the private investor's confidence if China expects to attract more private investment for infrastructure building.

These risks are especially true for foreign private investments, where there are extra restrictions such as foreign exchange control.[72]

Facilitation foreign exchange is essential in encouraging foreign private investors to enter into PFIPs. Foreign exchange control may hinder private investment from other countries. China has many restrictions with foreign exchange and has not allowed for any exemptions in the case of PFIPs.

2.3.2.5 Poor Protection on Public Interest

The public interests in PFIPs are not protected enough by laws in China.

Sometimes the risks to PFIPs are not from the host country, where the infrastructure is to be implemented, but from the concessioners. The PFIPs may fail because of the concessioner in two situations: the first is a serious breach by the concessioner, such as unsatisfactory quality, which leads the public authority to refuse to continue the concession. The second is the bankruptcy of the concessioners. There is the famous case *HuangQiao Pacific Electricity Power Co. LTD* in 2000.[73] HuangQiao Pacific Electricity Power Co. LTD, a project company, financed

---

Article 2 ....

"Unfair competition", in this Law, means activities made by managers who damage the others' legal rights and interests, disturb the order of social economy and violate the provisions of this Law.

71 Ke Yong Jian, Wang Shouqing & Chan Albert PC, *'Public-Private Partnership in China's Infrastructure Development: Lessons Learnt'*, in H. Wamelink, M. Prins & R Geraedlts (eds), Proc. of Int'l Conf. on Changing Roles: New Roles and New Challenges (TU Delft, Faculty of AREH, The Netherlands, Oct 5–9, 2009, pp 177–188).

72 The Regulation of the People's Republic of China on Foreign Exchange Administration (2008 Revision):

Article 8: Foreign currency is prohibited for circulation and shall not be quoted for pricing or settlement in the territory of the People's Republic of China…

Article 14: Purchase of foreign exchange for current account transactions shall be conducted with the designated foreign exchange banks, in accordance with the regulations issued by the State Council on the purchase of foreign exchange and making payments in foreign exchange, upon the presentation of valid documents and commercial bills.

73 Southern Weekly Newspaper, *'BOT failure: HuangQiao Case'* South weekly (GuangDong Province, China, 29th January 2003) page B13.

by Chinese HuangQiao Electricity Power Co. Ltd (US$7.6 million) and Australia Asia-Pacific Electricity Power Co. Ltd (US$8.5 million), was established in 1995 in Tai Xing City, Jiangsu Province, to construct electricity plants to power HuangQiao District. However, before the PFIP was completed, the Australian party withdrew their investment because of conflicts with Chinese partner, which resulted in the breakup of the project company. The projects had to be postponed until a new concession was awarded to a new concessioner.[74]

2.4 The Possibility of Legislative Reform

Given that the current Chinese laws are insufficient to protect PFIPs from the above risks, it is necessary to reform the Chinese laws on PFIPs. As a matter of fact, some essential objective conditions to enable the reform of current laws on PFIPs have been satisfied already, so it is possible to reform the laws.

First of all, Chinese politics is ready to have a law reform on PFIPs. Although China is a communist country, it has gradually allowed private investment to occur and has permitted private capital protection. A law reform on PFIPs would mean the Chinese government would further admit the legal status of private capital in the Chinese infrastructure market. As a matter of fact, the private financing of public infrastructure is greatly encouraged by the Chinese Public Sector. The development of private investment in China has gained support recently, following a series of encouraging political and policy initiatives issued at a central level over the past few years.[75] Although they are not formal legislation documents, they show the intent to remove political barriers, and that private investment is backed by certain legal measures.[76] These changes and improvements are also indicated in *'Doing Business 2013: Smarter Regulations for Small and Medium-Size for Enterprises'*, a report to the World Bank. Although China is in 91st place in the ease of doing business index (a high ranking on the index means the regulatory environment is more conducive to the starting and operation of a local firm), it is the 12th place in

[74]Ibid.

[75]Cao Fuguo, 'Regulating procurement of privately financed infrastructure in China: a review of the recent legislative initiatives and the emerging regulatory framework' (2007), Public Procurement law review (P.P.L.R. 2007, 3, 147–173).

[76]e.g. the Notice on Publishing the Opinions on Promoting and Guiding Private Investment, issued by the then National Planning Commission on December 11, 2001. Some Opinions On Some Policy Measure To Increase The Development Of Service Sectors In The 15th Five Year Period, issued by the then National Planning Commission in January 2002; Opinion On Promoting The Marketization Of Urban Public Utilities, issued by the Ministry of Construction on December 27, 2003; Measures On Urban Public Utilities Concession, issued by MOC in 2004; the Opinions On Encouraging, Supporting And Guiding The Development Of Non-State Sector Economies, issued by the State Council in 2005.

the most-improved economies list.[77] China has been adjusting its policies to catch up with the international developments in PFIPs in order to facilitate them.

Secondly, the Chinese judiciary is ready to have a law reform on PFIPs. China already has laws on PFIPs in some provinces. Although there are only provincial regulations[78] which are only valid in their corresponding provinces and have features which just fit their local requirements, the regulations under review as a whole could contribute to the reform of the legislative framework on Chinese PFIPs.[79] Moreover, the Chinese laws on franchises[80] have apparently gone beyond the phase of case-by-case regulation to a more comprehensive stage of regulation, which could offer useful reference in establishing legislation on PFIPs.

Finally, the Chinese market is ready to have a law reform on PFIPs. Once specific legislation on PFIPs is established, more PFIPs may come into the Chinese infrastructure market. China's infrastructure market is mature enough to accept an increased number of PFIPs, which would be brought by the legislative reform of PFIPs. With the development of the Chinese economy from a planned economy to a market economy, the Chinese infrastructure market has been occupied by private investors, rather than SOEs.[81][82] The market has been opened to private investors, with the exception of some special sectors such as the defence industry.

2.5 The Aims of the Reform of Chinese Legislation on PFIPs

Now that the existing provincial regulations on PFIPs have been assessed and deemed to be defective, and the objective conditions to reform the legislation on PFIPs have

---

[77] World Bank, *'Doing Business 2013: Smarter Regulations for Small and Medium-Size for Enterprises'* (1st June, 2012), <http://www.doingbusiness.org/~/media/GIAWB/Doing%20Business/Documents/Annual-Reports/English/DB13-full-report.pdf> accessed on 17th September, 2019.

[78] e.g. Urban Public Utilities Concession Regulation, issued by the province Shenzhen of China in 2004; Urban Infrastructure Concession Regulation, issued by the province Beijing of China in 2005; Public Utilities Concession Regulation, issued by the province Xinjiang of China in 2005.

[79] Cao Fuguo, 'Regulating procurement of privately financed infrastructure in China: a review of the recent legislative initiatives and the emerging regulatory framework' (2007), Public Procurement law review (P.P.L.R. 2007, 3, 147–173).

[80] e.g. Regulation on the Administration of Commercial Franchises, issued by the State Council in 2007; Measures for the Administration on the Franchise of Municipal Public Utilities, issued by Ministry of Construction in 2004; Administrative Measures for the Information Disclosure of Commercial Franchise, issued by Ministry of Commerce in 2007. Moreover, almost provincial regulations on PFIPs focus on concession rather than all aspects of PFIPs.

[81] SOEs stand for State-owned Enterprises which is a legal entity created by a government to undertake commercial activities on behalf of an owner government.

[82] The state-own enterprises monopolizing the infrastructure market has a lot of problems. E.g. the Beijing 5th Ring Road was provided by a SOE controlled by the Municipal Government based on bank loans. However audit found that the cost for the construction of the road was excessively high and later investigation disclosed a number of corruption cases.

been considered, this section will consider what the new legislation should aim to achieve if the legislation on PFIPs is to be reformed.

2.5.1 Facilitate PFIPs

The new Chinese legislation on PFIPs should facilitate PFIPs in China. It is obvious that legislation plays an important role in promoting private investment in public infrastructure projects. As the UNCITRAL Legislative Guide also points out:

> The law typically embodies a political commitment, provides specific legal rights and may represent an important guarantee of stability of the legal and regulatory regime.[83]

In light of their own specific national circumstances, various countries have drawn up appropriate legislative measures under which PFIPs are awarded and executed. The legislation on PFIPs should ensure that the public infrastructure may be financed by private investors, even foreign private investors. This basic provision is particularly important in China where public services used to be governmental monopolies. Therefore, the first aim of the new Chinese legislation on PFIPs should be to facilitate PFIPs.

2.5.2 Establish a National Comprehensive Legislation

The new Chinese legislation on PFIPs should be a nationally comprehensive legislation. This means three things, outlined below:

2.5.2.1 It Should Be a National Legislation

It should be national legislation rather than provincial regulation. Though some experts consider that "local regulation is more flexible in certain areas",[84] it is a trend in thinking about the development of PFIPs that the features of PFIPs are better decided upon by a unified national legislation on PFIPs than provincial regulations.

Firstly, national legislation is more stable than provincial regulations. National legislation is not easy to change or repeal. PFIPs are mostly long-term projects in which a stable legislative environment is very important. The participants, in particular foreign private investors operating on a certain preferential policy basis,

[83] *'Legislative Guide on Privately Financed Infrastructure Project'* (2001) UNCITRAL (A/CN.9/SER.B/4) (hereafter referred to as the Legislative Guide) p25 Chap. I, General Legislative and Institutional Framework, paras 10.

[84] Broomhill Ray, *'Neoliberal Globalismand The local State: A Regulation Approach'* (Journal of Australian Political Economy No 48).

would be affected if the regulations on PFIPs were changed in the middle of the project.

Secondly, national legislation could resolve conflicts between different provincial regulations. Infrastructure such as road and rail is generally constructed through cross-provincial projects. If the regulations on a single PFIP are different in different provinces, they can cause significant difficulties to concessioners trying to accommodate conflicting provincial regulations. Therefore, a unified national legislation could coordinate between different provinces using the same PFIP.

Thirdly, national legislation could offer better administrative coordination. The Legislative Guide says: "Privately financed infrastructure projects may require the involvement of several public authorities, at various levels of government."[85] Most PFIPs are large-scale projects which need coordination by various levels or bureaus of government, such as the Land and Resources Bureau, the Auditing Bureau, the Quality Control Bureau and so on. Therefore, a unified national legislation clarifying the authority and duties of each Bureau would lead to greater clarity in regulating PFIPs.

2.5.2.2 It Should Be a Comprehensive Legislation on PFIPs

PFIP legislation should be separated from other laws, so that it might focus on all aspects of PFIPs. A comprehensive legislation on PFIPs could offer a clear and competitive selection procedure and clarify the rights and responsibilities of the parties in PFIPs.

Firstly, the comprehensive legislation on PFIPs could offer a competitive selection procedure, which is appropriate for the special features of PFIPs rather than ascertained from the provisions in the Procurement Law or the Bidding Law. The Legislative Guide also says that the domestic laws on competitive selection procedures for the procurement of goods, construction or services may not be entirely suitable for PFIPs. International experience in the award of PFIPs has in fact revealed some limitations of traditional forms of competitive selection procedures.[86]

Secondly, comprehensive legislation on PFIPs, which clarifies the rights and responsibilities among the parties in PFIPs, could ensure the projects run smoothly. For example:

(1) To set out the roles of the different branches of government: the large-scale PFIPs need the co-operation of different government departments and a specific law could clarify the responsibilities and rights of each government branch.
(2) To set out the basis on which a Public Authority may provide support for various project risks, e.g. revenue guarantees; and limit the interference from government.
(3) To provide clarity on investors' rights if the PFIPs contract is terminated early, whether because of default by the Project Company or because the Public

[85]The Legislative Guide, Chap. I, General Legislative and Institutional Framework, paras 23.

[86]The Legislative Guide, Chap. III, on Selection of the concessioner, paras 19.

Authority wants to take the Facility back under the control by the Public Sector. In the latter case, a method of compensation should be offered to the Project Company to defray costs.

(4) To give lenders security in the PFIPs contract.[87]
(5) To confirm specific channels for resolving disputes that may arise.

2.5.2.3 A Contract Version on Project Agreement Could Be Attached

A contract version on project agreement could be attached to the national comprehensive legislation on PFIPs. This contract version would not be mandatory, but parties would be free to adopt it in full or in part with modifications in specific circumstances. This contract version could help to avoid misunderstandings over vague contract terms made by the parties themselves, and offer a generic form to parties to prevent items being omitted through negligence. In this respect, the United Kingdom's approach provides an interesting example. A series of versions of PFIP contracts were published by HM Treasury during 1999 to 2007.[88] The Standardisation of PFI Contracts Version 1 was published in July 1999;[89] the second and third editions were published in September 2002, and April 2004, together with an Addendum in December 2005;[90] and the Standardisation of PFI Contracts Version 4, was published in March 2007.[91] The Standardisation of PF2 Contracts (SoPC), which was issued in December 2012, is the latest version of the standard wording and guidance to be used by Public Sector bodies and their advisors when drafting PF2 contracts. It reflects the new model of contracting for projects for the delivery of infrastructure and services using public private partnerships and replaces Standardisation of PFI Contracts Version 4.[92]

[87] Yescomebe E. R., 'Public-Private Partnerships: Principles of Policy and Finance' (ELSEVIER 2007) P32.

[88] HM Treasure, *'Standardisation of PFI Contracts Version 4'* (March 2007) P1, <https://webarchive.nationalarchives.gov.uk/20130123191515/http://www.hm-treasury.gov.uk/d/pfi_sopc4pu101_210307.pdf> accessed on 26th July, 2019.

[89] Ibid.

[90] Ibid.

[91] Ibid.

[92] HM Treasure, *'Standardisation of PF2 Contracts'* (December 2012), <https://www.gov.uk/government/uploads/system/uploads/attachment_data/file/221556/infrastructure_standardisation_of_contracts_051212.pdf> accessed on 26th July, 2019; Infrastructure UK, *'PF2: A User Guide'* (December 2012), <https://www.gov.uk/government/uploads/system/uploads/attachment_data/file/207382/pf2_userguide.pdf> accessed on 26th July, 2019; The National Archive, <http://webarchive.nationalarchives.gov.uk/20130129110402/http://www.hm-treasury.gov.uk/infrastructure_ppp_contractual.htm> accessed on 26th July, 2019.

2.5.3 Balance the Interests of Private and Public

The new Chinese legislation on PFIPs should balance the interests of the Private and Public Sector. The Legislative Guide says:

> The advice provided in the Guide aims at achieving a balance between the desire to facilitate and encourage private participation in infrastructure projects, on the one hand, and various public interest concerns of the host country, on the other.[93]

The legislator has been greatly concerned that the government may on some occasions be vulnerable to exploitation by private operators seeking excessive profits. In particular, when the host government lacks finance to satisfy public requirements for infrastructures, they may accept unfair agreements, which may harm the public interest, to obtain investment from private investors.[94] This is particularly true when a judicial system is not in place: the regulations are poor, the project implementation process can be easily manipulated and a supervisory system is not yet established. These situations are likely in the Chinese context. Therefore, while it must consider the protection of private interest, the new legislation should also safeguard public interests.

However, although sovereignty and autonomy are important, Chinese legislation on PFIPs should also have the intention of protecting the private investor.

Firstly, the nature of PFIPs means that the private investor is the most important performer. The private investor has to deal with various problems in the design, construction and operation of the project. Moreover, the foreign private investor has to face more complex problems in China, such as material import custom duties and foreign exchange control.[95] Therefore, the legislation should offer more protection to private investors. It should deal with these specific problems for foreign private investor.

Secondly, the private investor needs more legislative protection because it is more vulnerable than the Chinese government. The public authority, which makes regulations and has administrative power, is the most powerful party in Chinese PFIPs. The private investor who commences PFIPs needs the concessions of the public authority and will be monitored even after it wins the concession.

Foreign private investors may be more vulnerable than local private investors. Although all private investors have similar concerns regarding public authorities,

---

[93] The Legislative Guide, Introduction and Background information on PFIPs, paras 4.

[94] Ke Y.J., Wang S.Q. and Chan A.P.C. '*Risk Allocation in Public-Private Partnership Infrastructure Projects: Comparative Study*', Journal of Infrastructure Systems, 16(4): 343–351.

[95] Regulations on the Foreign Exchange System of The People's Republic of China, adopted on 1st August, 2008:

Article 8: Foreign currency is prohibited for circulation and shall not be quoted for pricing or settlement in the territory of the People's Republic of China…

Article 14: Purchase of foreign exchange for current account transactions shall be conducted with the designated foreign exchange banks, in accordance with the regulations issued by the State Council on the purchase of foreign exchange and making payments in foreign exchange, upon the presentation of valid documents and commercial bills.

local private investors have more ways of protecting themselves than foreign private investors. The local private investors usually interact with the public authority in other areas of business, and they can even sometimes affect the decisions of the public authority through their personal impact. By contrast, foreign private investors may encounter discrimination in comparison with the local private investors. Even if foreign private investors try to obtain help from their home countries, it is impossible for these countries to intervene directly. They may only provide diplomatic support.

Compared with other parties in PFIPs, the private investor is lacks protection. The lender, who gives financial support to the investor, has insurance or a mortgage in the case of failure. The final customer, who represents "public interest", is backed by the host country. The private investor may only rely on the protection of legislation.

Thirdly, China is looking for more investment to meet its requirements for infrastructure. Legislation which offers more protection to foreign private investors on PFIPs could attract more foreign investment.

Finally, legislation which pays more attention to protecting foreign private investors will not affect Chinese sovereignty and autonomy. The profits of the foreign private investors are closely tied to the success of the PFIPS. Moreover, the final goal of the foreign private investor is not the ownership of the project but the profits from it.

It is worthy to note whether Chinese legislation on PFIPs should regulate the foreign public authorities and State-owned enterprises which finance Chinese public infrastructures.

The principle of sovereign immunity promotes the functioning of all governments by protecting states from the burden of defending themselves in litigation abroad.[96]

In China, there are no specific regulations on how to deal with sovereign immunity. The Civil Procedure Law of the People's Republic of China only gives a general principle that the solution to issues of sovereign immunity should be consistent with the relevant Chinese laws and the international treaties concluded or acceded to by China.[97] The *Regulations of the People's Republic of China Concerning Diplomatic Privileges and Immunities* only refers to the privileges and immunities of the diplomatic missions in China and their members rather than their sovereign immunity.[98] Thus far, no any case about sovereign immunity has been claimed in Chinese courts,

---

[96]Hill Jonathan & Chong Adeline, *'International Commercial Disputes: Commercial Conflict of Laws in English Courts'* (4th edition, Hart Publishing, Oxford and Portland, Oregon 2010) P28; Martin Dixon, Robert McCorquodale, & Sarah Williams, *'Cases and materials on International law'* (5th edition, Oxford University Press, 2011) P305.

[97]Civil Procedure Law of the People's Republic of China, amended for the second time in accordance with the Decision on Amending the Civil Procedure Law of the People's Republic of China as adopted at the 28th Session of the Standing Committee of the Eleventh National People's Congress on 31st August, 2012:

Article 239: Civil actions brought against a foreign national, a foreign organization or an international organization that enjoys diplomatic privileges and immunities shall be dealt with in accordance with the relevant laws of the People's Republic of China and the provisions of the international treaties concluded or acceded to by the People's Republic of China.

[98]Regulations of the People's Republic of China Concerning Diplomatic Privileges and Immunities, Adopted at the 17th Meeting of the Standing Committee of the Sixth National People's Congress,

so there is no juridical precedence in China. However, according to the international agreements[99] acceded to by China and the cases[100] in which China has claimed in other countries, China's stance in dealing with sovereign immunity is as follows:

China recognizes and supports the principle of sovereign immunity but the state-owned enterprises should be treated separately. Whether or not the state-owned enterprises have sovereign immunity is decided by their status. When the foreign public authorities or State-owned companies enter into the Chinese infrastructure market, if the foreign public authorities or State-owned companies finance the Chinese infrastructure as a general commercial investment, they should be regulated under legislation relating to PFIPs. Conversely, if they represent an effort by the public authority to finance Chinese infrastructure with political or diplomatic aims and without commercial profits, their behaviour should be regulated through diplomatic negotiation.

As the matter of fact, China and the UK share their views on sovereign immunity. After considering the scope of Sect. 20(1) of the State Immunity Act 1978[101] and article 31 of Schedule 1 to the Diplomatic Privileges Act 1964,[102] the UK High Court confirmed sovereign immunity does not extend to commercial activities in Apex Global Management Ltd v Fi Call Ltd and others [2013] EWHC 587 (Ch),[103] and the Court of Appeal re-confirmed the decision in the succedent appeal Al Saud and another v Apex Global Management Ltd [2013] EWCA Civ 642.[104] Therefore,

---

promulgated by Order No. 44 of the President of the People's Republic of China and effective as of September 5, 1986:

Article 1: The present Regulations are formulated for the purpose of defining the diplomatic privileges and immunities of the diplomatic missions in China and their members and facilitating the efficient performance of the functions of the diplomatic missions in China as representing States.

99 Vienna Convention on Diplomatic Relations 1961, done at Vienna on 18 April 1961, entered into force on 24 April 1964 (United Nations, Treaty Series, vol. 500, p. 95.); UN Convention on Jurisdictional Immunity of States and Their Property, adopted by the General Assembly of the United Nations on 2 December 2004, not yet in force, See General Assembly resolution 59/38, annex, Official Records of the General Assembly, Fifty-ninth Session, Supplement No. 49 (A/59/49). Though it is not yet in force but China has acceded on 14th September, 2005.

100 *Bechman v. Chinese People's Republic,* Hague yearbook of international law(1988) P 171, this case was reprinted in Materials on Jurisdictional Immunities of State and their property, United Nations Legislative Series 1982, UN Doc.ST/LEG/SER.B/20, pp 426–427; *Huguang Railway Bond Case,* Theroux, Eugene; Peele, B. T, *'China and Sovereign Immunity: The Huguang Railway Bonds Case',* P129.

101 Section 20(1) of the State Immunity Act 1978 gives the scope of the heads of state. It extends sovereign immunity to a sovereign or other head of state and "members of his family forming part of his household".

102 Article 31 of Schedule 1 to the Diplomatic Privileges Act 1964(transferred from Article 31(1) of the Vienna Convention on Diplomatic Relations) gives the exception of commercial activities.

103 *Apex Global Management Ltd v Fi Call Ltd and others [2013] EWHC 587 (Ch)* concerned a claim of sovereign immunity by two Saudi Arabian princes. The judge dismissed the Princes' applications claiming sovereign immunity from the claims made in Apex's petition.

104 *Al Saud and another v Apex Global Management Ltd [2013] EWCA Civ 642*, the Court of Appeal upheld a High Court decision, dismissing a claim of sovereign immunity made by two Saudi Arabian princes.

in the UK, sovereign immunity does not extend to cover any action relating to an individual's professional or commercial activity outside his official functions.[105]

2.5.4 Embody Marketisation

The new Chinese legislation on PFIPs should embody marketisation, i.e., competition in the market. The Legislative Guide points out:

> For monopolistic situations resulting from legal prohibitions rather than economic and technological fundamentals, the main legislative action needed to introduce competition is the removal of the existing legal barriers.[106]

In China, one limitation that should be removed from concession is the rule granting government the option not to choose to employ the means of concession for infrastructure, but may appoint the SOEs directly without any reasonable reasons. The other limitation that should be removed is the privileges of SOEs that some infrastructure projects, which are not in forbidden areas such as national defence, only award concession to SOEs.[107]

2.5.5 Approach International Standard

The new Chinese legislation on PFIPs should harmonise with international standards. A current report on the 'Quality of Concession Legislation in Early Transition Countries' may present a general scenario and comment:

> In response to this situation, the UNECE, with the support of key international partners, has established an International PPP Centre of Excellence. We are confident that the Centre will take countries to the next stage in PPP development, drawing on materials produced to a consistent and high standard by specialist Centres located all over the world that reflect the excellence in PPPs which countries should aspire to.[108]

Only if the Chinese legislation on PFIPs corresponds with international standards, can it protect foreign investors and attract more foreign investment into Chinese public infrastructure.

---

[105] Olswang LLP, Litigation and arbitration: top things you need to know—April/May 2013(31 May 2013), <http://www.olswang.com/articles/2013/05/litigation-and-arbitration-top-things-you-need-to-know-aprilmay-2013/> accessed on 28th July, 2019.

[106] The Legislative Guide, Introduction and Background information on PFIPs, paras 31.

[107] Cao Fuguo, *'Regulating procurement of privately financed infrastructure in China: a review of the recent legislative initiatives and the emerging regulatory framework'* (2007), Public Procurement law review (P.P.L.R. 2007, 3, 147–173).

[108] European Bank for Reconstruction and Development, *'Funding public infrastructure: challenges and horizons'* (Law in transition online, October 2012), P1 <http://www.ebrd.com/downloads/research/news/lit112_full.pdf> accessed on 28th July, 2019.

2.6 Conclusion

This chapter answers the 1st research question, namely whether China needs to reform its legislation on PFIPs.

First of all, this chapter describes some of the successful PFIPs in China. These cases cover various infrastructures built by PFIPs, since the first project in 1984. The benefits brought to China by PFIPs are summarised by analysing these cases. These benefits demonstrate that the legislation on PFIPs is worth improving because it has brought and will bring benefits to China.

Then, the current Chinese laws and regulations and legal documents on PFIPs are summarised. The existing Chinese regulations are found to be insufficient in reducing or avoiding the risks to PFIPs. Therefore, it is necessary to reform the Chinese legislation on PFIPs; otherwise the PFIPs in China may fail.

Thirdly, the objective conditions for reforming the Chinese legislation on PFIPs are analysed. It is found that the existing politics, judiciary and market are mature enough to reform Chinese legislation on PFIPs. Therefore, it is possible to reform Chinese legislation on PFIPs.

Finally, this chapter considers the aims of reforming Chinese legislation on PFIPs. It looks forward to the future benefits that may be brought by new legislation.

To summarise, China needs to reform its laws on PFIPs. The laws on PFIPs in China are worthy of reform because the PFIP model could bring benefits to China; it is necessary to reform these laws because their current shortcomings are hindering the development of PFIPs; the Chinese conditions would support the reform of legislation and the new legislation on PFIPs will facilitate the development of PFIPs in China and bring more benefits to both the Public Sector and (foreign) private investors.

Chapter 3 will compare some international agreements and treaties. It will be found that the aims of the Legislative Guide and Model Provisions made by UNCITRAL match the aims of the reform of Chinese legislation on PFIPs. That is one of the reasons why the Legislative Guide and Model Provisions should be used as guidelines when reforming the Chinese laws on PFIPs. The next chapter will also discuss the reason why other countries' laws are given as a supplementary reference to Chinese law reform on PFIPs.

Chapter 3
The Guidance Made by UNCITRAL as International Standards

3.1 Introduction

In Chap. 2, PFIPs were shown to benefit the development of China, but that current laws on PFIPs in China are hindering their use. Moreover, as the objective conditions in China were also shown to be mature enough, Chap. 2 concluded that it was time to reform Chinese laws on PFIPs. The next question is what guidelines or experiences should be taken from international organizations or other countries so that this law reform can achieve the aims of the law makers, since China has no experience in establishing comprehensive legislation on PFIPs? The aim of this Chapter is to consider the guidelines of the international organizations and the experiences of other countries, which could become references for Chinese law reform on PFIPs.

There are two objectives in this chapter. The first objective is to prove that the Legislative Guide and Model Provisions on PFIPs made by UNCITRAL are the best guidelines for the law reform in China by comparing the advantages and disadvantages of the international agreements on PFIPs made by certain international organisations, and treaties on PFIPs subscribed to by China and other countries. The second objective is to confirm whether other countries' laws on PFIPs may be used as supplementary references for the law reform in China.

This chapter consists of three sections. Section 3.2 states the international agreements relating to PFIPs made by various international organisations (WTO, OECD, World Bank), the bilateral or multilateral treaties relating to PFIPs subscribed to by China, and analyses their disadvantages and limitations. Section 3.3 presents the background of the international organisation, UNCITRAL, and its Legislative Guide and Model Provisions. It then analyses and discusses why the Legislative Guide and the Model Provisions made by UNCITRAL are better placed to guide Chinese legislative reform on PFIPs. Section 3.4 states the reasons why the other countries' laws on PFIPs are used in this book as a supplementary reference for Chinese law reform and analyses why these are just used as supplementary references rather than as the principal guidelines.

S. Liang, *Legal Aspects of Privately Financed Infrastructure Projects (PFIPs) in China*,
https://doi.org/10.1007/978-981-15-6803-9_3

This chapter answers the second research question, namely why the Legislative Guide and Model Provisions made by UNCITRAL are chosen to be the standard to improve the Chinese legislation on PFIPs; and why the other countries' laws on PFIPs are used as a supplementary reference.

3.2 The International Agreements and Treaties Related PFIPs

With the synchronisation of global processes in politics and economics, and in order to improve co-operation and development, the harmonisation of laws has gradually been accepted and applied worldwide.[1] The harmonisation movement is most readily identified with the adoption of the United Nations on Convention on Contracts for the international Sale of Goods (CISG) in 1980.[2] Harmonisation is also required in investment laws, as expressed by Keba Mbaye during the mission led by the former president of the CCJA[3] in 1992: "We do not want investment because we do not know which law will govern our assets."[4] In the harmonisation of aspects of International Investment Law, some international agreements have been drafted by international institutions, some regional treaties have been made by certain regions, and some bilateral treaties have been subscribed to by two countries.[5] These agreements and treaties are intended to establish a harmonised standard so that the investment laws in different countries can approach harmonious accord. However, although these agreements and treaties have contributed to the harmonisation of International Investment Law, they cannot be used to guide the reform of Chinese legislation on PFIPs because of their specificity and limitations. The Legislative Guide and the Model Provisions made by the UNCITRAL are different from other international agreements or treaties.

---

[1] Laryea Emmanuel, *'Why Ghana should implement certain international legal instruments relating to international sale of goods transactions'* (A.J.I.C.L. 2011, 19(1), 1–37) P4.

[2] Jarvin Sigvard, *'The role of international commercial arbitration in the modern world'* (Arbitration 2009, 75(1), 65–70) P68.

[3] The Common Court of Justice and Arbitration (CCJA) is the court of the Organization for the Harmonization of Business Law in Africa (OHADA), one of the most successful regional legal harmonization efforts on the Continent. Unlike the other continental regional integration groups, OHADA does not seek to conform national law to an overarching treaty and successive regulations and directives, which allow national legislature some leeway. Instead, OHADA uses the integration method of issuing binding uniform acts that automatically supercede all prior and future inconsistent national laws.—The official website of African International Court and Tribunals (AICT) <http://www.aict-ctia.org/courts_subreg/ohada/ohada_home.html> accessed on 9th March 2020.

[4] *'Knowing how to accept poverty: an interview with President Kéba Mbaye'*, remarks collected by François Katendi and Jean-Baptiste Placca, L'autre Afrique, <http://www.afrology.com/eco/kebam> accessed on 9th March 2020; Boris Martor, 'Public-Private Partnerships' (IBLJ 2008), endnote 2.

[5] Dolzer Rudolf and Schreuer Christoph, *'Principles of international investment law'* (Oxford University Press,2008)P21.

They regulate all aspects of behaviour in PFIPs and give detail guidelines to improve legislation on PFIPs.

3.2.1 WTO

The World Trade Organization (WTO) is the only global international organisation that deals with the rules of trade between nations. The goal of this organisation is to help producers of goods and services, exporters, and importers conduct their business.[6] Due to its status and its positive impact on international trade, the WTO, it was hoped, would break down investment barriers between nations. However, the WTO has made very few contributions to the harmonisation of International Investment Law.

The WTO established a working group on Trade and Investment during the 1996 Ministerial Conference in Singapore. However, this working group was short-lived and achieved little by way of multilateral agreement. During the Cancun meeting in October 2004, which was intended to be the mid-term review of the Doha Round,[7] the WTO Members took the dramatic decision to stop negotiation on trade and investment. As a result, the WTO Members abandoned the working group on trade and investment.[8]

The only multilateral agreement on investment issued by WTO is the Agreement on Trade Related Aspects of Investment Measures (hereafter referred to as "TRIM"). This agreement recognizes that certain investment measures restrict and distort trade. It provides that no contracting party shall apply any TRIM inconsistent with Articles III (national treatment[9]) and XI (prohibition of quantitative restrictions[10]) of the

[6]World Trade Organization Website, <http://www.wto.org/english/thewto_e/whatis_e/whatis_e.htm> accessed on 30th May 2019.

[7]The Doha Round is the latest round of trade negotiations among the WTO membership. The Round was officially launched at the WTO's Fourth Ministerial Conference in Doha, Qatar, in November 2001. Its aim is to achieve major reform of the international trading system through the introduction of lower trade barriers and revised trade rules. The work programme covers about 20 areas of trade. WTO website, <http://www.wto.org/english/tratop_e/dda_e/dda_e.htm> accessed on 28th July, 2019. However, Doha Round negotiations took in excess of ten years but it was not completed or concluded with a consensus so far (as it failed). Parties to the Round arrived at a "stalemate" and could not agree or consent to each other's terms. The Round highlights the fact that not all negotiations are successful (that is, resulting in a concluded treaty), and neither is it necessarily a speedy process. Westlaw insight, *'analysis key areas of complexity or uncertainty'*.

[8]Matsushita M., Schoenbaum T.J. & Mavroidis P.C., *'The World Trade Organization: Law, Practice, and Policy'* (2nd ed, Oxford University Press, 2006) P836.

[9]National Treatment: It means treating foreigners and locals equally. If a state grants a particular right, benefit or privilege to its own citizens, it must also grant those advantages to the citizens of other states while they are in that country.

[10]Quantitative Restrictions: Explicit limits on the physical amounts of particular commodities that can be imported or exported.

GATT.[11] To this end, a list of TRIMs agreed to be inconsistent with these articles is appended to the agreement. The list includes measures which require particular levels of local procurement by an enterprise ("local content requirements"[12]) or which restrict the volume or value of imports such an enterprise can purchase or use to an amount related to the level of products it exports ("trade balancing requirements"[13]).[14] In light of the content of the TRIMs, it is obvious that TRIMs only apply to investments related to trade in goods.

The above analysis of the WTO and the content of TRIMs shows that the agreements on investment issued by WTO are not applied to all kinds of international investment but only to those investments related to trade. There is no reference to PFIPs. Therefore, it is impossible to use these agreements to guide the reform of Chinese legislation on PFIPs. However, the principles of TRIMs about fairness, anti-discrimination and removal of barriers to investment are exemplary for the discussions on PFIPs.

3.2.2 OECD

The Organisation for Economic Co-operation and Development (OECD) is another important international institution. It has 34 members and 25 non-members, who participate as regular observers or participants in OECD Committees. About 70 non-members are engaged in OECD working parties, schemes or programmes.[15] The mission of the OECD is to promote policies that will improve the economic and social well-being of people around the world.[16] Though the OECD has contributed more to the harmonisation of international investment than the WTO, and has established some measures relating to PFIPs, these are only scattered and do not provide specific and systematic guidance on PFIPs.

The Multilateral Agreement on Investment (MAI), proposed by the OECD in 1995, was meant to provide a general protection of "fair and equitable treatment and full and constant security. In no case shall a Contracting Party accord treatment

[11] General Agreement on Tariffs and Trade 1994.

[12] Local Content Requirements: A requirement that goods sold in a country contain a certain minimum of domestic value added.

[13] Trade Balancing Requirements: an enterprise's purchases or use of imported products be limited to an amount related to the volume or value of local products that it exports.

[14] World Trade Organization Website, *'Agreement on Trade Related Aspects of Investment Measures'*, <http://www.wto.org/english/docs_e/legal_e/ursum_e.htm#eAgreement> accessed on 30th May 2019.

[15] China is not the member of OECD, but it is the Enhanced engagement country of OECD. In May 2007, OECD countries agreed to invite Chile, Estonia, Israel, Russia and Slovenia to open discussions for membership of the organisation and offered enhanced engagement to Brazil, China, India, Indonesia and South Africa.

[16] The Organisation for Economic Co-operation and Development Website, <http://www.oecd.org/home/0,3675,en_2649_201185_1_1_1_1_1,00.html> accessed on 31th May 2019.

less favourable than that required by international law."[17] The MAI was seen by the OECD as a harmonisation exercise, and an attempt to address the fragmented nature of investment protection through BITs.[18] However, it provoked intense opposition from Non-Governmental Organisations (NGOs) on the grounds that it would weaken the regulatory capacity of host States, in favour of investor protection.[19] Efforts to conclude it collapsed in 1998.

The MAI does not directly refer to PFIPs, but its references to Foreign Direct Investment (FDI)[20] may be overlap with the functions of PFIPs in some cases. When the foreign private investor is one of the investors in a Special Purpose Vehicle (SPV),[21] which undertakes the responsibility of conducting and operating public infrastructure and is allowed to charge the public or public authorities for use, this investor is participating in a PFIP. This is also a FDI. The foreign private investor sets up an enterprise in the form of a joint venture or using foreign capital. While this company obtains profits through financing and operating a public infrastructure, the foreign private investor acquires profits through the operation of the company rather than through a secondary market (such as the stock market). This form of investment is not only a FDI but also a PFIP. Therefore, although the MIA does not specify practice for PFIPs and it has failed in practice, the concepts it puts forward on investment liberalisation, investment protection and dispute settlement[22] are worth considering in the reform of Chinese legislation on PFIPs.

In 1976, the OECD adopted the Declaration on International Investment and Multinational Enterprises, which was rewritten and annexed by the OECD Guidelines for Multinational Enterprises in 2000.[23] The guidelines constitute voluntary recommendations to multinational enterprises in areas such employment, human

---

[17]OECD, *'The Multilateral Agreement on Investment draft consolidated text'* (DAFFE/MAI(98)7/REV1, 22nd April 1998), <http://www1.oecd.org/daf/mai/pdf/ng/ng987r1e.pdf> accessed on 29th September 2019; OECD, *'Fair and Equitable Treatment Standard in International Investment Law'* (2004) in 'OECD Working Papers on International Investment, 2004/03', <http://dx.doi.org/10.1787/675702255435> accessed on 29th September 2019.

[18]McLachlan Campbell, *'Investment treaties and general international law'* (I.C.L.Q. 2008, 57(2), 361–401) P368–369.

[19]Salzman JE, *'Decentralized Administrative Law in the Organization for Economic Cooperation and Development'* (2005) 68 Law & Contemporary Problems 189, 196–200.

[20]FDI stand for Foreign Direct Investment, which refers to an investment made to acquire lasting interest in enterprises operating outside of the economy of the investor.

[21]SPV (special purpose vehicle): a special purpose entity is a legal entity (usually a limited company of some type or, sometimes, a limited partnership) created to fulfil narrow, specific or temporary objectives. The Project Company as an SPV cannot carry out any other business that is not part of the project. E. R. Yescombe, *'Public-Private Partnerships: Principles of Policy and Finance'* (ELSEVIER 2007) P109.

[22]Matsushita M., Schoenbaum T.J. & Mavroidis P.C., *'The World Trade Organization: Law, Practice, and Policy'* (2nd ed, Oxford University Press, 2006) P834.

[23]The Guidelines are reprinted in 40 ILM (2001) P143. S Tully, *'The 2000 Review of the OECD Guidelines for Multinational Enterprise'* (2001), 50 I.C.L.Q, P394.

rights, environment, fighting bribery, science and technology, competition, taxation, information disclosure and consumer interests.[24]

PFIPs are implemented through SPVs,[25] which have to face problems relating to environments, labour rights and so on. Although these guidelines are not specific to SPVs in PFIPs, this content could also be considered in the reform of Chinese legislation on PFIPs.

The OECD Istanbul Centre, i.e. the Centre for Private Sector Development in Istanbul, has been the place where knowledge and experience is exchanged between OECD member countries and other partner countries in Eastern Europe, Central Asia and the Caucasus since 1994. The Private Sector continues to play a key role in the transformation to market-based economies. Therefore, creating a framework which is conducive for Private Sector development is a priority for many Transition Economies and the OECD is committed to supporting these efforts. The mission of this centre is to promote sustainable economic development and poverty alleviation through Private Sector development in OECD partner countries with particular focus on economic and social policy areas, making use of policy dialogue, peer review backed by high quality analytical work, and the willingness of policy makers to exchange good practices.[26]

It is worth noting that the Basic Elements of a Law on Concession Agreement,[27] published by The OECD Istanbul Centre use the UNCITRAL Legislative Guide as the starting point for its report. The OECD convened an expert group that would formulate basic elements in light of international experience, so as to insure that project financing becomes a more viable option for much needed infrastructure financing in the region. This document sets out in legislative language the guiding principles of a modern law on concession agreements and comments on these principles in light of best international practice. This study contributes to the facilitation of Private Sector investment in the infrastructure of countries in economic transition.[28]

It could easily be concluded that the OECD has a specific remit to research PFIPs and has published relevant legal documents. To some extent, these legal documents represent the opinion of the OECD members and contribute to the harmonisation of the laws on PFIPs. They are worthy of reference in the reform of Chinese legislation on PFIPs.

---

[24]Dolzer Rudolf and Schreuer Christoph, *'Principles of international investment law'* (Oxford University Press,2008) P24.

[25]SPV (special purpose vehicle): a special purpose entity is a legal entity (usually a limited company of some type or, sometimes, a limited partnership) created to fulfil narrow, specific or temporary objectives. The Project Company as an SPV cannot carry out any other business that is not part of the project. E. R. Yescombe, *'Public-Private Partnerships: Principles of Policy and Finance'* (ELSEVIER 2007) P109.

[26]OECD Istanbul Center: Centre for Private Sector Development Istanbul Brochure.

[27]OECD, Multilateral Centre for Private Sector Development Istanbul, *'Basic Elements of a Law on Concession Agreement'* (19/09/2002).

[28]Ibid.: Preface.

In 2010, the OECD offered a new concept—dedicated public-private partnership units.[29] Dedicated public-private partnership units include any organisation set up with the full or partial aid of the government to ensure that necessary competencies to manage third-party provision of goods and services are made available and clustered together within government. The establishment of dedicated units serves to enhance the capacity of government to manage the risks associated with a growing number and value of public-private partnerships successfully. Although a relatively recent phenomenon, in 2009 over half of all OECD member countries reported the existence of a dedicated unit of some kind.[30]

Dedicated public-private partnership units have not been established in China yet. However, it could be considered for addition into Chinese legislation on PFIPs when the provisions on monitoring government administration are drafted.

The above analysis of the OECD and its relevant measures shows that the OECD has contributed much more than the WTO to the harmonisation of International Investment Law. The OECD's MIA considers all aspects of investment. Particularly, the OECD has specific measures that focus on PFIPs. Despite the OECD's efforts and useful ideas, it is not systematic enough to guide the reform of Chinese legislation on PFIPs, especially with regard to substantive provisions.

3.2.3 *World Bank*

The World Bank is a vital source of financial and technical assistance to developing countries around the world. Its mission is to fight poverty with lasting results and to help people help themselves and their environment by providing resources, sharing knowledge, building capacity and forging partnerships in the Public and Private Sector.[31] In comparison with the OECD, the World Bank only focuses on the procedures of dispute settlement in PFIPs rather than on substantive agreements on the regulation of PFIPs.

In the World Bank, it was the then General Counsel, Aron Broches, who initiated and drove the debates on the possible scope of international consensus. Broches concluded that

> …the best contribution of the Bank was to provide for effective procedures for impartial settlement of disputes, without attempting to seek agreement on substantive standards.

It sounds that this approach seemed to break the logic that any system of dispute settlement would have to be based on a set of substantive rules that could be applied.

---

[29] OECD, 'Dedicated Public-Private Partnership Units: A Survey of Institutional and Governance Structures' (2010).

[30] Ibid., P3.

[31] World Bank Website, <http://web.worldbank.org/WBSITE/EXTERNAL/EXTABOUTUS/0,,pagePK:50004410~piPK:36602~theSitePK:29708,00.html> accessed on 3th July 2019.

Broches argued that, from a pragmatic point of view, such a substantive agreement on international investment law was neither necessary nor productive.[32]

At first sight, the Broches concept ('procedure before substance') seemed to be a limited and modest one. However, he began the design of what was to become, in 1965, the Convention on the Settlement of Investment Dispute between States and Nationals of Other States (ICSID Convention) establishing the International Centre for Settlement of Investment Disputes (ICSID). The five features of ICSID make it to be the boldest innovative step in the modern history of international cooperation concerning the role and protection of foreign investment: (a) foreign companies and individuals can directly bring a suit against their host state; (b) state immunity[33] is severely restricted; (c) international law can be applied to the relationship between the host state and the investor; (d) the local remedies[34] rule is excluded in principle; and (e) ICSID award are directly enforceable within the territories of all states parties to ICSID.[35]

The above analysis of the World Bank shows that the World Bank pays more attention to dispute settlement than to substantive provisions. Although the ICSID was proved successful when in subsequent decades more and more investment treaties, bilateral and multilateral, referred to the ICSID as a forum for dispute settlement, this concept ('procedure before substance') cannot be used to guide the reform of Chinese legislation on PFIPs because it does not prevent the disputes (it only resolves them). A completed legislation should be applied both to prevent disputes from arising and settle disputes if they do arise.

3.2.4 Bilateral Treaties Between China and Other Countries

Bilateral investment treaties (BITs) are agreements between two countries for the reciprocal encouragement, promotion and protection of investments in each other's territories by companies based in either country.

32Dolzer Rudolf and Schreuer Christoph, '*Principles of international investment law*' (Oxford University Press, 2008) p. 20.

33The doctrine and rules of state immunity concern the protection which a state is given from being sued in the courts of other states. Hazel Fox, '*The Law of State Immunity*', (2008 Oxford University Press).

34The local remedies rule is that a State should be given the opportunity to redress an alleged wrong within the framework of its own domestic legal system before its international responsibility can be called into question at international level. A. A. Cancado Trindade, '*The application of the rule of exhaustion of local remedies in international law 1*' (1983). <http://www.asil.org/ajil/Udombana.pdf>.

35Shihata I, '*Towards a Greater Depoliticization of Investment Disputes: The Roles of ICSID and MIGA*' in The Wold Bank in a Changing World (1991) P309.

The number of BITs has grown worldwide. In 2010 alone, 54 new BITs were signed. By the end of 2010, there were 2,807 BITs in total.[36] According to the statistics of UNCTAD,[37] China has signed 127 BITs on 1st June 2011, since its first BIT was signed with Norway on 21st November 1984.[38] China has signed BITs with almost all economies and only follows Germany in total BITs signed (with 136 BITs).

Generally, BITs have a similar basic structure that covers the following areas. Firstly, the treaty begins with a prefatory statement as to the aims of the treaty, which are usually the reciprocal encouragement and protection of investment flows between the two states. Secondly, it is followed by identification of the types of property which are protected and the nature of the link of nationality to one of the parties which entitles the foreign investor to the protection of the treaty. Thirdly, the standard of treatment to be accorded to the foreign investor is established, such as national treatment, most-favoured-nation treatment, and fair and equitable treatment. Fourthly, the right to the repatriation of profits is asserted. Fifthly, there are statements on the compensation in the event of expropriation or damage to the investment during wars and civil riots. The standard of compensation in the event of a takeover of the foreign investor's property is identified. Finally, the mechanisms for dispute settlement (both state-state and investor-state) arising from the investment are stated. The above items are the standard contents in most BITs. In light of the specific conditions of the treaty, there are variations in the statements of rules that are to be applied between the parties in each of these areas.[39]

The above analysis of BITs shows that the contents of BITs may be flexible in light of the specific situation shared by the bilateral parties, but they are too flexible and numerous to be used as a guideline for law reform in China. What Chinese law reform needs is a systematic set of guidelines to guide all aspects of the law reform on PFIPs, rather than the resolution of one specific issue. According to the World Investment Report 2011 by UNCTAD, BITs have a vital weakness:

> It has come close to a point it is too big and complex to handle for governments and investors alike, yet remains inadequate to cover all possible bilateral investment relationships which would require a further 14,100 bilateral treaties.[40]

---

[36]UNCTAD, *'World Investment Report 2011: non-equity modes of international production and development'*, P100(with Figure III. 2).

[37]UNCTAD stands for United Nations Conference on Trade and Development, which was established under United Nations' system in Geneva in 1964. UNCTAD promotes the development-friendly integration of developing countries into the world economy. UNCTAD has progressively evolved into an authoritative knowledge-based institution whose work aims to help shape current policy debates and thinking on development, with a particular focus on ensuring that domestic policies and international action are mutually supportive in bringing about sustainable development.

[38]UNCTAD, *'Total number of Bilateral Investment Treaties concluded, 1 June 2011'*, <http://www.unctad.org/Templates/Page.asp?intItemID=2344&lang=1> accessed on 1st September 2019.

[39]Sornarajah M., *'The international law on foreign investment'* (3rd ed, Cambridge University Press, 2010) P187–188.

[40]UNCTAD, *'World Investment Report 2011: non-equity modes of international production and development'*, Px.

However, when the Chinese laws on PFIPs are reformed, these BITs should be considered, in case there is conflict between the PFIP law and some of China's existing BITs.

To sum up, the above international agreements (made by WTO, OECD and World Bank) and BITs (signed by China) can be referred to in the Chinese legislation on PFIPs, but they cannot guide the reform of Chinese legislation on PFIPs because of their limitations. By contrast, the Legislative Guide and Model Provisions made by UNCITRAL can guide the reform of Chinese legislation on PFIPs, as will be analysed and discussed in the following section.

3.3 UNCITRAL and Its Legislative Guide and Model Provisions

When compared with the above international investment agreements made by the various international organisations and the bilateral investment treaties made between China and other countries, the Legislative Guide and Model Provisions made by UNCITRAL proves itself to be the most suitable guideline in supporting the reform of Chinese law on PFIPs.

3.3.1 Background of UNCITRAL

UNCITRAL itself is highly prestigious. UNCITRAL was established in 1966 by the United Nations General Assembly through Resolution 2205 (XXI). The mandate of this organisation is to work towards the progressive harmonisation and unification of international economic laws, so the guidelines offered by UNCITRAL would permit reform of Chinese laws on PFIPs to approach international standards.

In an increasingly economically interdependent world, the importance of an improved legal framework for the facilitation of international trade and investment is widely acknowledged. UNCITRAL plays an important role in developing that framework in pursuit of its mandate to further the progressive harmonisation and modernisation of International Trade Law by preparing and promoting the use and adoption of legislative and non-legislative instruments in a number of key areas of commercial law.[41]

The areas covered by UNCITRAL include dispute resolution, international contract practices, transport, insolvency, electronic commerce, international

[41]UNCITRAL, *'The UNCITRAL Guide: Basic Facts about the United Nations Commission on International Trade Law'* (United Nations Vienna, 2007) P1.

payments, secured transactions, procurement and the sale of goods.[42] The legislative guidelines offered by UNCITRAL in these areas favour the progressive harmonisation and unification of international economic laws.

3.3.2 Reasons for Choosing UNCITRAL

3.3.2.1 The Framework of UNCITRAL Organisation for Harmonisation

UNCITRAL's framework is suited to making its guidelines achieve the maximum harmonisation of legislative instruments.

UNCITRAL is composed of members selected from among States Members of the United Nations (UN) and ensures that the various geographic regions and the principal economic and legal systems of the world are represented. The 60 member States include 14 African States, 14 Asian States, 8 Eastern European States, 10 Latin American and Caribbean States and 14 Western European and other States. The General Assembly elects members for terms of six years; every three years the terms of half of the members expire.[43]

China, a member of UN, was also selected to be a member of UNCITRAL. China joined UNCITRAL in 1983 and this membership will expire in 2013.[44] As a result, there is interaction between China and UNCITRAL. Chinese delegations, through regional legislative instruments, specific consultation and language, support UNCITRAL in drafting legislative instruments, so as to add Chinese elements to the UNCITRAL legislative instrument. This could be reciprocated if UNCITRAL legislative instruments, which involve harmonisation considerations, were to offer guidelines to the development of Chinese laws.

---

[42]Ibid.

[43]Pursuant to General Assembly resolution 2205 (XXI) of 17 December 1966, members of the Commission are elected by the General Assembly for a term of six years, the term of half of the members expiring every three years. By its resolution 3108 (XXVIII) of 12 December 1973, the Assembly increased the membership of the Commission from 29 to 36 States. By its resolution 57/20 of 19 November 2002, the Assembly further increased the membership of the Commission from 36 States to 60 States. In order to maintain the system of electing half of the membership every three years, of those 24 additional members, 13 have a three-year term expiring on the day preceding the opening of the fortieth regular annual session, in 2007, and 11 have a six-year term expiring on the day preceding the opening of the forty-third regular annual session, in 2010, with the result that of the 60 members of the Commission, the membership of 30 States expires in 2007 and the remaining 30 States expires in 2010.

[44]UNCITRAL website, <http://www.uncitral.org/uncitral/en/about/origin_history.html> accessed on 05 September 2019.

3.3.2.2 The Work Methods of UNCITRAL for Harmonization

The work methods of UNCITRAL may also provide guidelines to achieving the maximum harmonisation of legislative instruments.

UNCITRAL cooperate with other international organisations active in the field of International Economic Law. Those international organisations, both within and outside the United Nations system, include the World Trade Organization (WTO); the Organization for Economic Cooperation and Development (OECD); the World Bank; UNCTAD and so on. As was previously discussed in Sect. 3.2, these international organisations have their own advantages, which might be used in the reform of Chinese laws on PFIPs. UNCITRAL has close links with these international organisations, could facilitate the exchange of ideas and information, avoiding a duplication of effort and promoting efficiency, consistency and coherence in the modernisation and harmonisation of International Trade Law.[45] In this case, UNCITRAL could offer the best guidelines for the reform of Chinese laws.

UNCITRAL considers suggestions from a wide variety of parties when it drafts its legislative instruments. These instruments are negotiated through an international process involving a variety of participants, including the member States of UNCITRAL, which bring different legal traditions and levels of economic development; non-member States; Intergovernmental Organisations; and Non-Governmental Organisations. Thus, these texts offer solutions appropriate to different legal traditions and to countries at different stages of economic development.[46] In this case, UNCITRAL could offer guidelines which involve high harmonisation but may also be acceptable to China.

UNCITRAL offers technical assistance to law reform, which is not only helpful for the countries requiring assistance but also involves harmonisation to a certain extent. UNCITRAL undertakes a range of technical assistance activities to promote its work and the use and adoption of the legislative and non-legislative texts it has developed to further the progressive harmonisation and unification of International Trade Law. One such activity is to undertake a law reform assessment to assist Governments to review existing legislation and assess their need for law reform in the commercial field.[47] In this case, should China start to reform its laws on PFIPs, UNCITRAL could offer China essential and efficient technical assistance to achieve an international standard.

It is noteworthy that, as Processor McCormack has argued, the UNCITRAL Secured Transactions Guide and the UNCITRAL Insolvency Guide are very similar to US law because of the US influence on their drafting through organisations such as

[45]UNCITRAL, '*The UNCITRAL Guide: Basic Facts about the United Nations Commission on International Trade Law*' (United Nations Vienna, 2007) P10.

[46]Ibid., P1.

[47]Ibid., P22.

CFA.[48] The UK influence is similarly observable, as influenced through the London-based INSOL.[49][50] Although some academics complain that UNCITRAL may be too US or West-dominated, which may hurt the interests of developing countries, this does not negatively affect the Legislative Guide and Model Provisions on PFIPs in this case. Firstly, China also has had some influence in the drafting of the Legislative Guide and Model Provisions on PFIPs. The UNCITRAL Secretariat invited Chinese experts to the two drafting sessions,[51] and even the recent UNCITRAL International Colloquium on PPPs[52] invited Professor Cao as a keynote speaker. Secondly, although the US and the UK and their related organisations participated in the drafting of the Legislative Guide and Model Provisions on PFIPs, the relatively unprejudiced international organisations such as the World Bank and the OECD had more influence.[53] Finally, neither the Legislative Guide nor the Model Provisions on PFIPs are mandatory prescriptions. They provide a point of reference, so China could choose those recommendations it needs and abandon others.

3.3.3 Background of the Legislative Guide and Model Provisions Made by UNCITRAL

UNCITRAL believed that guidelines on the legislation of PFIPs could help countries improve their laws on PFIPs to facilitate the development of PFIPs. This led to

---

[48]The Commercial Finance Association (CFA) founded in 1944, is the international trade association dedicated to the asset-based lending and factoring industries. The CFA has nearly 300 member companies and 16 chapters located throughout the United States, Mexico and Canada.

[49]International Association of Restructuring, Insolvency & Bankruptcy Professionals (INSOL), is a world-wide federation of national associations for accountants and lawyers who specialise in turnaround and insolvency.

[50]Gerard McCormack, 'Secured credit and the harmonisation of law, the UNCITRAL Experience' (Edward Elgar, USA 2011) P182–186.

[51]UNCITRAL, 33rd session, A/CN.9/471—*Privately financed infrastructure projects: draft chapters of a legislative guide on privately financed infrastructure* projects, P1, para 1–4: The Commission requested the Secretariat to seek the assistance of outside experts, as required, in the preparation of future chapters and invited Governments to identify experts who could be of assistance to the Secretariat in that task……; The Commission requested the Secretariat to continue the preparation of future chapters, with the assistance of outside experts……; UNCITRAL, 34th session, A/CN.9/488—*Possible work on privately financed infrastructure projects*, P2, para 5–6: there were more than 70 registered participants at the Colloquium, including Government officials, bankers and Private Sector lawyers from more than 20 States……The participants represented a broad range of practical experience and the perspectives of different legal systems.

[52]UNCITRAL International Colloquium on Public-Private Partnerships (PPPs) took place on 2–3 May 2013, Vienna: to produce a recommendation to United Nations Commission on International Trade Law (UNCITRAL) on possible future works in the area of PPPs.

[53]UNCITRAL, '*Concept Note Prepared for French Business Association (MEDEF) And World Bank group meeting March 2013*' <http://www.uncitral.org/pdf/english/colloquia/public-private-partnerships-2013/Frilet_Concept-note.pdf> accessed on 30th July, 2019.

drafting the Legislative Guide and the Model Provisions. The content of the Legislative Guide and the Model Provisions were drawn up over seven years' discussion, between the 29th Commission Session and the 36th Commission Session.

3.3.3.1 Why Did UNCITRAL Get Involved in PFIPS?

After recommendations by many States and the consideration of a report (A/CN.9/424)[54] prepared by the Secretary-General, the UNCITRAL decided to prepare a legislative guide on PFIPs[55] at its 29th session in 1996.

3.3.3.1.1 The Attraction of Joining Private Investors and Public Infrastructure

The UNCITRAL noted that the interest in various forms of private participation in public infrastructure projects had risen in many States, particularly in developing countries.

Firstly, the PFIP model could save public funding. Since the private investor finances the project, the successful implementation of such projects would enable States to achieve significant savings in public expenditure. In this case, the resources that would have been invested in infrastructure could be reallocated to meet more pressing social needs.[56]

Secondly, the host government could benefit from the Private Sector's expertise in operating and managing such projects. The private investor undertakes to complete a construction and to operate the facility for a certain period of time with a view to reclaiming its costs with reasonable profits. Thus, the private investor has a clear interest in the feasibility and design of the facility. At the same time, the host government also expects in particular to achieve efficient gains and high standards of service, which may not be provided by State monopolies.[57]

---

[54]UNCITRAL, 29th session, A/CN.9/424-*Possible Future Work: Build-Operate-Transfer projects.*

[55]The exactly words here should be "build-operate-transfer (BOT) and related types of projects" which was used before 30th session. However, in order to maintain consistency in this book, the advanced word "PFIPs" which was created and confirmed in 30th session is used here.

[56]UNCITRAL, 29th session, A/CN.9/424-*Possible Future Work: Build-Operate-Transfer projects*, P3, para 4–5; UNCITRAL, 29th session, A/51/17-*Report of the United Nations Commission on International Trade Law on its twenty-ninth session*, P53, para 228; UNCITRAL, 30th session, A/52/17-*Report of the United Nations Commission on International Trade Law on its thirty session*, P46, para 228.

[57]UNCITRAL, 29th session, A/CN.9/424-*Possible Future Work: Build-Operate-Transfer projects*, P3–4, para 5–6; UNCITRAL, 30th session, A/52/17-*Report of the United Nations Commission on International Trade Law on its thirty session*, P46, para 228.

3.3.3.1.2 The Advantages of a Favourable Legal Framework on PFIPs

The UNCITRAL noted that a favourable legal framework for PFIPs is necessary and important when PFIPs are implemented.

Firstly, a favourable legal framework fosters the confidence of national or foreign potential investors, and attracts more private investment into public infrastructure. PFIPs require substantial investment from private sources which is generally obtained by borrowing from commercial banks and other financial institutions. However, the repayment of borrowed funds and the return on the investment takes place over an extended period. Thus, the lenders and the investors look for clear guarantees by the host government that it will encourage long-term private investments and that such investments will be protected from expropriation or nationalisation without fair compensation. The way that the host government gives such guarantees is by providing a favourable legal framework that encourages private investment and protects the return on the investment.[58]

Secondly, a favourable legal framework protects public interests.[59] The final customers of the infrastructures are the people. A favourable legal framework ensures that the private investor provides a proper service.

Thirdly, a favourable legal framework makes it easier to negotiate specific PFIPs. In the absence of such legislation, the contract documents have to cover various issues and guarantees that should be covered by legislation. It adds complexity to the negotiations.[60]

3.3.3.1.3 The Necessity of Legislative Guidance

The UNCITRAL noted that it would be useful to provide legislative guidance to States preparing or modernising legislation relevant to PFIPs, and it has the capability to do this.

Firstly, many countries require legislative guidance in improving their legislation to tackle the problems found in PFIPs. PFIPs usually involve contractual arrangements of considerable complexity and may require lengthy negotiations. Work by the UNCITRAL in this area would help such States in tackling identifiable problems. In particular, it would be useful to provide legislative guidance to States preparing or modernising their legislation on PFIPs.[61]

Secondly, UNCITRAL has done a lot of preliminary work in preparing legislative guidance on PFIPs. The Secretariat examined other international organisations' work

---

[58] UNCITRAL, 29th session, A/CN.9/424-*Possible Future Work: Build-Operate-Transfer projects*, P8, para 22–23.

[59] UNCITRAL, 30th session, A/52/17-Report of the United Nations Commission on International Trade Law on its thirty session, P46, para 229.

[60] UNCITRAL, 29th session, A/CN.9/424-*Possible Future Work: Build-Operate-Transfer projects*, P8, para 23.

[61] UNCITRAL, 29th session, A/51/17-Report of the United Nations Commission on International Trade Law on its twenty-ninth session, P53, para 228.

on PFIPs, such as that of UNIDO, the EC and the World Bank[62] and examined the legislative and regulatory texts on PFIPs from twenty-four countries.[63]

Thirdly, UNCITRAL has been considered to be the best international organisation to provide the legislative guidance on PFIPs to various countries. It was noted that organisations that had done work in the area of PFIPs were not working to provide comprehensive guidance to national legislators regarding PFIPs. Given UNCITRAL's universal representation and its record in preparing trade law texts, there was a general agreement that UNCITRAL was the appropriate body to undertake such work, but that it needed to avoid a possible overlap with work being done by other international organisations.[64]

To sum up, UNCITRAL founded a PFIP model that could benefit the development of a country, and a favourable legislative framework that could ensure these benefits and avoid some risks carried by PFIPs. Therefore, UNCITRAL decided to provide comprehensive legislative guidance to assist States who are preparing or modernising their legislation on PFIPs.

3.3.3.2 Why Were Two Legal Documents on PFIPs with the Same Effect Drafted by UNCITRAL—The Legislative Guide on PFIPs and the Model Provisions on PFIPs?

The structure of the Legislative Guide is a set of legislative recommendations, followed by an explanatory discussion of the pertinent issues and the possible options available. The present Model Legislative Provisions were prepared by UNCITRAL as an addition to the Legislative Guide on PFIPs. The texts of the Legislative Guide and the Model Legislative Provisions were combined into one single publication to retain the legislative recommendations contained in the Legislative Guide as a basis of the development of the Model Legislative Provisions.[65]

The 30th Commission session in Vienna in 1997 had before it the first document comprising a table of contents setting out the topics proposed to be covered by the legislative guide, followed by annotations in some detail concerning the issues to be discussed therein.[66] After this, the Commission commenced work towards the preparation of a Legislative Guide on PFIPs.[67] The structure and content of the Legislative Guide were discussed repeatedly in the 30th session, the 31st session,

[62]UNCITRAL, 29th session, A/CN.9/424-*Possible Future Work: Build-Operate-Transfer projects*, P5–7, para 11–21.

[63]Ibid., P9, para 30.

[64]UNCITRAL, 29th session, A/51/17-Report of the United Nations Commission on International Trade Law on its twenty-ninth session, P53, para 228.

[65]UNCITRAL, 36th Session, A/58/17-*Report of the United Nations Commission on International Trade Law on its thirty-sixth session,* P37–38, para 171.

[66]UNCITRAL, 30th Session, A/CN.9/438-*Privately-Financed Infrastructure Projects: Draft Chapters of a legislative guide on privately-financed infrastructure projects.*

[67]UNCITRAL, 30th Session, A/52/17-*Report of the United Nations Commission on International Trade Law on its thirtieth session,* P46, para 230.

and the 32nd session. The Legislative Guide on PFIPs was finally confirmed and adopted by UNCITRAL on 29th June 2000 in its 33rd session.

At the early stages of the preparation of the Legislative Guide, the Commission was expected to formulate more concrete guidance in the form of model legislative provisions or even in the form of a model law dealing with specific issues. The reason why the UNCITRAL preferred a Legislative Guide is mainly attributable to a lack of consensus as to which of the various issues dealt with in the Legislative Guide might be suitable subjects for Model Legislative Provisions.[68] When arguing whether the Model Legislative Provisions should be drafted instead of the Legislative Guide, the opposing view was that PFIPs involved a number of Public Law and policy issues and that it would therefore be difficult to attempt to formulate model provisions that have to consider the differences between legal systems and the variety of policy options. Moreover, these opponents considered that it more important to offer sufficient flexibility to legislators in countries wishing to promote private investment in infrastructure. For that purpose, UNCITRAL decided that a clear set of legislative recommendations followed by explanations and the possible options, as in the Legislative Guide, might be more useful than a set of model provisions that legislators might find difficult to apply to domestic conditions.[69]

The proposal to make Model Legislative Provisions on PFIPs had been reiterated in 33rd session, after the Legislative Guide had been adopted and published. The draft of Model Legislative Provisions was discussed and reviewed during the 34th session, the 35th session, and the 36th session. The Legislative Model Provisions were finally confirmed and adopted by UNCITRAL in 2003 in its 36th session.

The reason why the Model Legislative Provisions on PFIPs was drafted soon after the Legislative Guide was adopted is that the UNCITRAL considered the requisite conditions to formulate more concrete guidance to be in place. The immediate decision to prepare a model law or model legislative provisions should not be interpreted as a sign of dissatisfaction by the Commission with the work on Legislative Guide that had just been accomplished.[70]

Firstly, over the course of the 3 years' work in drafting the Legislative Guide on PFIPs, a clearer understanding had developed within UNCITRAL with regard to the issues involved and the options available. As a matter of fact, the Legislative Guide adopted by the Commission reflected their common understanding and represented a good starting point for future work aimed at providing more concrete guidance, e.g. the Model Legislative Provisions. More concrete guidance would meet a pressing need, in particular in countries with economies in transition and in developing countries.[71]

[68]UNCITRAL, 33rd session, A/55/17- *Report of UNCITRAL on the work of its thirty-third session*, P86, para 375.

[69]UNCITRAL, 31st session, A/53/17- *Report of UNCITRAL on the work of its thirty-first session*, P20, para 203.

[70]UNCITRAL, 33rd session, A/55/17-*Report of UNCITRAL on the work of its thirty-third session*, P86, para 378.

[71]UNCITRAL, 33rd session, A/55/17- *Report of UNCITRAL on the work of its thirty-third session*, P86, para 375.

Secondly, UNCITRAL had done enormous work in answering questions of the desirability and feasibility of preparing a model law or model legislative provisions on selected issues covered by the Legislative Guide,[72] and this affirmed the work to draft the Model Legislative Provisions was necessary.[73]

During the second week of the 34th session of the UNCITRAL Commission in Vienna from 2 to 4 July 2001, a Colloquium on Privately Financed Infrastructure: Legal Frameworks and Technical Assistance was organised by the Secretariat of UNCITRAL with the co-sponsorship and organisational assistance of the Public-Private Infrastructure Advisory Facility (PPIAF).[74] This Colloquium had two aims. Firstly, it presented the best legislative and regulatory practices, as well as assessing the needs of recipient countries for assistance in establishing a legislative and regulatory framework for public-private partnerships. Secondly, the participant countries were invited to make recommendations on the desirability and, especially, the feasibility of a model law or model legislative provisions on PFIPs.[75]

In the Colloquium, the debate on whether a model law or model legislative provisions on PFIPs was desirable or feasible was very intense. The countervailing view was that the preparation of a model law was neither feasible nor desirable. As to feasibility, it was recalled that some projects had failed because of the significant disparity of approach in different legal systems. As to desirability, the draft of the Model Legislative Provisions might conflict with the Legislative Guide, which was already adopted, and would therefore negatively affect the considerable work behind the widely disseminated Legislative Guide.[76] However, several participants, who supported preparing the Model Legislative Guide, stated that there was significant demand for such a model law. It was noted that the Legislative Guide represented a good starting point, but that more concrete guidance, in the form of model legislative provisions, was desirable, especially for those countries with little or no experience in the field of PFIPs.[77] It was also noted that the prompt undertaking of such work would take advantage of the experience gathered throughout the process that led to the adoption of the Legislative Guide. This would allow the work to be achieved easily and effectively within a reasonable amount of time. There was no conflict between

---

[72] Ibid., para 379.

[73] UNCITRAL, UNCITRAL Executive Report: International Colloquium- *Privately Financed Infrastructure: Legal Framework and Technical Assistance* <http://www.uncitral.org/pdf/english/news/pfip-7-01colloquium-e.pdf> accessed on 5th January 2020.

[74] The Public-Private Infrastructure Advisory Facility (PPIAF) was created in 1999 to act as a catalyst to increase Private Sector participation in emerging markets. It is a multi-donor technical assistance facility aimed at helping developing countries improves the quality of their infrastructure through Private Sector involvement and assisting government to support the creation of a sound enabling environment for private service provision. <http://www.ppiaf.org/ppiaf/page/about-us#WhatisPPIAF?> accessed on 5th January 2020.

[75] UNCITRAL, UNCITRAL Executive Report: International Colloquium- Privately Financed Infrastructure: Legal Framework and Technical Assistance <http://www.uncitral.org/pdf/english/news/pfip-7-01colloquium-e.pdf> accessed on 5th January 2020.

[76] UNCITRAL, 34th session, A/CN.9/488-*Possible work on privately financed infrastructure projects*, P4, para 20.

[77] Ibid., para 17.

preparing the Model Legislative Provisions and the efforts undertaken to disseminate the Legislative Guide.[78] Although the views on how to deal with the Model Legislative Provisions varied, its feasibility was agreed upon by the propositions group.[79]

Although it was difficult to achieve an agreement between the two parties, the consequence was that the UNCITRAL Commission decided to continue its work on preparing the Model Legislative Provisions.[80]

Thirdly, the UNCITRAL Working Group I[81] was entrusted in 34th Session with the specific task of drafting core model legislative provisions in the field of PFIPs.[82] At the beginning of this task, the Working Group I was invited to formulate a specific part of the Model Legislative Provisions, namely the selection of the concessioner.[83] However, the Working Group I was of the view that Model Legislative Provisions on other parts might be desirable as well.[84] Therefore, the Model Legislative Provisions covered most of the subject matter addressed in the legislative recommendations of the Legislative Guide. The Model Legislative Provisions had been drafted during the 4th and 5th session of Working Group I and adopted by UNCITRAL in 2003 in its 36th session.

It is worth noting that the Model Legislative Provisions, which provides more concrete guidance, has not replaced the Legislative Guide in its entirety, nor have the model provisions been thoroughly combined with the recommendations contained in Legislative Guide. The Model Legislative Provisions is a supplement to the Legislative Guide. It cannot supplant the Guide.[85]

Firstly, the Model Provisions need the notes from the Legislative Guide in order to be explained and understood. According the discussions in the 4th and 5th sessions

---

[78]UNCITRAL, 35th session, A/CN.9/505-*Report of the Working Group on Privately Financed Infrastructure Projects at its fourth session*, P3, para 16.

[79]UNCITRAL, 34th session, A/CN.9/488-*Possible work on privately financed infrastructure projects*, P4, para 19.

[80]UNCITRAL, 34th Session, A/56/17-*Report of the United Nations Commission on International Trade Law on its thirty-forth session,* P69, para 369.

[81]Official Records of the General Assembly, 33th Session, Supplement No. 17 (A/33/17), para 67, reproduced in UNCITRAL Yearbook, vol. IX: 1978, part one, chap. II, sect. A. In 2005: There are six UNCITRAL working groups: I (Procurement); II (Arbitration); III (Transport Law); IV (Electronic Commerce); V (Insolvency Law); and VI (Security Interests). The working group titles reflect broad subject areas and may encompass the development of different texts in a particular subject area. For example, the subject area of the Working Group on Electronic Commerce includes electronic commerce generally, electronic signatures and electronic contracting. Working Group I were working on Time-limits and Limitation (Prescription) between 1969–1971; working on Privately Financed Infrastructure Projects between 2001–2003; working on Procurement from 2004 to present.

[82]Ibid.

[83]UNCITRAL, 34th Session, A/56/17-*Report of the United Nations Commission on International Trade Law on its thirty-forth session,* P69, para 369.

[84]UNCITRAL, 35th session, A/CN.9/505-*Report of the Working Group on Privately Financed Infrastructure Projects at its fourth session*, P3–24, para 18–174.

[85]Ibid., P24, para 176.

of Working Group I, the draft model provisions were not a departure from, but rather a development of, the policies and principles upon which the Legislative Guide was based. Thus, the draft model provisions did not replace the Legislative Guide in its entirety, and were to be understood and applied in light of and with the assistance of the explanatory notes contained in the Guide.[86]

Secondly, although the draft model provisions covered most of the subject matter addressed in the legislative recommendations, there were matters dealt with in some legislative recommendations that were not addressed in any of the draft model provisions, such as recommendations 3 and 5-13. That circumstance alone excluded the possibility of replacing the legislative recommendations with the draft model provisions.[87] Therefore, even in the Model Provisions, the full text of the legislative recommendations 1-13 as originally adopted by the Commission in 2000 remains in Part 1 of the Model Provisions.

Thirdly, some issues neither arise in the recommendations of the Legislative Guide nor the provisions in the Model Provisions. These issues are only explained and discussed in the notes of the Legislative Guide, such as that on sovereign immunity.[88] The countries who expect to establish or reform their laws on PFIPs in light of the Legislative Guide and the Model Provisions should consider all of these documents.

Therefore, the preamble of the Model Legislative Provisions clearly spells out that the legislators in recipient countries need to consider the whole of the contents of the Legislative Guide, whether or not expressly dealt with in the Model Legislative Provisions.[89]

To sum up, so far UNCITRAL has drafted two relevant guidelines: the Legislative Guide (2000) and the Model Legislative Provisions (2003). Both of them have the same effect.

3.3.4 The Reasons to Choose the Legislative Guide and Model Provisions Drafted by UNCITRAL

Both the Legislative Guide on Privately Financed Infrastructure Projects and Model Provisions on Privately Financed Infrastructure Projects were issued by UNCITRAL. In addition to representatives of member States of the Commission, representatives of many other States and of a number of international organisations, both intergovernmental and non-governmental, actively participated in the preparatory work. When

[86]UNCITRAL, 36th session, A/CN.9/521-*Report of the Working Group on Privately Financed Infrastructure Projects on the work of its fifth session,* P5, para 18.

[87]Ibid., P6, para 19.

[88]Son Seungwoo, 'Legal Analysis on Public-Private Partnerships regarding Model PPP Rules' (June 2012, UNCITRAL Visiting Scholar (2011.7.26 - 2012.7.25.), Faculty of Law at the Dankook University in Republic of Korea) P33.

[89]UNCITRAL, 'Model Legislative Provisions on Privately Financed Infrastructure Projects' (2003), Preamble.

the Legislative Guide and Model Provisions are considered as guides to the reform of Chinese laws on PFIPs, it will be found that they not only satisfy the aims of the reform of Chinese legislation on PFIPs, referred to in Sect. 2.5 in Chap 2, but they also could overcome the shortcomings of Chinese laws on PFIPs, referred to in Sect. 2.3.2 in Chap 2.

3.3.4.1 Facilitate PFIPs

The final aim of the reform of Chinese laws on PFIPs is to facilitate PFIPs, which is the original aim for drafting the Legislative Guide and Model Provisions. As is written in the Foreword to the Legislative Guide:

> For host countries wishing to promote PFIPs it is recommended that the following principles be implemented by the law.[90]

Law could be considered to be a political commitment to provide legal rights and guarantee policy stability. Therefore, an efficient legislative framework could attract private investment and facilitate PFIPs.

The Legislative Guide and Model Provision could help China establish a legislative framework to protect private investment. The Legislative Guide contains a set of recommended legislative principles entitled "Legislative Recommendations". The Model Provisions issued afterwards was also written on the basis of these recommendations. The legislative recommendations are intended to assist in the establishment of a legislative framework favourable to PFIPs.[91]

The Legislative Guide and Model Provisions could help China review its laws to attract private investment. The Legislative Guide is intended to be used as a reference by legislators when they prepare new laws or review existing laws and regulations. For that purpose, the Guide helps identify areas of law that are typically most relevant to private capital investment in public infrastructure projects and discusses the content of those laws which would be conducive to attracting private capital, national and foreign.[92]

3.3.4.2 Unified Legislation

The aim of reform of Chinese laws on PFIPs and the principles in the Legislative Guide and Model Provisions emphasize long-term sustainability.

One of the reasons why the Chinese legislation on PFIPs needs to be reformed is current Chinese provincial laws on PFIPs cannot ensure consistency between the public authorities, since they sometimes contradict each other. Meanwhile, the

---

[90] *'Legislative Guide on Privately Financed Infrastructure Project'* (2001)UNCITRAL (A/CN.9/SER.B/4) (hereafter referred to as the Legislative Guide) Foreword, P xi.

[91] The Legislative Guide, Introduction and background information on PFIPs, P2, para 5.

[92] Ibid., P3, para 7.

Legislative Guide and Model Provisions consider it important to ensure that the host country has the institutional capacity to undertake the various tasks entrusted to public authorities involved in infrastructure projects through their phases of implementation.[93]

It is noteworthy that, although the Legislative Guide and Model Provisions do not mention the "establishment of national legislation" directly, all four legislative frameworks analysed in them imply a unified legislation at a national rather than provincial level. Firstly, it adopts specific legislation in respect of individual projects.[94] In other words, even if the infrastructure project crosses difference provinces in the host country, only one legislative body manages the project. Secondly, it awards concessions to the Private Sector for the provision of public services. The Government is authorized by general legislation to award the Private Sector a concession in which a public service, which has economic value and is originally offered by the Public Sector, is allowed to be exploited by private entities.[95] In other words, the standard by which concessions are awarded is fixed by general legislation and cannot be changed in different regions without permission. Thirdly, it adopts sector-specific legislation, taking into account the market structure in each sector.[96] In other words, in the specific sector the legislation should have coherence in the host country rather than depending upon provincial regulation in different regions. Fourthly, it enacts regulations, setting forth more detailed rules to implement the general provisions of domestic laws on PFIPs.[97] In other words, a unified general provision should be made first.

3.3.4.3 Comprehensive Legislation on PFIPs

China need to establish a comprehensive legislation on PFIPs, and the Legislative Guide and Model Provisions offer a pattern and choices for this legislation.

The new Chinese legislation on PFIPs needs be separated from other laws in order to focus on PFIPs. The legislative recommendations in the Legislative Guide and Model Provisions deal with matters that need to be addressed in legislation specifically concerned with PFIPs, but they do not deal with other areas of law which also have an impact on Privately Financed Infrastructure Projects. Moreover, the successful implementation of PFIPs typically requires various measures beyond the establishment of an appropriate legislative framework, such as adequate administrative structures and practices, organisational capability, technical expertise, appropriate human and financial resources and economic stability. Although some of

[93]The legislative Guide, Chap. I on General legislative and institutional framework, P24, para 6.

[94]Ibid., P25, para 11.

[95]Ibid., P25, para 11.

[96]Ibid., P26, para 12.

[97]Ibid., P26, para 14.

these matters are covered to some extent, they are not fully addressed in the legislative recommendations.[98]

The new Chinese legislation on PFIPs should cover all aspects of PFIPs. The Legislative Guide contains seventy one recommendations covering all aspects of PFIPs. The Model Provisions, which was drafted afterwards, consist of five parts on the basis of these recommendations: I. General Provisions; II. Selection of the concessioner; III. Contents and implementation of the concession contract; IV. Duration, extension and termination of the concession contract; V. Settlement of disputes. Therefore, the Legislative Guide and the Model Provisions offer a clear and competitive selection procedure and clarify the rights and responsibilities of the parties in PFIPs.

During the reform of Chinese legislation on PFIPs, the contents of the Legislative Guide and Model Provisions could be applied in light of different requirements. The Legislative Guide and Model Provisions do not provide a single set of model solutions to address these concerns, but it helps the country to evaluate different approaches available and to choose the one most suitable to the national or local context.

3.3.4.4 Balancing the Interests Between Private and Public

The new Chinese legislation on PFIPs should balance the interests between the Private and Public Sector. The advice provided in the Legislative Guide also aims at achieving a balance between the desire to facilitate and encourage private participation in infrastructure projects, on the one hand, and the various public interest concerns of the host country, on the other. The Legislative Guide lists and discusses a number of concerns of fundamental public interest and private interest which should be considered in the new Chinese legislation.

Points of public concern include matters such as the continuity of the provision of public services; adherence to environmental protection, health, safety and quality standards set by the host country; fairness of prices charged to the public; non-discriminatory treatment of customers or users, full disclosure of information pertaining to the operation of infrastructure facilities and the flexibility needed to meet changing conditions, including the expansion of the service to meet additional demand.[99]

Fundamental concerns of the Private Sector, in turn, usually include issues such as the stability of the legal and economic environment in the host country; the transparency of laws and regulations, and predictability and impartiality in their application; enforceability of property rights against violations by third parties; assurances that private property is respected by the host country and not interfered with other than for reasons of public interest and only then if compensation is paid; and freedom

[98]The Legislative Guide, Introduction and background information on PFIPs, P2, para 6.

[99]Ibid., P2, para 4.

of the parties to agree on commercial terms that ensure a reasonable return on invested capital commensurate with the risks taken by private investors.[100]

3.3.4.5 Embody Marketisation

The Chinese legislation reform on PFIPs aims to break monopoly and enhance competition in this market. Market competition is also advocated in the Legislative Guide and Model Provisions. The Legislative Guide and Model Provisions consider essential elements of national policies to include the level of competition sought for each infrastructure sector, the way in which the sector is structured and the mechanisms used to ensure adequate functioning of infrastructure markets.[101]

In China, competition between concessioners has no clear protection and there is still unfair competition between the common Private Sector and SOEs[102] which monopolize Chinese infrastructure projects. The government may prefer the SOEs to profit rather than the Private Sector. Then the SOEs may find it easier to get the concession because the concession is awarded by the government. Although this prejudice may not be shown directly, there is no doubt that the SOEs would at least get more information and support from the government, which could help them to get the concession.

Therefore, when referring to the Legislative Guide and Model Provisions, Chinese legislation to promote private investment in infrastructure should be accompanied by measures destined to introduce competition between public service providers or to prevent monopolistic conditions where competition is not feasible.

3.3.4.6 International Standards

Chinese legislation reform on PFIPs aims for Chinese legislation on PFIPs to achieve an international standard to attract more foreign private investment. The mission of the Legislative Guide and Model Provisions is to promote the transparency of laws on PFIPs so that private investment can clarify their investment options and have reasonable expectations about their profits. The transparency of laws and administrative procedures is of particular importance when foreign investment is sought, since foreign companies may be unfamiliar with the country's practices for the award of infrastructure projects.[103]

---

[100] Ibid.

[101] Ibid., P6, para 21.

[102] SOEs stand for State-owned Enterprises which is a legal entity created by a government to undertake commercial activities on behalf of an owner government.

[103] The legislative Guide, Chap. I on General legislative and institutional framework, P24, para 4.

3.4 Other Countries' Laws on PFIPs

In this book, some countries' laws about PFIPs are referenced. When compared with the various countries' domestic laws which reflect the specific demands of these countries, the guidelines made by UNCITRAL represent the commonly accepted international standard. Therefore, in Chinese law reform, the other countries' laws are considered as a reference only when the Legislative Guide and the Model Provisions made by UNCITRAL have gaps in their guidelines or their recommendations do not fit China's specific situation. In other words, the other countries' laws on PFIPs are not used as the primary guidelines to the Chinese law reform but as a supplement for situations when the guideline has gaps or is unavailable.

3.4.1 Extraordinary Opinions

The countries which have extensive experience of PFIPs may have some extraordinary opinions on making laws on PFIPs.

Some countries have extensive experience in PFIPs. There were a number of countries using the PPP model as early as the Eighteenth and Nineteenth Centuries.[104] With the development and improvement of PPPs, Britain even invented PFIs in 1992.[105] There are a lot of successful examples on PFIPs in these countries. For example, the M6 toll road in Britain which connects Birmingham and the Black Country was constructed and is operated by the private company—Midland Expressway Limited.[106] The Channel Tunnel which connects Britain and France is financed by a joint-owned British and French private company—Eurotunnel General Limited.[107] Since these countries have been using the PFIP model, these cases offer practical examples used in establishing the laws on PFIPs in these countries, and therefore these countries have made a number of laws and regulations on PFIPs. In the UK for example, a series of PFIPs contract versions were published by HM Treasury during 1999 to 2012.[108] The Standardisation of PF2 Contracts (SoPC), which was issued in December 2012, is the latest version of the standard wording and guidance used by Public Sector bodies and their advisors when drafting PF2 contracts. It reflects the new model of contracting for projects for the delivery of infrastructure

---

[104] Smith A.J., *'Privatized Infrastructure: the role of government'* (1999) Thomas Telford, P8–10.

[105] Yescombe E. R., *'Public-Private Partnerships: Principles of Policy and Finance'* (ELSEVIER 2007) P9.

[106] *'Question and Answer Equivalent project relief'* published in Construction Newsletter(2006); the website <https://www.m6toll.co.uk/about-us/> accessed on 21st May, 2019.

[107] Veditz Leslie A, *'The Channel Tunnel: A Case Study'* (Washington, D.C: National Defense University 1993).

[108] HM Treasure, *'Standardisation of PFI Contracts Version 4'* (March 2007) P1, <http://webarchive.nationalarchives.gov.uk/20130129110402/http://www.hm-treasury.gov.uk/d/pfi_sopc4pu101_210307.pdf> accessed on 26th July, 2019.

and services using public private partnerships.[109] There is no standardisation contract version offered by UNCITRAL. If China expects to offer standardisation contracts to private investors in PFIPs, the standardisation contracts used in the UK could be referenced.

3.4.2 Supplemental Reference Rather Than Primary Guideline

Other countries' laws cannot be used as the primary guidelines in Chinese law reform but they may be used as a supplementary reference.

The countries' domestic laws on PFIPs focus on the specific situations in these countries, which may be not be appropriate to the specific circumstances in China. The UK, for instance, does not have a specific law on PFIPs, but regulations on PFIPs are scattered in some relevant policies and guidelines. Although China could reference the UK's model in the Standardisation of Contracts on PFIs, China, which needs a nationally comprehensive legislation on PFIPs, would find it impossible to use British laws as a guideline. Japanese law provides a further example. It issued the Law Relating the Promotion of Realization of Public Facilities by Using Private Funds of 1999 as a comprehensive law on PFIPs to regulate their relevant behaviours systematically.[110] However, neither the Japanese law nor other countries' laws deal with China-specific problems such as the state-owned land. They only offer alternative suggestions. By contrast, the Legislative Guide and the Model Provisions made by UNCITRAL represent commonly accepted international standards. They consider all aspects of PFIPs and various solutions to possible problems that might arise. It does not provide a single set of model solutions to address these concerns, but helps countries which need reform their laws on PFIPs to evaluate the different approaches available and to choose the one most suitable to its specific national context.[111] Therefore, the other countries' laws on PFIPs should not become the primary guide to Chinese law reform, but remain a supplementary reference.

---

[109]HM Treasure, *'Standardisation of PF2 Contracts'* (December 2012), <https://assets.publishing.service.gov.uk/government/uploads/system/uploads/attachment_data/file/221556/infrastructure_standardisation_of_contracts_051212.pdf> accessed on 26th July, 2019; Infrastructure UK, *'PF2: A User Guide'* (December 2012), <https://www.gov.uk/government/uploads/system/uploads/attachment_data/file/207382/pf2_userguide.pdf> accessed on 26th July, 2019;The National Archive, <http://webarchive.nationalarchives.gov.uk/20130129110402/http://www.hm-treasury.gov.uk/infrastructure_ppp_contractual.htm> accessed on 26th July, 2019.

[110]Wang Tie Shan, 'Comparative research on PFI project between Britain and Japan' (2008) IEC, No1: 49.

[111]*'Legislative Guide on Privately Financed Infrastructure Project'* (2001)UNCITRAL (A/CN.9/SER.B/4), Introduction and Background information on PFIPs, paras 4.

3.5 Conclusion

This chapter answers the 2nd research question, namely why choose the Legislative Guide and Model Provisions made by UNCITRAL as the guidelines to improve the Chinese legislation reform on PFIPs, and why use other countries' laws on PFIPs as a supplementary reference.

Firstly, this chapter states that, in addition to the Legislative Guide and Model Provisions made by UNCITRAL, there are other international agreements relating to Privately Financed Infrastructure Projects (PFIPs) made by international organisations, such as the WTO, the OECD and the World Bank. Moreover, some bilateral or multilateral treaties relating to PFIPs are subscribed to by China and other countries. These international agreements and treaties have contributed to the harmonisation of laws on PFIPs, so that the countries are in agreement on the issues relating to PFIPs. However, these international agreements and treaties cannot be used to guide the reform and improvement of the host countries' laws on PFIPs because of various limitations and disadvantages.

Secondly, the Legislative Guide and Model Provisions made by UNCITRAL are considered for their appropriateness in guiding the Chinese legislation reform on PFIPs. On the one hand, the organisation UNCITRAL, which works towards the progressive harmonisation and unification of international economic laws, is reliable. On the other hand, the Legislative Guide and Model Provisions, which have recommendations for the treatment of all aspects of PFIPs, address all the aims of Chinese legislation reform. Therefore, they are considered to be the best guideline to inform Chinese legislation on PFIPs.

Thirdly, some countries' laws on PFIPs may be useful as a supplementary reference because these countries have extensive experience in PFIP practice and related laws. These countries' laws on PFIPs could not guide Chinese law reform, since they focus on their own situations. However, they could be used to remedy the gaps in the guidelines in the Legislative Guide and Model Provisions.

To sum up, after comparing the advantages and disadvantages among these international agreements and treaties, the Legislative Guide and Model Provisions made by UNCITRAL serves as the best guide to Chinese legislation reform on PFIPs. Meanwhile, some countries' laws on PFIPs may be used as a supplementary reference.

The next chapters of this book will discuss in detail how the Legislative Guide and Model Provisions will guide the Chinese legislation reform on PFIPs. Following the structure of the Legislative Guide and Model Provisions, the rest of the book will be divided into four parts: legislative framework, concessioner selection, project agreement and dispute settlement. Chapter 4 will discuss, referring the guidelines of Legislative Guide and Model Provisions, how to reform the general legislative and institutional framework on PFIPs in China.

Chapter 4
General Legislative and Institutional Framework

4.1 Introduction

This chapter will discuss Chinese law reforms on PFIPs in terms of the general legislative and institutional framework required, according to the guidelines of the Legislative Guide and Model Provisions made by UNCITRAL and supplementary references to other countries' laws.

The aim of this chapter is to review the current Chinese legislative and institutional framework on PFIPs, and to propose a more appropriate legislative and institutional framework to facilitate the development of PFIPs in China.

There are two objectives for this chapter. The first objective is to prove that the best way to use the Legislative Guide and Model Provisions is to use its structure to discuss Chinese law reform on PFIPs while making the use of their content optional. The second objective is to point out the defects in current Chinese legislative and institutional frameworks and improve them by considering the principles in terms of the legislative and institutional framework on PFIPs offered by Legislative Guide and Model Provisions.

This chapter consists of two sections. Section 4.2 presents the history behind the structure of the Legislative Guide and the Model Provisions and suggests new Chinese legislation on PFIPs may benefit from using this structure. This section also points out that using the content of the Legislative Guide and the Model Provisions is optional. Section 4.3 lists the four principles necessary to establishing the general legislative and institutional framework offered by Legislative Guide and the Model Provisions—transparency, fairness, long-term sustainability and eliminating undesirable restrictions. This section reviews whether the current Chinese framework satisfies these four principles. The British regulations about regulatory institutions and customer interest are also used as supplementary reference.

This chapter answers the third research question, with reference to the Legislative Guide and Model Provisions and with supplementary reference to the laws of other countries; namely, how should the general legislative and institutional framework on PFIPs in China be improved?

S. Liang, *Legal Aspects of Privately Financed Infrastructure Projects (PFIPs) in China*,
https://doi.org/10.1007/978-981-15-6803-9_4

4.2 How to Use the Legislative Guide and the Model Provisions to Guide Chinese Law Reform on the General Legislative and Institutional Framework of PFIPs

4.2.1 Flexibility Principle and Concise Principles

The Legislative Guide includes a clear set of legislative recommendations followed by an explanatory discussion of the pertinent issues and the possible options available.[1] The Model Legislative Provisions also gives a set of model provisions corresponding to the recommendations in the Legislative Guide and each provision references its corresponding recommendation and paragraphs of explanations in the Legislative Guide.[2]

The Legislative Guide and the Model Provisions are made up of recommendation, provisions and explanatory discussion, based on two principles fixed by UNCITRAL on how to draft legal documents on PFIPs:

Firstly, the Legislative Guide was drafted with the flexibility principle in mind. The subject matter dealt with in the Guide touched upon a number of public law and policy issues and that it would therefore be difficult to attempt to formulate model provisions that adequately took into account the differences between legal systems and the variety of policy options. Thus the Guide stressed the importance of affording sufficient flexibility to legislators in countries wishing to promote private investment in infrastructure.[3]

Secondly, the Legislative Guide was drafted with the principle of concision in mind. After considering the different views expressed, the Commission requested the Secretariat to draft the legislative recommendations in the form of concise legislative principles, thereby reducing the number of recommendations.[4]

Therefore, when China uses the Legislative Guide and the Model Provisions as guidelines in its law reform, it is not mandatory that China copies all recommendations and provisions into its new legislation. It may choose any recommendations and provisions which it needs in the law reform.

---

[1]UNCITRAL, 31st session, A/53/17- *Report of UNCITRAL on the work of its thirty-first session*, P20, para 203.

[2]UNCITRAL, 34th session, A/CN.9/488-*Possible work on privately financed infrastructure projects*, P4, para 19; UNCITRAL, 35th session, A/CN.9/505-*Report of the Working Group on Privately Financed Infrastructure Projects at its fourth session*, P3–24, para 18–174; UNCITRAL, 35st session, A/57/17- *Report of UNCITRAL on the work of its thirty-fifth session*, para 231–232.

[3]UNCITRAL, 31st session, A/53/17- *Report of UNCITRAL on the work of its thirty-first session*, P20, para 203.

[4]Ibid., para 204.

4.2.2 The Structure of the Legislative Guide and the Model Provisions

The structure of both of the Legislative Guide and the Model Provisions are similar. The first part includes general items on general legislative and institutional frameworks, followed by chapters on the details of selection of the concessioner, concession contract (plus the duration, extension and termination of the project agreement) and settlement of dispute.

The structure of the Legislative Guide and the Model Provisions was discussed many times in the UNCITRAL meetings and the current structure is considered to be the most suitable. One of the documents submitted to the 30th Commission Session of UNCITRAL included annex I, which contains a table of contents setting out the topics to be covered by the legislative guide.[5] This content was divided into eleven chapters in the 31st Commission Session.[6] The Commission, in its 32nd Session, was informed that the overall structure of the legislative guide should be changed by combining some of its chapters. The result was eight chapters (I, "General legislative considerations", II, "Project risks and government support", III, "Selection of the concessioner", IV, "The project agreement", V, "Infrastructure development and operation", VI, "End of project term, extension and termination", VII, "Governing law", VIII, "Settlement of disputes").[7] The final structure of seven chapters was confirmed in the 33rd Commission Session of UNCITRAL (I, "General legislative and institutional framework", II, "Project risks and government support", III, "Selection of the concessioner", IV, "Construction and operation of infrastructure", V, "Duration, extension and termination of the project agreement", VI, "Settlement of disputes", VII, "Other Relevant Areas of Law"). It can be seen that though the structure of the Legislative Guide changed during the discussions, it still maintained a connection between the general legislative framework and various issues in detail.

Considering China has never established a comprehensive legislation on PFIPs, the new Chinese legislation on PFIPs could follow the structure of the Legislative Guide and Model Provisions: first to discuss the general legislative framework (in this chapter), and then separately discuss the details pertaining to concessioner selection, project agreements and dispute settlement.

[5]UNCITRAL, 30th Session, A/CN.9/438-Privately-Financed Infrastructure Projects: Draft Chapters of a legislative guide on privately-financed infrastructure projects, P4.

[6]UNCITRAL, 31st Session, A/CN.9/444-Privately Financed Infrastructure Projects - Draft chapters of a legislative guide on privately financed infrastructure projects, P3–7, para 6–30.

[7]UNCITRAL, 32nd Session, A/54/17-*'Report of UNCITRAL on the work of its thirty-second session'*, P3, para 15.

4.3 How to Use the General Principles of the Legislative Guide and the Model Provisions to Guide Chinese Law Reform on the General Legislative and Institutional Framework of PFIPs

The general guiding principles are expressed in Recommendation 1 of the Legislative Guide:

> The constitutional, legislative and institutional framework for the implementation of privately financed infrastructure projects should ensure transparency, fairness, and the long-term sustainability of projects. Undesirable restrictions on private sector participation in infrastructure development and operation should be eliminated.

It is clear that the Legislative Guide considers the four issues of transparency, fairness, long-term sustainability and eliminating undesirable restrictions to be the general guiding principles to the establishment of a legal framework for PFIPs.

The original draft[8] from the Secretary-General did not express such clear general guiding principles but it did indicate that it is necessary to eliminate undesirable restrictions in constitutional provisions so as to give power to contracting authorities to award concessions.

However, in the Report by UNCITRAL on the work of its 32nd Session,[9] a proposal was made that the draft should outline the general principles that should inspire a domestic legislative framework for privately financed infrastructure projects, in particular the principles of transparency, fairness, openness and competition. Therefore, the general guiding principles were refined and clearly expressed in Recommendation 1 of the Legislative Guide and formally adopted in succeeding documents. When the Model Provisions was developed as an addendum to the Legislative Guide in the 35th session of UNCITRAL, these general guiding principles were emphasised in Model Provision 1.[10]

The following discussion assesses whether these general principles are also embodied in current Chinese laws on PFIPs. If so, it will examine whether they are

[8]UNCITRAL, 32nd session, A/CN.9/458/add.2—*Privately Financed Infrastructure Projects: Draft Chapters of a legislative guide on privately financed infrastructure projects—Chapter I. General Legislative Considerations*, p 3: (1) The law should provide the contracting authorities in the host country with the necessary power to award concessions for infrastructure development and operation. It is advisable to review existing constitutional provisions so as to eliminate undesirable restrictions to Private Sector participation in infrastructure development and operation, or unnecessary limitations to the use of public property by private entities and obstacles to private ownership of infrastructure.

[9]UNCITRAL, 32nd session, A/54/17-*'Report of UNCITRAL on the work of its thirty-second session'*, P6, para 44.

[10]UNCITRAL, Model Provisions, Model provision 1. Preamble: …considers it desirable to establish a favourable legislative framework to promote and facilitate the implementation of privately financed infrastructure projects by enhancing transparency, fairness and long-term sustainability and removing undesirable restrictions on Private Sector participation in infrastructure development and operation.

applied appropriately; if not, it will address how these principles should be applied and how they might reform current Chinese laws on PFIPs.

4.3.1 Transparency

According to the Legislative Guide, transparency in a legal framework for PFIPs means clear and readily accessible laws with efficient procedures that can be easily applied.[11] It involves two aspects: firstly, transparent laws and administrative procedures offer clear and readily accessible laws and efficient procedures, so that the potential private investors can predict and estimate the costs and risks of their investment and thus offer the most advantageous terms. Secondly, transparent laws and administrative procedures foster openness through provisions requiring the publication of administrative decisions, in order to prevent corruption or improper actions and decisions in the contracting authority or its officials.

In order for the private investor better to estimate the risks,, the Legislative Guide emphasises rules relating to project risk and government support, in addition to the rules on the behaviour within PFIPs. The Legislative Guide does not advise statutory provisions that limit the negotiators' ability to achieve a balanced allocation of project risks, as appropriate to the needs of individual projects.[12] However, the Legislative Guide does advise that legislation has explicit legislative authorisation to provide certain government support.[13] This is very important when foreign investment is sought, since foreign companies may be unfamiliar with the country's laws on PFIPs. By clarifying the risks and supports, foreign private investors will have more confidence to join a project.

Both the Legislative Guide and the Model Provisions point out the importance of information disclosure, but they do not offer this resolution in detail. In the follow chapters, however, information disclosure is implicitly dealt with in suggestions on the processes of concessioner selection, and project construction and operation.

In current Chinese laws on PFIPs, the transparency principle is implicit in provincial regulations to some extent but it is not framed clearly enough. In China, there are only provincial regulations on PFIPs, and no comprehensive national legislation (as was discussed in Chap. 2). These deficiencies are evident if the most typical provincial regulation is taken for example: Urban Infrastructure Concession Regulation (Beijing) 2005 (hereafter referred to as "Beijing Regulation").

Firstly, the transparency principle is not directly expressed in the general provisions of the Beijing Regulation. Article 5 of the Beijing Regulation[14] states that

---

[11]The legislative Guide, Chap. I on General legislative and institutional framework, P23–24, para 4.

[12]The legislative Guide, Chap. II on Project risks and government support, P42, para 21.

[13]The legislative Guide, Chap. II on Project risks and government support, P47, para 36.

[14]Beijing Regulation 2005, Chapter 1 General Provisions, Article 5: the implement of urban infrastructure concession should follow the principles of fair, honest and priority to public interest.

fairness, honest and priority of public interest are the general guiding principles for PFIPs, but it does not mention transparency. Although some provisions in the Beijing Regulation imply transparency, the transparency principle is explicit.

Secondly, the Beijing Regulation only provides for a very general legal framework to govern private finance in infrastructure, so it does not offer clear and readily accessible laws and efficient procedures for certain aspects. On the one hand, some vague words are used in this Regulation, which means that more work is needed to do to fix their significance. For example, Article 3 lists the specific sectors where concession may be taken as a means to provide infrastructure services, but a vague item at the end of Article 3 says the Municipal Government may also designate other sectors where concessions may be arranged. How the Municipal Government is to designate these sectors is not addressed. On the other hand, the procedure governing concessioner selection is not clear either. For example, a reference to "other competitive procedures" in concessioner selection[15] means that both the Bidding Law and also the Procurement Law may be applied (as analysed in Sect. 2.3.2.3 in Chap. 2). Another example in the Beijing Regulation is the failure to explain the pre-award process for deciding a concession project. It only says that the concession project should satisfy the requirements of city development[16] (The pre-award process and the concessioner selection process will be analysed in detail in Chap. 5). Therefore, much work is left over in relation to the explanation and implementation of the Regulation, the careful preparation of the PIP[17] and the negotiation of the concession agreement.[18]

Thirdly, the disclosure of administrative information is hardly referred to in the Beijing Regulation. Although the Regulation requires the relevant department of the administration to supervise the concession project, it does not require the administrative department to disclose their decision or the results of this supervision to public. By contrast, it stresses the concessioner's obligation to disclose information to both administration and the public in Article 39. Publishing the concessioner's information is important, but the administrative information disclosure is also important to both the concessioner and the public.

Transparency of laws and administrative procedures is of particular importance to foreign investment, since foreign companies may be unfamiliar with the country's practices in awarding infrastructure projects.[19] Therefore, the legal framework governing future PFIPs in China should be explicit in reference to the transparency principle, and offer clear and readily accessible laws and efficient procedures.

---

[15]Beijing Regulation 2005, Chapter 2 Award procedures, Article 11.

[16]Beijing Regulation 2005, Chapter 2 Award procedures, Article 8.

[17]Implementation Plan for the Project (PIP): After a concession project is determined, the contracting authority shall prepare a project implementation plan, which lays out the basis for the award process and provides for the substance of the concession agreement.

[18]Cao Fuguo, *'The emerging legal framework for private finance in infrastructure in China: a preliminary review of the Beijing Concession Regulation'* (2006), (P.P.L.R. 62).

[19]The legislative Guide, Chap. I on General legislative and institutional framework, P23–24, para 4.

4.3.2 *Fairness*

In the Legislative Guide, the fairness of a legal framework for PFIPs means it should take into account the various (and sometimes possibly conflicting) interests of the Public Sector, the Private Sector and the customers, and seeks to achieve an equitable balance between them.[20] The interest of Public Sector is to ensure public interest, including continuous provision of essential services and promoting the development of national infrastructure. The interest of the private investors is their business profits. The interest of the customers is access to adequate services with a high quality and an affordable price.

In current Chinese laws on PFIPs, the fairness principle is accepted and applied in provincial regulations. The current Chinese regulations are intended to protect both public interest and private interest. However, the regulations only emphasise the balance between public interests and private interests, whereas the interests of the customer is not reflected upon at all. For example, the beginning of the Beijing Regulation states that the Regulation aims at protecting social and public interests, ensuring safety and the quality provision of public goods and services, and protecting the legitimate interests of concessioners.[21]

4.3.2.1 Protection of Public Interests

The Legislative Guide lists those public interests that should be considered by the legislators when drafting legislation on PFIPs. These include continuity in the provision of public services; adherence to environmental protection, health, safety and quality standards set by the host country; fairness of the prices charged to the public; non-discriminatory treatment of customers or users; full disclosure of information pertaining to the operation of infrastructure facilities; and flexibility to meet changing conditions, including the expansion of the service to meet additional demand.[22]

In China, there are measures in provincial regulations designed to protect public interest, including the regulation of the project quality and safety;[23] the withdrawal of concession in emergency situation;[24] control of the service fee and the concessioner charge.[25]

It seems that the current Chinese regulations on protecting the public interest are consistent with the guidelines of the Legislative Guide and Model Provisions.

---

[20] Ibid., P24, para 5.

[21] Beijing Regulation 2005, Chapter 1 General Provisions, Article 1.

[22] The Legislative Guide, Introduction and background information on PFIPs, P2, para 4.

[23] Beijing Urban Infrastructure Concession Regulation 2005 Article 19; Xinjiang Regulation, Article 5; Shenzhen Regulation, Article 4.

[24] Beijing Urban Infrastructure Concession Regulation 2005 Article 21; Shenzhen Regulation, Article 36.

[25] Beijing Urban Infrastructure Concession Regulation 2005 Article 20; Xinjiang Regulation, Article 22; Shenzhen Regulation, Article 20.

However, one exceptional situation should be noted: all current Chinese Provincial Regulations establish the "principle of public interest precedence", which means when conflicts arise between public interest and private interest, public interests is given priority for protection.[26] When the Chinese laws on PFIPs were not sufficiently advanced to regulate PFIPs, the government was, on occasion, vulnerable to exploitation by the private operator investors seeking excessive profits.[27] Therefore, the "principle of public interest precedence" was useful for protecting Chinese public interest. However, this principle is inconsistent with the spirit of the Legislative Guide and Model Provisions made by UNCITRAL. Although the Legislative Guide and Model Provisions require the protection of the public interest[28] and allow for the termination of projects for reasons of public interest,[29] they still emphasise the spirit of "equitable balance between the interests"[30] rather than the priority of certain interests over others. China's efforts to attract more private finance to satisfy the infrastructure demand mean it should abandon the "principle of public interest precedence", and instead, to maintain consistency with the spirit of the Legislative Guide and Model Provisions. This will emphasise the "equitable balance between the interests", and give exceptions to the contracting authority's termination rights and relative compensation rules.[31]

4.3.2.2 Protection of Private Interests

The Legislative Guide also lists those private investor's interests that should be considered by the legislator when drafting legislation on PFIPs: stability of the legal and economic environment in the host country; transparency of laws and regulations, and predictability and impartiality in their application; enforceability of property rights against violations by third parties; assurances that private property is respected by the host country and not interfered with other than for reasons of public interest and only then if compensation is paid; and freedom of the parties to agree on

[26]Beijing Urban Infrastructure Concession Regulation 2005

Article 5: The principles of fairness, honesty and priority of public interests shall be followed for implementing concession of urban infrastructure.

Cao Fuguo, *'Regulating procurement of privately financed infrastructure in China: a review of the recent legislative initiatives and the emerging regulatory framework'* (2007), Public Procurement law review (P.P.L.R.2007, 3, 147–173) P152.

[27]Shen Jiyong, Wang ShouQing, Qiang Maoshan, *'The Political Risks in China's BOT/PPP Project: a case study'*, Chinese Businessmen Investment and Finance, pp. 50–56, No. 1, 2005.

[28]The Legislative Guide, Introduction and background information on PFIPs, P2, para 4.

[29]The legislative Guide, Chap. V on Duration, extension and termination of the project agreement, Section D on Termination, paras 26.

[30]The legislative Guide, Chap. I on General legislative and institutional framework, P23–24, para 5.

[31]The legislative Guide, Chap. V on Duration, extension and termination of the project agreement, Section D on Termination, paras 14–27.

commercial terms that ensure a reasonable return on invested capital commensurate with the risks taken by private investors.[32]

In China, there are also measures in the provincial regulations designed to protect the interests of private investors, including the transparency of laws and regulations on the award process, and predictability and impartiality in their application. In respect of concession contracts by the Government, there are regulations on strengthening the co-ordination between governments; on government support and commitment; on protection of commercial secret; and on compensation payable in the case of policy change.[33]

In practice, the balance of public interests and private interest is a consequence of negotiation; thus the achievement of the balance of interest objectives depends very much on the selection and negotiations process and the resulting contract between the contracting parties.[34]

4.3.2.3 Protection of Customer Interests

The Legislative Guide and Model Provisions particularly refer to the customers' right to adequate services with proper quality and price.

The current Chinese Provincial Regulations do not consider the customer interests to be a primary objective, although, in Beijing Regulation Article 20,[35] the customer rights are more or less protected. Customer interest is so related to the development of a consumer society that it is no surprise that efforts to declare consumer protection failed in the Chinese Provincial Regulations, where a consumer society is not a primary consideration. Although it is difficult to separate customer interest from government interest because the government represents a public interest that includes the customer interest, customers have to safeguard their interests in cases where the government and the private investor conspire to harm customer interests.[36] As a matter of fact, consumers can play an important role in supervising the operation of public services. However, the Legislative Guide does not offer the details how to protect the customers' interest, even though the protection of customer interest is considered to be one of its objectives. In this case, it is welcome that some advances

[32] The Legislative Guide, Introduction and background information on PFIPs, P2, para 4.

[33] Beijing Urban Infrastructure Concession Regulation 2005 Article 6, 11, 15, 16, 17, 18,19, 29, 30, 32.

[34] Cao Fuguo, *'Regulating procurement of privately financed infrastructure in China: a review of the recent legislative initiatives and the emerging regulatory framework'* (2007), Public Procurement law review (P.P.L.R.2007, 3, 147–173) P153.

[35] Beijing Regulation 2005, Chapter 3 Rights and obligations, Article 20: The concessionaire must provide a universal and non-discriminatory service to the consumers within the area defined in the concession agreement. When new users request connection to the infrastructure facilities supplying water, gas or heating, or infrastructure facilities established for sewage disposal, the concessionaire operating the facilities may not charge a connection fee to such new users.

[36] Peng Tao, *'PPP' practice in China and Composition of PPP' Legal Framework'*, Zheng Fa Lun Cong (No. 6, Dec. 10, 2006) P83.

have been achieved. Some countries' regulations require the establishment of a utilities committee, such as a consumer mechanism in the British counterpart. In the United Kingdom, several consumer voice mechanisms have been established in light of relevant Utilities Regulations as in, for example, the Consumer Council for Water (hereafter refers to CCWater) in the water industry.[37] The organisation of CCWater makes sure that the water consumers' collective voice is heard in national water debates and that consumers are important in the water industry.[38]

To sum up, the fairness of legal framework for PFIPs is both the means by which Governments regulate and ensure the provision of public services to their citizens and the means by which public service providers and their customers may protect their rights. Therefore, the legal framework for the further PFIPs in China should do more to balance public and private interests. Additionally, the protection of customer interests is necessary in further Chinese legislation on PFIPs.

4.3.3 Long-Term Sustainability

In the Legislative Guide and Model Provisions, long-term sustainability of legal frameworks governing PFIPs means that domestic legislation on infrastructure development should ensure the long-term provision of public services, with increasing attention paid to environmental sustainability.[39] From a legislative perspective, it involves two aspects: Firstly, the legislation can ensure that the host country has the institutional capacity to undertake the various tasks entrusted to public authorities involved in infrastructure projects through the phases of implementation.[40] Secondly, the legislation can ensure a marketization to achieve a correct balance between competitive and monopolistic provision of public services.[41]

---

[37] Cao Fuguo, *'Regulating procurement of privately financed infrastructure in China: a review of the recent legislative initiatives and the emerging regulatory framework'* (2007), Public Procurement law review (P.P.L.R.2007, 3, 147–173) P152.

[38] The Consumer Council for Water (CCWater) represents water and sewerage consumers in England and Wales. It is to make sure that the consumers' collective voice is heard in national water debate and that consumers remain at the heart of the water industry. It also takes up consumers' complaints if they have tried and failed to resolve issues with their water companies. (It took over the original organization "Water Voice" on 1 October 2005.) <http://www.ccwater.org.uk/server.php?show=nav.1300> accessed at 26th November2019.

[39] The legislative Guide, Chap. I on General legislative and institutional framework, P24, para 6.

[40] Ibid.

[41] Ibid.

4.3.3.1 Institutional Capacity

In order to ensure the host country has the institutional capacity to undertake tasks through the phases of implementation, the Legislative Guide and Model Provisions indicate that three aspects should be considered when the host country makes domestic legislation on PFIPs.

4.3.3.1.1 Authority Sector

The legislation should identify the sectors of the host country that are empowered to award concessions and enter into agreements for the implementation of PFIPs.[42] In some countries, such as China, the Government's responsibility for providing public services cannot be delegated without prior legislative authorisation.[43] In this case, when the legislation allows Private Sector to offer public services, the first thing is to identify clearly the sectors authorised to award infrastructure projects and to act as contracting authorities. Once the concession is award by the authorised sector, it means the PFIP has been acknowledged by the host country and is protected by the laws, and it cannot be withdrawn arbitrarily. The Model Legislative Provisions further specifies this recommendation. It indicates that the host country should list all sectors empowered to award concessions and enter into agreements for the implementation of PFIPs.[44] It even gives suggestions as to how to list the authorised sectors. One alternative may be to provide a list of authorised sectors empowered to enter into concession contracts, either in Model Provisions or in a schedule to be attached thereto. Another alternative might be to indicate the levels of government that have the power to enter into those contracts, without naming relevant public authorities.[45] In a big country, such as China, which has 35 provinces, it would be impossible to list all the names of the authorised sectors. A more reasonable approach may be to list the levels of government that have the power to enter into those contracts.

The scope of authorised sectors to award concessions should also be identified by the legislation, in order to ensure that concessions are lawful and valid.

---

[42]The Legislative Guide, recommendation 2.

[43]The Constitution of the People's Republic of China, adopted on March 14, 2004

Article 99: Local people's congresses at various levels ensure the observance and implementation of the Constitution and the law and the administrative rules and regulations in their respective administrative areas. Within the limits of their authority as prescribed by law, they adopt and issue resolutions and examine and decide on plans for local economic and cultural development and for the development of public services…….

[44]Model provision 3: Authority to enter into concession contracts (see the Legislative Guide, recommendation 2 and chap. I, paras 15–18) The following public authorities have the power to enter into concession contracts 4 for the implementation of infrastructure projects falling within their respective spheres of competence:…………….

Model provision 4: Eligible infrastructure sectors (see the Legislative Guide, recommendation 4 and chap. I, paras 19–22) Concession contracts may be entered into by the relevant authorities in the following sectors:………………….

[45]The Model Legislative Provisions, Model provision 3, P5. footnote 5.

The "scope" includes the nature and purpose of the PFIP for which concessions may be awarded in the host country. The law should identify the sectors or types of infrastructure in respect to which concessions may be granted.[46] Some infrastructures projects related to national defence or security may be excluded from the scope. The law should also identify the activities available to the private investor. It may be the construction and operation of new infrastructure facilities and systems, or the operation and maintenance of existing ones.[47] Before the Legislative Guide was adopted, the opinion was expressed that the legislator should set out only a priority list of the sectors or types of infrastructure where concessions might be granted. However, the UNCITRAL commission points out in the accompanying notes[48] that there was more than one possible way of indicating sectors or types of infrastructure where concessions might be granted. Therefore, the UNCITRAL commission did not adopt this suggestion.[49] At the same time, the UNCITRAL commission also disagreed to adding more indications on the activities of implementation of PFIPs, which is a matter related to the various policy options available to the host country.[50] To sum up, the UNCITRAL commission expected the Legislative Guide to be more flexible on the scope of the nature and purpose of the infrastructure projects, leaving scope to the decision of the host country. The scope made by the host country in light of this feature may have more long-term sustainability.

The "scope" also includes the extent of the concession. The law should identify whether the right to provide the service is exclusive or whether the concessioner will face competition from other infrastructure facilities or service providers. Certain sectors have the characteristics of natural monopolies, in which case open competition is usually not an economically viable alternative. The decision whether or not to grant exclusivity rights to a certain project or category of projects should be taken in the light of the host country's policy on the sector concerned. Therefore, the Legislative Guide deals with the issue of exclusivity in a flexible manner.[51] However, there should be some principles in issuing exclusive concession.

It is preferable for the law to authorise exclusive concessions when it is deemed to be in the public interest. The contracting authority should be required to state the reasons for issuing an exclusive concession, prior to starting the selection procedure.[52] The UNCITRAL commission expected that the host country should have the flexibility to decide whether to grant an exclusive concession, but the decision must be based on the consideration of public interest and the authority must state the reasons.

---

[46] The Legislative Guide, recommendation 4.

[47] The Legislative Guide, recommendation 3.

[48] The Legislative Guide, Chap. I on General legislative and institutional framework, P27, para 18.

[49] UNCITRAL, 33th session, A/55/17- *Report of the United Nations Commission on International Trade Law on the work of its thirty-third session*, P60, para 205.

[50] UNCITRAL, 33th session, A/55/17- *Report of the United Nations Commission on International Trade Law on the work of its thirty-third session*, P60, para 203.

[51] The legislative Guide, Chap. I on General legislative and institutional framework, P28, para 20–21.

[52] The legislative Guide, Chap. I on General legislative and institutional framework, P28, para 22.

To sum up, the enactment of express legislative authorisation can confirm the authorised sectors and the scope of the authority to award concessions on PFIPs. It is important to foster the confidence of private investors and ensure the long-term sustainability of PFIPs.

4.3.3.1.2 Regulatory Sector

The legislation should identify the regulatory sectors of the host country empowered to regulate the implementation of PFIPs. The issue of authority to regulate infrastructure services does not been noted in the Model Legislative Provisions. But it is analysed and discussed as an important part of the Legislative Guide.[53]

Since the first PFIPs, the activities in their implementation have been subject to a regulatory regime that may consist of a regulatory sector, substantive rules, procedures, and review.

The term "regulatory sector" refers to the institutional mechanisms required to implement and monitor the rules governing the activities of infrastructure operators.[54] One key issue concerning the regulatory sector is whether there is an independent body to supervise the whole process of the PFIPs.[55] The efficiency of the regulatory regime in most cases depends on the objectivity with which regulatory decisions are taken. Thus, it requires that regulatory sectors should be able to take decisions without interference or inappropriate pressures from infrastructure operators and public service providers.[56] On this basis, the legislation should have some regulations to ensure these kinds of interference or pressure are avoided, as in, for example, a conflict of interest when the regulatory officials also work for the infrastructure operator. It is noteworthy that the separation of the regulatory sector from the authorised sector is not expressly dealt with in the recommendations of the Legislative Guide, but that the notes of the Legislative Guide indicate that a regulatory sector joined with the authorised sector may affect the way they regulate the provision of service.[57] To some extent, it implies that the Legislative Guide prefers a totally independent regulatory sector.

The efficiency and credibility of regulatory sector's work require transparency and objectivity in the regulatory rules and procedures. Rules and procedures should be objective and clear so as to ensure fairness, impartiality and timely action by the regulatory sectors.[58] For the purpose of transparency, the law should require that the rules and procedures should be made public. Regulatory decisions should state

---

[53]The Legislative Guide, recommendation 7–11.

[54]The legislative Guide, Chap. I on General legislative and institutional framework, P31, para 31.

[55]Cao Fuguo, *'Regulating procurement of privately financed infrastructure in China: a review of the recent legislative initiatives and the emerging regulatory framework'* (2007), Public Procurement law review (P.P.L.R.2007, 3, P163).

[56]The legislative Guide, Chap. I on General legislative and institutional framework, P32, para 37.

[57]The legislative Guide, Chap. I on General legislative and institutional framework, P33, para 40.

[58]The legislative Guide, Chap. I on General legislative and institutional framework, P35, para 46.

the reasons on which they are based and should be made accessible to interested parties, through publication or other appropriate means.[59] The Legislative Guide even points out that the regulatory sectors could publish an annual report of their regulatory decisions and activities.[60] Additionally, for the purpose of objectivity, the law could require that the regulatory sector's important decisions should be based upon wide consultation, either in the form of a public hearing or the consultation of papers by interested groups.[61] The requirements of transparency and objectivity in the regulatory rules and procedures also reflect the principles of the Legislative Guide and Model Legislative Provisions.

If the decision made by the regulatory sector is wrong, the law should provide a channel to review the decision. This is a safeguard to ensure the transparency and objectivity of regulatory procedures. Recommendation 10 of the Legislative Guide clearly points out that the law should establish transparent procedures whereby the concessioner may request a review of regulatory decisions by an independent and impartial body, including court review, and should set forth the grounds on which such a review may be based.[62] However, it is noteworthy that overturning the regulatory sector by way of court decision may be not feasible in China. In China, the regulatory sector in PFIPs is often an administrative sector, so the decision made by the regulatory sector is treated as an administrative action. Although court review is one of the ways to review administrative action, not all administrative actions are easy to review by court in China. Some claims of administrative action are mandatorily required to have administrative reconsideration before court review.[63] Some claims of administrative action are final, as ruled by administrative reconsideration, which means there is no chance to access them by way of court review.[64] Therefore, if the new legislation on PFIPs expects to ensure the actions of the regulatory sector to be

[59]Ibid.

[60]The legislative Guide, Chap. I on General legislative and institutional framework, P35, para 47.

[61]The legislative Guide, Chap. I on General legislative and institutional framework, P35, para 48.

[62]The Legislative Guide, recommendation 10.

[63]For example, the Administrative Reconsideration Law of the People's Republic of China 2009;

Article 14: A citizen, legal person, or any other organization that refuses to accept a specific administrative act of a department under the State Council, or the people's government of a province, an autonomous region, or a municipality directly under the Central Government, shall apply for administrative reconsideration to the department under the State Council, or the people's government of the province, the autonomous region, or the municipality directly under the Central Government that undertook the specific administrative act. The applicant who refuses to accept the administrative reconsideration decision may bring a suit before a people's court; or apply to the State Council for a ruling, and the State Council shall make a final ruling according to the provisions of this Law.

[64]For example: the Administrative Reconsideration Law of the People's Republic of China 2009

Article 30: ……According to the decisions of the State Council or the people's governments of provinces, autonomous regions and municipalities directly under the Central Government to prospect and confirm or adjust administrative divisions into districts, or to requisition lands, an administrative reconsideration decision, which is made by the people's governments of provinces, autonomous regions and municipalities directly under the Central Government, to confirm ownership and right to use of natural resources, such as land, mineral resources, rivers, forests, mountains, grasslands, unclaimed land, beaches, maritime waters, is a final ruling.

reviewed by court, it should either: ensure the regulatory sector is more independent, so that its actions are not administrative and may be sued freely by the concessioner; or remove the legal barriers from the Chinese laws so that administrative action may be sued freely by the concessioner.

The Legislative Guide does not give suggestions on what kind of regulatory sector should be established. However, Britain offers a specific example in this regard: Britain has established a mechanism to regulate PFIPs, which includes three kinds of institutions. The OGC (Office of Government Commerce) issues the regulation and policies on PFIPs[65]; the PUK (Partnership UK)[66] and the PRG (Project Review Group)[67] give support on issues of finance; OGC's GP (Gateway Process),[68] Audit Commission[69] and Local Partnerships[70] monitor PFIPs. In contrast, China has no regulatory sectors that only focus on PFIPs. The regulatory sectors on infrastructure in China are divided by the different types of the infrastructure, irrespective of whether the infrastructure is financed by public or private funding. For example, roads in China are regulated by Ministry of Communications of the People's Republic of China and its subordinate bodies; hospitals are regulated by Ministry of Health of the People's Republic of China; schools are regulated by Ministry of Education of the People's Republic of China and its subordinate bodies, etc. If China expects to develop PFIPs, it needs to establish regulatory sectors specific to PFIPs. These

[65]OGC is now a part of the new Efficiency and Reform Group within the Cabinet Office. It used to belong to the HM Treasury. OGC has offered guidance on certain financing issues in PFI contracts. <http://webarchive.nationalarchives.gov.uk/20120503092022/ http://www.dh.gov.uk/en/Managingyourorganisation/NHSprocurement/Publicprivatepartnership/Privatefinanceinitiative/InvestmentGuidanceRouteMap/DH_4133031> accessed on 26th May, 2019.

[66]Partnerships UK plc. (PUK) was an organisation responsible for furthering public-private partnerships in the United Kingdom. It was a public limited company formed in 2000, owned jointly by HM Treasury and the Private Sector. In June 2010, Infrastructure UK (IUK) was established as a separate unit within the Treasury to work alongside the Private Sector on major infrastructure projects. As a result, it was announced in May 2011 that PUK was to be dissolved.

[67]The PRG oversaw the approval process for local authority PFI projects that received Government support through the previous PFI credit system. The Treasury has revised its project approval processes as part of a wider programme of strengthened spending control. These revisions aim to provide a more coherent approvals and assurance framework, and make the tools the Treasury uses to approve Major Projects more consistent across Government. These revisions have included bringing the assurance and approvals processes previously completed by the PRG into a standardised Treasury Approval Point (TAP) process. <http://www.hm-treasury.gov.uk/ppp_projectreview_group.htm> accessed on 26th May, 2019.

[68]The OGC Gateway Process examines programmes and projects at key decision points in their lifecycle. It looks ahead to provide assurance that they can progress successfully to the next stage. <http://www.dfpni.gov.uk/cpd-coe-ogcgateway0-strategic-assessment.pdf> accessed on 26th May, 2019.

[69]It role is to protect the public purse. <http://www.audit-commission.gov.uk/> accessed on 26th May, 2019.

[70]Local Partnerships is a company that is uniquely and jointly owned by HM Treasury and the Local Government Association. It provides commercial expertise on matters of infrastructure, legal and contractual complexity and act for the benefit of the Public Sector. <http://www.localpartnerships.org.uk/> accessed on 26th May, 2019.

are beneficial for establishing a guarantee system to help private investors obtain loans from banks and they are favourable for dealing with problems in PFIPs in a professional manner.[71]

To sum up, the Legislative Guide does not advocate the establishment of any particular model or administrative structure. It only illustrates the different options that have been used in various domestic legislative measures to set up regulatory frameworks for PFIPs. The UNCITRAL commission expected host countries to establish the regulatory regime in light of its specific requirements, to fit for long-term sustainability of PFIPs in that host country.[72]

4.3.3.1.3 Administrative Coordination

The legislation should ensure administrative coordination. PFIPs are generally huge and complicated, which require the public authorities to be responsible for issuing approvals, licences, permits and so on. PFIPs may include the involvement of several public authorities, at various levels of government. Thus, it is necessary to coordinate the activities of public authorities for the implementation of PFIPs.[73] The Legislative Guide strongly recommends establishing a central unit within the host country's administration with the overall responsibility for formulating policy and providing practical guidance on PFIPs.[74] This ensures institutional capacity in the implementation of PFIPs.

To sum up, if the law cannot ensure institutional capacity in the implementation of PFIPs, it limits the efficiency of PFIPs and results in reduced service quality and increased costs for users, which negatively affects the long-tem sustainability of PFIPs at the end.

4.3.3.2 Marketization

In order to ensure the long-term sustainability of PFIPs, the legislation on PFIPs needs not only to ensure the institutional capability in the host country, but also to ensure marketization that balances competitive and monopolistic provision of public services.[75]

Competition is beneficial to the long-term sustainability of PFIPs. Competition may reduce overall costs and provide more back-up facilities for public services. In

---

[71] Tie Shan Wang, 'Comparative research on PFI project between Britain and Japan' (2008) IEC, No1: 49.

[72] The legislative Guide, Chap. I on General legislative and institutional framework, Section E. Authority to regulate infrastructure services, para 32.

[73] The Legislative Guide, recommendation 6.

[74] The legislative Guide, Chap. I on General legislative and institutional framework, P29, para 24.

[75] The legislative Guide, Chap. I on General legislative and institutional framework, P24, para 6.

certain sectors, competition has also helped to increase the productivity of infrastructure investment, to enhance responsiveness to the needs of customers and to obtain a better quality of public service, thus improving the business environment for all sectors of the economy.[76]

A service provider operating under monopolistic conditions is typically able to fix prices. Even when the price is regulated by public authority, it does not benefit the quality of service since the monopolist may decrease the quality to compensate for the lower cost. This means the consumers may have to pay more and the provider has no motivation to improve its service, which may have negative repercussions for the whole economy. However, monopolies may be supported by legislation for special reasons, despite their negative economic effects. One such case is found in natural monopolies. When the services attend to an increase of demand, additional units decrease the costs of production.[77] The other is found in legal monopolies. A price below cost is set to achieve policy objectives, such as public services for senior citizens or low-income earners in the form of state welfare.[78]

To sum up, in order to ensure the long-term sustainability of PFIPs, legislation on PFIPs is required to balance competitive and monopolistic provision of public services in the market. Legislation on PFIPs should not only protect competition, but also certain monopolies as it affects public interest.

4.3.4 Eliminating Undesirable Restrictions

According to the Legislative Guide and Model Provisions, eliminating undesirable restrictions for PFIPs means these restrictions on Private Sector participation in infrastructure development and operation should be eliminated.[79] The Legislative Guide and Model Provisions offer the guidelines on three forms of undesirable restriction, which may be eliminated when countries establish legislation on PFIPs.

4.3.4.1 Eliminating Undesirable Restrictions in Constitution

Undesirable restrictions on PFIPs should be eliminated from constitutional rules. As the Constitution is the foundation to laws and policies, all specific laws and policies on PFIPs made by the country should follow its principles. Some constitutions state that public service delivery is reserved for the Public Sector, while other constitutions authorise the State to award concessions to Private Sector for the development

[76]The legislative Guide, Chap. I on General legislative and institutional framework, P24, para 6.

[77]The legislative Guide, Introduction and background information on privately financed infrastructure projects, P7, para 24(a).

[78]The legislative Guide, Introduction and background information on privately financed infrastructure projects, P8, para 26.

[79]The Legislative Guide, recommendation 1.

and operation of infrastructure and the provision of public services. Therefore, for countries wishing to develop PFIPs, it is important to review existing constitutional rules so as to identify possible restrictions on the implementation of PFIPs.[80]

The review of existing constitutional rules was discussed in detail during the drafting of the UNCITRAL Legislative Guide. One opinion was that it would not be appropriate for the guide to recommend the review of constitutional rules as it is a politically sensitive process in many countries. There were also concerns that the review of constitution rules is a complicated procedure. The objective of the Legislative Guide was to encourage Private Sector investment, which is a matter of specific laws and relevant policies rather than the Constitution. However, the opponents of these views pointed out that the guide is addressed to legislators and policy makers in countries interested in promoting PFIPs. The legislators and policy makers should be concerned with the various potential legal difficulties for the implementation of PFIPs, especially constitutional restrictions.[81]

As a result, constitutional review is considered in Recommendation 1 of the Legislative Guide and the Model Provision 1 of the Model Provisions. That means the UNCITRAL Commission aimed to support the review of constitutions to eliminate undesirable restrictions. Firstly, "Constitution" was added into the opening words of the recommendation 1 in the 33rd Commission Session when the draft of the Legislation Guide was discussed.[82] The UNCITRAL Commission agreed that removing undesirable restrictions should be achieved at the constitutional level. Secondly, constitutional review is recommended clearly and explained in detail in the notes to the Legislative Guide.[83]

It is worth noting that constitutional review is very important to certain Communist countries such as China. In Capitalist countries, the main matter under consideration is the balance between private investment and public interest. In Communist countries, private investment in public infrastructure may become a political problem. Generally, constitutions in Communist countries claim that public infrastructure is reserved exclusively for the state and for all the people in the country. In other words, even if private investors invest in public infrastructure, they are not entitled to use the facilities or ask for profits in light of the Constitution. This may discourage many private investors from forming PFIPs. However, if this restriction is removed from the Constitution, legislators may be concerned by possible changes to the character of the state. In this case, the Legislative Guide and the Model Provisions have not given suggestions as to removing "socialisation" as an undesirable restriction from Communist Constitutions. But the Legislative Guide clearly points out that its content does not cover "privatisation" transactions related to public infrastructure. It claims

[80]The legislative Guide, Chap. I on General legislative and institutional framework, P25, para 8.

[81]UNCITRAL, 32nd session, '*Report of UNCITRAL on the work of its thirty-second session*', A/54/17 P7, para 50–51.

[82]UNCITRAL, 33th session, '*Report of UNCITRAL on the work of its thirty-third session*', A/55/17 P59, para 200.

[83]The legislative Guide, Chap. I on General legislative and institutional framework, P25, para 8.

that "privatisation" gives rise to legislative issues that are substantively different from legislative issues pertaining to PFIPs.[84]

4.3.4.2 Eliminating Undesirable Restrictions in Land Laws

Undesirable restrictions on PFIPs should be eliminated from land laws. Since the infrastructure is most often built on land, restrictions on the ownership of land may lead to the reluctance of private investors to invest, and it also may form an obstacle to the operation of PFIPs. For this problem too, the Legislative Guide and Model Provisions do not give suggestions in the recommendations or provisions. But during the draft proceedings, it was proposed that the host country should consider adopting legislative provisions to authorise the authority sector to make available to the concessioner such public land that may be required for the execution of the project.[85]

Eliminating undesirable restrictions in Chinese land laws is very difficult. The primary reason is that China forbids the private ownership of land. The Constitution of the People's Republic of China clearly states that Chinese land is owned by the state or collectives[86] rather than by any individual or organization.[87] In the other words, it means the land is not allowed to be traded in the market. The land required in infrastructure projects may not be obtained by the private investors themselves. This kind of land ownership regime is a fundamental policy in China and it is not expected

---

[84]UNCITRAL, 31st session, '*Report of UNCITRAL on the work of its thirty-first session*', A/53/17 P4, para 25.

[85]UNCITRAL, 32nd session, A/CN.9/458/Add.2–'Privately Financed Infrastructure Projects: Draft Chapters of a legislative guide on privately financed infrastructure projects - Chapter I. General Legislative Considerations' P2, para (2)(c); 31st session, A/CN.9/444/Add.2-'Privately Financed Infrastructure Projects - Draft chapters of a legislative guide on privately financed infrastructure projects - Chapter I. General Legislative Considerations' P9, para 16.

[86]Collective ownership is a special kind of ownership system in Chinese rural areas. The rural areas have hundreds collectives such as People's Communes, Agricultural Producers Cooperatives and other forms of cooperatives economy under collective ownership by the working people. Generally, these collectives are divided by region. Every rural people works as a member of one collective and all Chinese rural land belongs to these collectives.

[87]The Constitution of the People's Republic of China, adopted on March 14, 2004:

Article 10: Land in the cities is owned by the state.

Land in the rural and suburban areas is owned by collectives except for those portions which belong to the state in accordance with the law; house sites and privately farmed plots of cropland and hilly land are also owned by collectives.

The state may, in the public interest, requisition land for its use in accordance with the law.

No organization or individual may appropriate, buy, sell or lease land or otherwise engage in the transfer of land by unlawful means.

The Land Administration Law of the People's Republic of China (2004 Amendment), adopted on August 28th, 2004:

Article 2 The People's Republic of China resorts to a socialist public ownership i.e. an ownership by the whole people and ownerships by collectives, of land. In ownership by the whole people, the State Council is empowered to be on behalf of the State to administer the land owned by the State. No unit or individual is allowed to occupy, trade or illegally transfer land by other means.......

to be changed in the next few decades. Therefore, this kind of undesirable restriction may not be eliminated. The current Chinese law allows the private investor to acquire the rights of land use and land easement required for an infrastructure project.[88] Therefore, the law reform in this regard need only eliminate undesirable restrictions that hinder the rights of land use and land easement required by private investors in infrastructure projects. Or, to make the process easier, the new Chinese legislation on PFIPs could clearly claim that the authority sector has the responsibility to make available to the concessioner such land that may be required for the execution of the project.[89]

4.3.4.3 Eliminating Undesirable Restrictions in Foreign Exchange Laws

The undesirable restrictions on PFIPs should be eliminated from the rules relating to foreign exchange laws. In PFIPs, the private investors may be from countries or areas where a different currency is used. In this case, the private investor may encounter a number of problems with regard to foreign exchange, such as foreign currency payment, foreign currency income, foreign exchange guarantees, foreign debt, etc. If there are too many undesirable restrictions on foreign exchange in the host country, the investor may be discouraged from investing. Although the Legislative Guide and Model Provisions do not give the host country clear suggestions on how to remove undesirable restrictions from the foreign exchange laws as they pertain to PFIPs, they require the host country to establish law to support foreign exchange in PFIPs. For example, they require the host country make legislation to facilitate the issue of licences under foreign exchange regulations.[90] They emphasise that restrictions on foreign exchange may bring high exchange rate risks to private investors.[91] They suggest the private investor should have foreign exchange guarantees in host countries which do not have freely convertible currencies.[92] They require host countries to available legislation of foreign exchange for foreign private investors to transfer their capital.[93]

---

[88]The Land Administration Law of the People's Republic of China (2004 Amendment), adopted on August 28th, 2004

Article 2: ......Land use right may be transferred by law.......

[89]The legislative Guide, Chap. IV on Construction and operation of infrastructure: legislative framework and project agreement, Section C The project site, assets and easements, paras 27.

[90]The Legislative Guide, Chap. I, General Legislative and Institutional Framework, Section D, Administrative coordination, para 27.

[91]The Legislative Guide, Chap. II on Project risks and Government support, Section B on Project risks and risk allocation, para 19.

[92]The Legislative Guide, Chap. II on Project risks and Government support, Section C on Government support, para 49.

[93]The Legislative Guide, Chap. VII, Other relevant areas of law, Section B, Other relevant areas of law, para 5.

China is a country with very strict foreign exchange administration. It does not have freely convertible currencies. The Regulation of the People's Republic of China on Foreign Exchange Administration clearly outlines that the foreign private investment in PFIPs shall go through registration formalities at foreign exchange control agencies.[94] The Private Sector may not find it easy to get loans from banks in the private investors' home countries. The project company implementing the infrastructure project in China is often registered in China. According to the Regulation of the People's Republic of China on Foreign Exchange Administration, a Chinese company taking a loan from a foreign bank must be registered and follow relevant restrictions.[95] Moreover, the private foreign investor may not be free to offer guarantees on their PFIP.[96]

If China expects to attract more foreign private investments into its domestic public infrastructure, its laws should be as convenient as possible for foreign exchange. Otherwise, the foreign private investor may be discouraged from investment because of the risks of unpredictable foreign exchange.

4.4 Conclusion

This chapter answers the 3rd research question, namely how the Chinese general legislative and institutional frameworks on PFIPs may be improved, based on the guidelines from the Legislative Guide and Model Provisions and making supplementary reference to other countries' laws.

Section 4.2 analyses the structure of the Legislative Guide and the Model Provisions, which are considered for use in new Chinese legislation on PFIPs. The structure first gives recommendations on the general legislative and institutional frameworks, followed by recommendations on the specific areas of concessioner selection,

---

[94]The Regulation of the People's Republic of China on Foreign Exchange Administration (2008 Revision) adopt 5th August, 2008:

Article 16: Overseas organs and individuals that directly invest in China shall go through registration formalities at foreign exchange control agencies after have been approved by relevant competent department.

[95]Ibid.

Article 18: The state carries out the scale administration of foreign loan. Entities or individuals that borrow foreign loans shall observe relevant provisions of the state and go through registration formalities at foreign exchange control agencies……

Article 43: Where any entity or individual has acts including borrowing of foreign loans, issuance of bonds or providence of external guarantees without approval in violation of provisions on foreign loan control, foreign exchange control agencies shall give a warning and impose a fine of less than 30% of the illegal funds.

[96]Ibid.

Article 19: Entities or individuals that offer external guarantees shall apply to foreign exchange control agencies and the latter shall make decisions on whether granting an approval or not according to the assets and liabilities of the applicants.

contracts in PFIPs and dispute settlement. It is considered to be the most proper structure for new Chinese legislation on PFIPs. Additionally, this section indicates that the use of the recommendations in the Legislative Guide and the Model Provisions is optional and the Chinese law does not need to copy them.

Section 4.3 discusses the four principles offered by the Legislative Guide and the Model Provisions to guide the Chinese law reform on the Legislative and institutional framework on PFIPs.

Regarding the principle of transparency, the Legislative Guide and the Model Provisions require a clear and readily accessible law and adequate information disclosure about administrative decisions. Taking the Beijing Regulation as an example, it showed that some provisions in this regulation are vague and barely touch on information disclosure. Therefore, the new Chinese legislation on PFIPs needs offer clarity in its legal documentation and include provisions on information disclosure.

Regarding the principle of fairness, the Legislative Guide and the Model Provisions require a point of balance between public interests, private interests and customer interests. Through reviewing the Chinese law on PFIPs, it was found that the current Chinese law has the "public interest precedent principle". This principle harms the balance point so it should be removed from Chinese laws. There is no customer interest referred to in current Chinese laws on PFIPs, and this should be added into the Chinese new legislation. The British Water Voice offers a particularly good example of how to protect the customer interest, which could be considered in reference to Chinese law reform.

Regarding the principle of long-term sustainability, the Legislative Guide and the Model Provisions require the legislation on PFIPs to confirm the authority and regulatory sectors, and ensure administrative coordination among them. China already has some provisions regarding this feature, but still has space to improve this in further law reform. British regulations about regulatory insinuation are also referenced here.

Regarding the principle of eliminating undesirable restrictions, the Legislative Guide and the Model Provisions require the removal of all undesirable restrictions from laws on PFIPs. Here the chapter discussed three laws (Constitution Law, Land Law and Foreign Exchange Law) from which serious undesirable restrictions need to be removed.

Following this discussion of the general legislative and institutional frameworks, the next chapter, Chap. 5, will discuss concessioner selection.

Chapter 5
The Concessioner Selection Procedure in Privately Financed Infrastructure Projects (PFIPs)

5.1 Introduction

In a PFIP, selecting the concessioner is an important step. As has already been discussed, China has no specific legislation on PFIPs. Furthermore, no specific legal selection procedure is applied to ensure an appropriate private concessioner is selected in Chinese PFIPs. PFIPs have special requirements for concessioner selection procedures which may need specific selection procedures rather than general selection procedures. Thus, there are a lot of potential problems in the concessioner selection procedures of PFIPs in China. In order to ensure the project's success, protect the private investor's interests and avoid corruption, it is necessary to ensure the fairness and transparency of the concessioner selection procedure. The recommendations in Legislative Guide and the Model Provisions made by UNCITRAL represent the international standard for legislation regarding PFIPs. These recommendations could be tied to current laws in China, with regard to specific situations that might guide the establishment of Chinese laws regarding concessioner selection in PFIPs. This Chapter argues that Chinese laws on selecting the concessioner in PFIPs should be improved.

The aim of this chapter is to discuss how to reform Chinese laws on concessioner selection procedure in PFIPs, so that the selection procedure could achieve the levels of fairness and transparency set out in the Legislative Guide and Model Provisions.

There are four objectives in this Chapter. The first objective is to discuss how to reform the Chinese laws on the determination of infrastructure project plans and on market access so that private investors have an equal opportunity to participate in the selection procedure. This will ensure fairness and transparency in the pre-selection stage. The second objective is to confirm that a reasonable process for selecting concessioners in PFIP offers competitive selection procedures as its primary model, while uncompetitive selection procedures under negotiation may be recognised in exceptional circumstances. It also considers how to establish new Chinese legislation on the concessioner selection of PFIPs to ensure fairness and transparency in both the competitive selection procedures and the uncompetitive selection procedures. The

S. Liang, *Legal Aspects of Privately Financed Infrastructure Projects (PFIPs) in China*,
https://doi.org/10.1007/978-981-15-6803-9_5

third objective is to discuss how to reform Chinese laws about the complaint and review mechanism in concession selection procedures to ensure transparency in the post-selection stage. The fourth objective is to discuss whether the Chinese concessioner selection procedures on PFIPs should accept an unsolicited proposal model and how to ensure this kind of special selection procedure is fair and transparent.

This chapter consists of four sections. As with the flowchart below, the structure of this Chapter follows the three stages of the concessioner selection procedure of PFIPs: the preparation before the selection (Fig. 5.1: blue), the selection (Fig. 5.1: black) and the dispute settlement after the selection (Fig. 5.1: red). Additionally, there is a special concessioner selection procedure for PFIPs, namely the unsolicited proposal procedure (Fig. 5.1: green).

Section 5.2 shows that the pre-selection stage (Fig. 5.1: blue part) should be fair and transparent. There are two matters relating to this issue. The first is whether an infrastructure project should be provided. In China, the decision to build a public infrastructure is taken by the authority sectors, while the Private Sector is not entitled to suggest an infrastructure is necessary. Public opinion is also ignored, which means neither institutions nor individuals have clear legal channels to express their desire for infrastructure. The second is whether a private investor is allowed access to an infrastructure project. Generally, the public authority in the host country decides whether to issue a concession to a private concessioner rather than a State Own Entity (SOE) on the basis of both economic and political requirements.[1] Therefore, the situations in which a private investor may be considered should be clearly defined in the legislation, in case the public authority directly appoints a SOE and does not give the private investor sufficient opportunity to compete for projects. However, the Legislative Guide and Model Provisions[2] do not consider how the law authorises private investors to access the host countries' markets, so the EU is referenced in this regard to discuss a possible avenue for Chinese law reform.

Section 5.3 argues that the selection of the private concessioner (Fig. 5.1: black) should be based on a fair and transparent competition. The aim of this selection is to select an appropriate concessioner for PFIPs. Therefore, a competitive selection procedure is essential. Competitive procedures not only help to achieve value for money for both the contracting authority and the general public users of the infrastructure, but help to prevent corruption. Further analysis needs to be made of how to set up a proper competitive selection to select appropriate private concessioners in PFIPs. PFIPs need not only fairness and transparency but also economy and efficiency, so the laws should provide suitable regulations on competitive selection procedures.[3] However, in certain circumstances, concessions may be awarded without competitive procedure. The law should clarify these exceptional circumstances in order to

[1] Cao Fuguo, *'Regulating procurement of privately financed infrastructure in China: a review of the recent legislative initiatives and the emerging regulatory framework'* (2007), Public Procurement law review (P.P.L.R.2007, 3, 147–173) P157.

[2] Neither the Legislative Guide nor the Model Provisions refer to the pre-selection stage.

[3] *'Legislative Guide on Privately Financed Infrastructure Project'* (2001)UNCITRAL (A/CN.9/SER.B/4) (hereafter referred to as the Legislative Guide) the Legislative Guide, Chap. III on Selection of the concessioner, paras 18.

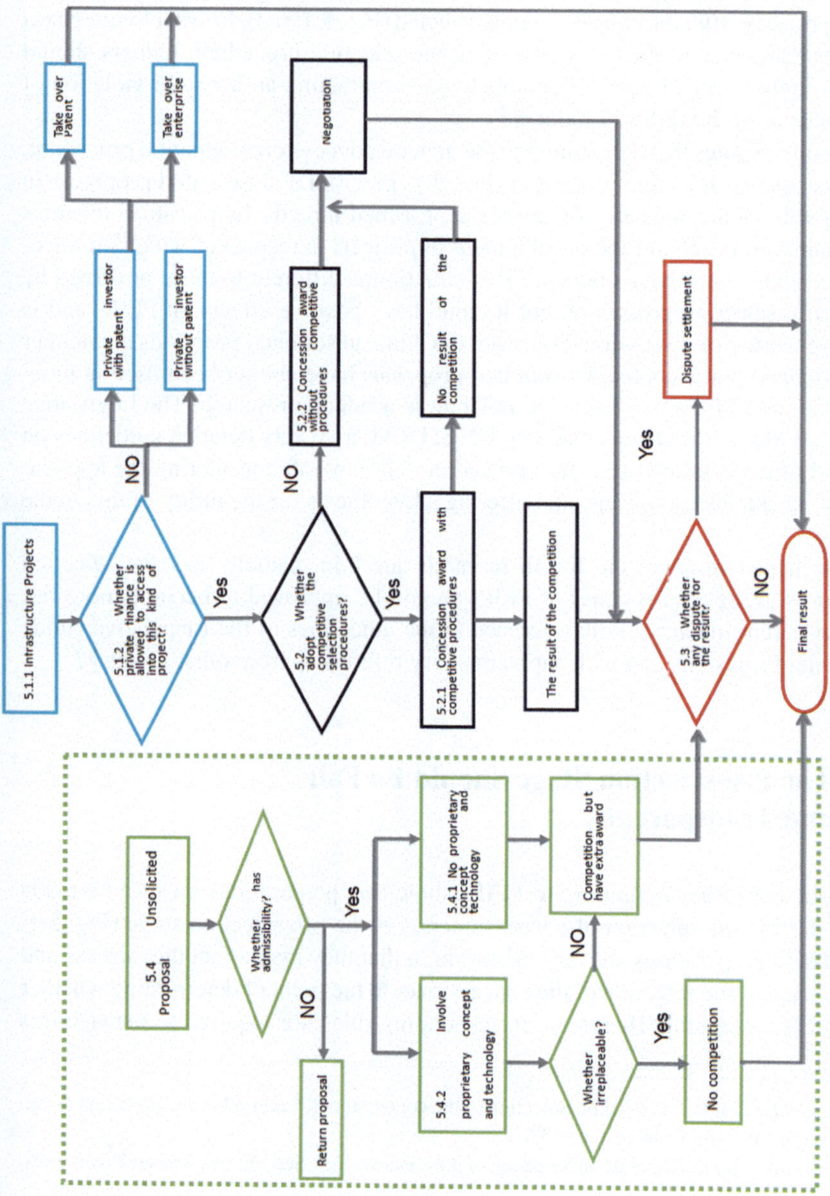

Fig. 5.1 The structure of concessioner selection procedure

ensure the fairness and transparency of the procedure.[4] The Legislative Guide and the Model Provisions made by UNCITRAL give detailed guidelines on how to regulate the concessioner selection procedure for PFIPs.

Section 5.4 discusses how disputes on the selection result or the procedure may be settled properly, after the concessioner is selected (Fig. 5.1: red). In order to safeguard a proper adherence to the rules governing the selection procedure, bidders should have the right to seek review of actions by the contracting authority in violation of those rules or of the rights of bidders.[5]

Section 5.5 notes that, in addition to the general concessioner selection procedure, there is a special selection procedure (Fig. 5.1: green), i.e. unsolicited proposals in which public authorities are sometimes approached directly by private companies who submit proposals for the development of projects in respect of which no selection procedures have been opened.[6] This situation is different to those governed by the general selection procedure, but it could have positive effects on PFIPs and is therefore worthy of discussion. However, in China, unsolicited proposals are neither acknowledged nor accepted. Unsolicited proposals have neither been used in practice in Chinese PFIPs nor discussed in Chinese academic research. The Legislative Guide and Model Provisions made by UNCITRAL give very detailed guidelines on this kind of concessioner selection procedure.[7] It is worth considering the applicability of unsolicited proposals, and offering a hypothesis for the utility of this in the future.

This chapter answers the fourth research question, namely how the selection procedures of the concessioner of PFIPs should be improved to become more fair and transparent in China, with reference to the guidelines of the Legislative Guide and Model Provisions and with supplementary references from other country?

5.2 The Pre-selection Stage Should Be Fair and Transparent

The particular issues pertaining to PFIPs show that preparations have to be made before starting the selection of concessioners, i.e. the pre-selection stage (Fig. 5.1: blue). These preparations are very important in that they may affect the fairness and transparency of the selection of the concessioner to the point of determining whether the PFIP is successful. Therefore, corresponding rules are required to manage this

[4]The Legislative Guide, Chap. III on Selection of the concessioner, Section D on Concession award without competitive procedures, paras 89.

[5]The Legislative Guide, Chap. III on Selection of the concessioner, Section I on Review Procedures, paras 127.

[6]The Legislative Guide, Chap. III on Selection of the concessioner, Section E on Unsolicited Proposal, paras 97.

[7]The Legislative Guide, Chap. III on Selection of the concessioner, Section E on Unsolicited Proposal, paras 97–117.

preparation process. As the pre-selection stage of PFIPs, the primary preparations are as follows.

5.2.1 Determination of an Infrastructure Project

Before selecting the concessioners, the first thing is to decide whether an infrastructure project should be launched. The cost of infrastructure is very high, so redundant infrastructure would waste a lot of resources. However, if there is insufficient infrastructure, public requirement will not be satisfied. In China, the public authority decides whether infrastructure should be built. In this case, there are no procedures to involve public opinion[8] or participation in the project decision. Therefore, private investors who are interested in building infrastructure have no access to offer initial suggestions as to potential infrastructure development not considered by the public authority. In fact, one of the initial steps that should be taken in relation to a proposed infrastructure project is to conduct a preliminary assessment of its feasibility, including the economic, political and environmental impact. Some countries' experience shows that it is useful to provide for some public participation in the preliminary assessment of the project's environmental impact and the various options available to minimise this impact.[9]

Chinese legislators agree that all infrastructure project proposals should be initiated by government alone. However, the Legislative Guide hints that UNCITRAL supports private investor participation in the initial determining phases of a project. The Legislative Guide considers one such situation: when the public authority has not considered an infrastructure or cannot implement the infrastructure because of certain technological limitations, a private investor could initially contact the public authority if the private investor considers the infrastructure to be essential or the investor has special capabilities to implement the project. If it is proved that there is public interest in pursuing the project, the project should be launched.[10] The Legislative Guide catalogues this situation as an "Unsolicited proposal". As a matter of fact, the concept of "Unsolicited proposals" has been discussed by Chinese scholars, but a move to address the issue of unsolicited offers in the Chinese regulations was not

[8] Cao Fuguo, *'Regulating procurement of privately financed infrastructure in China: a review of the recent legislative initiatives and the emerging regulatory framework'* (2007), Public Procurement law review (P.P.L.R. 2007, 3, 147–173).

[9] The Legislative Guide, Chap. III on Selection of the concessioner, Section A on General Remarks, paras 30.

[10] The Legislative Guide, Chap. III on Selection of the concessioner, Section E on Unsolicited proposals, paras 106.

accepted.[11] The "unsolicited proposal" is not discussed in this section but it will be analysed in detail in Sect. 5.5.

5.2.2 Determination of the Market Access of Private Finance

Once it is determined that an infrastructure project will be launched, the next step is to consider whether private finance should be allowed to participate in the project.

Market access to infrastructure projects is more difficult to determine than that to general goods and services because of the characteristics of infrastructure and its importance. Some special infrastructure projects pertaining to national defence and some special industries related to the national economy should not accessible to private finance. Only state-owned entities should have market access. In some case, the government may maintain preferential policies to support small and Medium-sized enterprises (SMEs).[12] Even the UNCITRAL, which strongly supports PFIP development, agrees in the Legislative Guide that countries should limit market access to infrastructure project in light of specific situations.[13] However, the Legislative Guide also clearly states that the countries' legislation should clarify the market access permission or the market access limitation, to prevent the public authorities abusing their rights, which might result in private investor not accessing other infrastructure project markets.[14]

When considering the scope of market access to infrastructure projects, countries may treat foreign private investment more circumspectly than domestic private investment. Countries generally have specific regulations on how foreign private investment joins their infrastructure project market.

There are two typical ways in which to manage the movement of foreign private finance into the host country's infrastructure project market. The first is to produce a catalogue of industries available to foreign investment, as has been done in China.[15] All foreign investment in China is then divided into three categories: encouraged,

[11] Cao Fuguo, *'Regulating procurement of privately financed infrastructure in China: a review of the recent legislative initiatives and the emerging regulatory framework'* (2007), Public Procurement law review (P.P.L.R.2007, 3, 147–173) P157.

[12] Linarelli John, *'The limited case for permitting SME procurement preferences in the agreement on government procurement'*, edited Arrowsmith Sue, Anderson Robert D., The WTO Regime on Government Procurement: Challenge and Reform (Cambridge 2011) P444.

[13] The Legislative Guide, Introduction and Background information on PFIPs, Section A Introduction, paras 4.

[14] The legislative Guide, Chap. I on General legislative and institutional framework, Section C Scope of authority to award concessions, paras 18.

[15] On 24 December 2011, the Chinese National Development and Reform Commission ("NDRC") and the Ministry of Commerce ("MOFCOM") jointly issued a new Guideline Catalogue of Industries for Foreign Investment (Amended 2011) ("2011 Catalogue"). The new Catalogue came into effect on 30 January 2012. It replaced the old Catalogue of 31 October 2007 ("2007 Catalogue").

restricted and prohibited. Foreign investment is subject to approval and registration by the relevant Chinese authorities. The category of a project influences of the degree to which authorities are in charge of the project and also determines access to certain incentives.[16] This way lists the areas of market access, whether access is allowed or not allowed, the degree to which access is allowed, and all this is confirmed by checking the catalogue. The advantage of this way is that both the authorities and the potential private foreign investors can ascertain whether a particular kind of infrastructure project is open to foreign private finance, while the disadvantage is that the catalogue is not comprehensive and cannot list all the kinds of projects.

The second is to create a leverage to balance market access between the host country and home country of the foreign private investor, as is found in the EU. The European Commission had, after several attempts over many years, finally managed to garner enough support to propose a 'tool' that would increase EU leverage in public procurement negotiations by penalising non-EU countries whose markets were closed.[17] The core principle of this way of doing things is that the host country can refuse foreign private investment in its infrastructure project market if the home country of the foreign private investor closes its own infrastructure project market to the investors of the host country. The advantage of this way is that it is flexible and looks like a relatively fair solution to the different market access policies in different countries, while the disadvantage is that it is difficult to implement in practice because it is unrealistic to expect a contracting authority to turn down low bids from foreign private investors that offer better value for money than others.

It is difficult to say whether it is better to give a catalogue of guidelines or use leverage. However, in the current situation of market access in the EU and China, there seems to be "unbalanced trade" between EU and China. On the one hand, the "inadequate protection of intellectual property" and "the fact that China's standards are not in accordance with international rules" are the reasons for EU firms' hesitancy about entering the Chinese market.[18] On the other hand, it is unrealistic to stop EU states looking to provide services and build infrastructure at the lowest possible price, particularly in times of economic crisis. Often these prices are offered by countries such as China.[19] This "unbalanced trade" is not helpful to the long-term development of investment markets, for the EU or for China. As a matter of fact, no matter which way market access is awarded, the aim remains to facilitate foreign investment and develop the economy without prejudicing national interest. The EU, as a union for almost its members are developed countries, is looking for fair opportunities to join infrastructure project markets, while China, as a developing country, is looking

---

[16]C'M'S Cameron McKenna LLP, *'China revised the guideline catalogue of industries for foreign investment'*, Law-now China on 31/01/2012 <http://www.law-now.com/law-now/2011/chinafdijan2012.htm> accessed on 7th August 2019.

[17]Magazine Mlex, *'Bar tenders from abroad'* (Issue 10-Europe, July–September 2012), P14.

[18]French MEP Marielle de Sarnez report to Committee on International Trade of European Parliament, *'EU and China: Unbalanced trade?'* (2010/2301(INI)) <http://www.europarl.europa.eu/oeil/popups/ficheprocedure.do?lang=en&reference=2010/2301%28INI%29> accessed on 2nd September 2019.

[19]Magazine Mlex, *'Bar tenders from abroad'* (Issue 10-Europe, July-September 2012), P17.

to acquire advanced technology, and research and development through awarding market access.[20] Therefore, a fairer solution would be to set up an international agreement on market access so that all member countries could base legislation on the same standard. Thus, it would be useful if China were to improve its legislation on PFIPs by referencing the Legislative Guide and the Model Provisions made by UNCITRAL, which consists of many countries including EU countries.

If private finance is allowed to access these kinds of projects, then it could move onto the selection procedure (Fig. 5.1, the black). By contrast, if the private finance is not allowed to access into this kind of project, unless there were special circumstances, the private investor would be excluded from building the project. Here is one such special circumstance. If private finance is not allowed to access this kind of project but the private investor holds a patent for an essential technology or the private investor has better management or technology skills for this project, the authority has to try to acquire the technology and skills, following legal procedures which should avoid expropriation without compensation.[21] The authority or its agents could purchase the patent or take over the whole private entity.[22] (Figure 5.1, the blue)

5.3 The Selection Stage Should Be Fair and Transparent

After the decision to launch the PFIP in the pre-selection stage, the next step is to select a proper concessioner (Fig. 5.1: black). Successful delivery of a concession project depends on whether a proper concessioner is selected. Therefore, the selection of concessioner is very important. Only an appropriate selection procedure will select the best concessioner to ensure the successful delivery of the PFIP.

This selection procedure should be suitable for use in relation to infrastructure projects that involve an obligation, on the part of the selected private entity, to undertake physical construction, repair or expansion works in the infrastructure with a view to subsequent private operation. It is not the selection procedure for selecting providers of public services through licensing or similar procedures, or of merely disposing of State property through capital increases or offerings of shares.[23]

Generally, the selection procedures of concessioner of PFIPs should be the same as the award procedure for other public contracts (e.g. traditional government procurement) and should attain the fundamental objectives of rules governing

---

[20]Ibid.

[21]Sims Alexandra, *'The public interest defense in copyright law: myth or reality?'* (2006), European Intellectual Property Review (E.I.P.R. 2006, 28(6), 335–343) P341: "expropriation without compensation is prima facie unconstitutional".

[22]Wadlow Christopher, *'The great pharmaceutical patent robbery, and the curious case of the Chemical Foundation'* (2010), Intellectual Property Quarterly (I.P.Q. 2010, 3, 256–292).

[23]The Legislative Guide, Chap. III on Selection of the concessioner, Section A on General Remarks, paras 4.

the award of public contracts: economy,[24] efficiency,[25] integrity,[26] confidence,[27] transparency.[28,29]

It seems that a competitive selection procedure could achieve the above five fundamental objectives. The formal procedures, and the objectivity and predictability that characterise the competitive selection procedures generally provide optimal conditions for economy, efficiency, integrity, confidence and transparency.[30] In most cases, economy is best achieved by means of procedures that promote competition among bidders. Competition provides them with incentives to offer their most advantageous terms and it can encourage them to adopt efficient or innovative technologies or production methods in order to do so. Competitive procedure not only helps to achieve value for money for both the contracting authority and the general public users of the infrastructure, but also helps to prevent corruption.[31] Compared with other selection procedures, the substantive rules and the procedures of competition are disclosed and easy to ascertain so that the competitive selection procedure is more transparent.

A competitive selection procedure is also supported by many international organisations, whose rules often affect the launch and the success of PFIPs. The use of competitive selection procedures in PFIPs has been recommended by UNIDO,[32]

---

[24] "Economy" refers to the selection of a concessioner that is capable of performing works and delivering services of the desired quality at the most advantageous price or that offers the best commercial proposal.

[25] "Efficiency" refers to selection of a concessioner within a reasonable amount of time, with minimal administrative burdens and at reasonable cost both to the contracting authority and to participating bidders.

[26] "integrity" refers to the selection system will usually contain provisions designed to ensure fair treatment of bidders, to reduce or discourage unintentional or intentional abuses of the selection process by persons administering it or by companies participating in it and to ensure that selection decisions are taken on a proper basis.

[27] "confidence" refers to the public confidence in the selection procedure and in the Public Sector in general. Bidders will often refrain from spending the time and sometimes substantial sums of money to participate in selection proceedings unless they are confident that they will be treated fairly and that their proposals or offers have a reasonable chance of being accepted.

[28] "transparency" refers to the transparency of laws and procedures governing the selection of the concessioner, which will help to achieve a number of the policy objectives already mentioned.

[29] The Legislative Guide, Chap. III on Selection of the concessioner, Section A on General Remarks, paras 5–16; UNCITRAL Model Law on Public Procurement (2011), Preamble.

[30] The Legislative Guide, Chap. III on Selection of the concessioner, Section A on General Remarks, paras 18.

[31] Cao Fuguo, 'Regulating procurement of privately financed infrastructure in China: a review of the recent legislative initiatives and the emerging regulatory framework' (2007), Public Procurement law review (P.P.L.R. 2007, 3, 147–173) P159.

[32] United Nations Industrial Development Organization (UNIDO). UNIDO is the specialized agency of the United Nations that promotes industrial development for poverty reduction, inclusive globalization and environmental sustainability.

which has formulated detailed practical guidance on how to structure those procedures.[33] The World Bank[34] advocates the use of competitive selection procedures through controlling loan offers. If the concessioner is not selected according to the competitive procedure accepted by the World Bank, the World Bank may refuse to provide the loan. The World Bank provides that a concessioner selected pursuant to bidding procedures acceptable to the World Bank is generally free to adopt its own procedures for the award of contracts required to implement the project. If the concessioner was not selected pursuant to those competitive procedures, the award of subcontracts has to be done pursuant to competitive procedures acceptable to the World Bank.[35] Although this rule is principally used for procurement, it is also applicable to PFIPs that apply for loans from the World Bank. UNCITRAL, which made the Legislative Guide and the Model Provisions, also prefers competitive selection procedures.[36]

However, besides the five fundamental objectives, i.e. economy, efficiency, integrity, confidence and transparency, the selection procedures of concessioners in PFIPs have other particular requirements in light of the special features of PFIPs, which should be considered when establishing legislation on the selection procedure of concessioner in PFIPs. Firstly, although competitive procedure can help achieve the objective of economy, open competition, without a pre-selection phase, is not advisable for the award of PFIPs, i.e. the bidders to be invited should be limited. The award of PFIPs involves complex, time-consuming and expensive proceedings, so it is unnecessary ask qualified bidders who have already paid high preparation costs to compete with unrealistic proposals or proposals submitted by unqualified bidders.[37] Secondly, in PFIPs the contracting authority only proposes demands rather than methods, so the selection procedure used in PFIPs should emphasise the output expected from the project (that is, the services or goods to be provided) rather than the technical details of the works to be performed or means to be used to provide those services.[38] Thirdly, the selection procedure used in PFIPs should evaluate a number of factors of bidders, in addition to the global price offered for the construction and operation works, concerning the capability of ensuring the long-term stability of

---

[33]UNIDO, "Guidelines for Infrastructure Development through Build-Operate-Transfer (BOT) Projects" (1996) P96.

[34]World Bank established in 1944. The World Bank provides low-interest loans, interest-free credits, and grants to developing countries. These support a wide array of investments in such areas as education, health, public administration, infrastructure, financial and Private Sector development, agriculture, and environmental and natural resource management.

[35]International Bank for Reconstruction and Development, "*Procurement under IBRD and IDA Loans*" (Washington, D.C., 1996) para 3.13 (a).

[36]UNCITRAL, 32nd session, *'Report of UNCITRAL on the work of its thirty-second session'*, A/54/17 P6, para 98.The Legislative Guide, Recommendation 14; The Model Provisions, Chap. II on Selection of the concessioner, Model provision 5.

[37]The Legislative Guide, Chap. III on Selection of the concessioner, Section A on General Remarks, paras 20.

[38]The Legislative Guide, Chap. III on Selection of the concessioner, Section A on General Remarks, paras 21–22.

construction and operation of the PFIPs.[39] Fourthly, the complexity and long duration of PFIPs makes it unlikely that the contracting authority and the bidder will agree on the terms of a draft project agreement without negotiation, so the selection procedure used in PFIPs should allow for this kind of negotiation.[40] But these negotiations should be carried out in transparent and fair manner.

In light of the features of PFIPs, the normal competitive selection procedure cannot completely fit the concessioner selection of PFIPs, which needs some amendments (e.g. the addition of a pre-selection phase). Additionally, the competitive selection procedure is at times a bit rigid, so directly negotiation between the contracting authority and the bidder should be allowed in exceptional cases.[41]

Therefore, according to the above analysis and discussion concerning the concessioner selection procedure of PFIPs, the conclusion is: the use of competitive selection procedures works as a primary model, while the award without competitive procedures formulated through negotiation may be recognised in exceptional cases. The competitive selection procedure should be adjusted in light of the special requirements for concessioner selection in PFIPs, while the award without competitive procedure and under negotiation should follow the legal tradition of the country concerned. However, no matter whether competitive selection procedures or negotiation are used, both should be based on the principle of fairness and transparency. In China, the Chinese Bidding Law claims to apply to all bidding activities within the territory of China, but the rigidity of the Chinese Bidding law may not be appropriate to satisfy the requirements of complex concession projects.[42] For example, the negotiation phases, which are needed more or less in selection procedure of PFIPs,[43] are totally forbidden in the Chinese Bidding Law.[44] Thus, the improvement of the Chinese legislation on PFIPs should try to include this standard.

[39]The Legislative Guide, Chap. III on Selection of the concessioner, Section A on General Remarks, paras 23–24.

[40]The Legislative Guide, Chap. III on Selection of the concessioner, Section A on General Remarks, paras 25–26.

[41]Lesguillons Henry, *'Selecting a project company'* (I.B.L.J. 1998, 6, 603–622) P606–613.

[42]Cao Fuguo, 'Regulating procurement of privately financed infrastructure in China: a review of the recent legislative initiatives and the emerging regulatory framework' (2007), Public Procurement law review (P.P.L.R.2007, 3, 147–173) P170–171.

[43]Lesguillons Henry, *'Selecting a project company'* (I.B.L.J. 1998, 6, 603–622) P605.

[44]The Bidding Law of the People's Republic of China, adopted on August 30,1999; effect as of January 1, 2000:

Article 43: Before the determination of the bid winner, no negotiations may be conducted between the tenderee and any tenderers concerning the substantive contents such as bid price, plans, etc.

5.3.1 *Concession Award in Competitive Procedures*

Once PFIPs move into the concessioner selection phase, the priority choice is competitive procedure (Fig. 5.1: black). However, the rules of competitive procedure on concessioner selection of PFIPs need to keep in line with the particular requirements of PFIPs

5.3.1.1 Pre-selection of Bidders

The competitive procedure on concessioner selection of PFIPs must include a step on the pre-selection of bidders. The award of PFIPs typically involves complex, time-consuming and expensive proceedings, and the large-scale of most infrastructure projects reduces the possibility of obtaining proposals from a large number of suitably qualified bidders. The suitably qualified bidders may be averse to participate in selection procedures, if the competitive field is too large and they have to compete with unqualified bidders, which may raise the bidders' cost.[45] In fact, competitive procedure does not necessarily require the participation of a large number of bidders. For PFIPs, in particular, the contracting authority may wish to limit the number of bidders to a manageable number. Provided that appropriate procedures are in place, the contracting authority can still take advantage of effective competition even where the competitive base is limited.[46] Therefore, open tendering without a pre-selection phase is usually not advisable for the award of concessions in PFIPs. Some matters which may arise in the pre-selection of bidders are noteworthy:

The pre-selection of bidders in PFIPs is different from normal pre-selection. In the normal pre-selection of bidders, all bidders who meet the pre-selection criteria are automatically admitted to the tendering phase.[47] In the pre-selection of bidders in PFIPs, the contracting authority may wish to limit the number of bidders from whom proposals will be accepted, even if many bidders satisfy the qualification criteria.[48] Therefore, the pre-selection proceedings for PFIPs may involve elements of evaluation and selection. For example, a bidder may achieve all the pre-selection standards, but if required quota is full, it cannot pass pre-selection to offer a formal proposal, because this bidder is not valued as highly by the contracting authority as some other bidders. In some countries, they encourage domestic contracting authorities to limit the prospective proposals to the lowest possible number still sufficient to ensure meaningful competition (for example, three or four). However, some multilateral

[45]The Legislative Guide, Chap. III on Selection of the concessioner, Section A on General Remarks, paras 20.

[46]The Legislative Guide, Chap. III on Selection of the concessioner, Section A on General Remarks, paras 7.

[47]UNCITRAL, "*Model Law on Public Procurement*" (2011), Article 18: Pre-qualification proceedings.

[48]The Legislative Guide, Chap. III on Selection of the concessioner, Section B on Pre-selection of Bidders, paras 34.

financial institutions prohibit the use of pre-selection proceedings for the purposes of limiting the number of bidders to a predetermined number.[49] As a matter of fact, there are very high costs involved in making a formal proposal, so the bidder may be more willing to take the risk if the competition is restricted to a limited pool of qualified candidates. Additionally, some qualified bidders may be denied entry into the formal selection procedure during the pre-selection phase, because the government wishes to avoid market domination by bidders who may have already been awarded a concession within a given sector of the economy. However, for purposes of transparency, it is desirable that the law to provide adequate notice that the contracting authority reserves the right to reject a bidder on monopolistic grounds in any invitation to pre-selection proceedings.[50]

It is useful for foreign private investors to participate in selection proceedings. Foreign participation can not only expand the competitive base, it can also lead to the contracting authority and its country to acquire new technologies that are not available locally.[51] However, the country that wishes to benefit from foreign participation should ensure that its relevant laws and procedures are conducive to such participation. Firstly, the law of the country should identify the publications consulted by foreign private investors to find invitations to pre-selection proceedings. Invitations to pre-selection proceedings should be published in a language customarily used in international trade, in a newspaper of wide international circulation or in a relevant trade publication or technical or professional journal of wide international circulation.[52] Secondly, the law of the country should protect the legitimate rights and interests of foreign investors when it deals with domestic preferences[53] in pre-selection. Countries that wish to provide such domestic preferences should apply them in the form of special evaluation criteria,[54] rather than by the blanket exclusion of foreign suppliers. In any event, where domestic preference is envisaged, it should be announced in advance, preferably in the invitation documents.[55]

Given the large scale of most PFIPs, the private investors may participate in the pre-selection proceedings through consortia formed for that purpose. However, in

[49]The Legislative Guide, Chap. III on Selection of the concessioner, Section B on Pre-selection of Bidders, paras 48.

[50]The Legislative Guide, Chap. III on Selection of the concessioner, Section B on Pre-selection of Bidders, paras 39.

[51]The Legislative Guide, Chap. III on Selection of the concessioner, Section A on General Remarks, paras 8.

[52]E.g. the Legislative Guide made by UNCITRAL recommends a publication as *Development Business* (DB), published by the Department of Public Information of the United Nations Secretariat. *Development Business* is the official publication for consulting, contracting and export opportunities worldwide. <http://www.devbusiness.com/> accessed on 8 September 2019.

[53]The laws of some countries provide some preferential treatments for domestic entities or require foreign bidders that undertake to use national goods or employ local labor.

[54]Such preferential treatment is sometimes provided as a material qualification requirement (for example, a minimum percentage of national participation in the consortium) or as a condition for participating in the selection procedure (for example, to appoint a local partner as a leader of the bidding consortium).

[55]The Model Provisions, Provision 7 on Pre-selection criteria, Footnote 12.

order to ensure the stability of the consortia and to accomplish the project, the law should offer some rules to regulate certain problems arising from the use of consortia. One regulation is the prohibition that one company, directly or through subsidiary companies, joins more than one consortium to submit proposals for the same project. If one company joins into two or more consortia to bid the some project, there may be an information leak or collusion between competing consortia, thus undermining the credibility of the selection proceedings. A breach of this law should cause the disqualification of the consortium and of its all individual member companies.[56] Another regulation is the strict control of changes in the composition of bidding consortia. The contracting authorities may face the problem that the composition of bidding consortia during the pre-selection proceedings may change. As a general rule, only consortia composed of identical members to those passing the pre-selection phase should be allowed to participate in the formal selection phase, unless the contracting authority ensures that the new members have the same capabilities as the retiring members.[57]

5.3.1.2 Procedure of Selecting Final Proposal

After the pre-selection of bidders, the contracting authority will request proposals from the pre-selected bidders. The rules regulating this step should ensure the fairness and transparency of the competition between the proposals submitted by the pre-selected bidders, and that these will fit the specific needs of PFIPs.

The competition between proposals should be transparent, which means as much information concerning the selection of proposals needs to be disclosed as possible in light of relevant laws. Firstly, before the pre-selected bidders submit their final proposals, the contracting authority needs to issue the final request for proposals. The final request for proposal is a document that includes all information necessary to provide the basis for the final decision. This will enable bidders to submit proposals that meet the needs of the contracting authority and that the contracting authority can compare in an objective and fair manner. Thus, the content of the final request for proposal should be as detailed as possible. The Legislative Guide lists the basic content necessary for the final request for proposals: General information to prepare and submit proposals; Project specifications and performance indicators; contractual terms; and the criteria for evaluating the proposals.[58] Secondly, all bidders to whom the contracting authority provided the request for proposals must be notified of any

[56]The Legislative Guide, Chap. III on Selection of the concessioner, Section B on Pre-selection of Bidders, paras 42.

[57]The Legislative Guide, Chap. III on Selection of the concessioner, Section B on Pre-selection of Bidders, paras 49.

[58]The Legislative Guide, Recommendation 20; The Model Provisions, Chap. II on Selection of the concessioner, Model provision 11.

clarifications and modifications, together with the questions that gave rise to the clarifications.[59] Thirdly, the contracting authority should keep an appropriate record of key information concerning the selection proceedings should the bidders and public wish to review the decision afterwards.[60] Fourthly, the agreement on contractual terms should be notified to any third parties in time, especially financiers such as banks who offer to finance the project.

Although the competition of proposals should be transparent, it is nevertheless also necessary to protect a degree of confidentiality by law. Before issuing the final request for proposals, the contract authority may need to negotiate with the preselected bidders because in some case it may not be feasible for the contracting authority to formulate its requirements in sufficiently detailed and precise project specifications or performance indicators. The contracting authority may discuss any aspect of a proposal with its respective bidder. The contracting authority should protect these proposals from disclosure to competing bidders. Any discussions need to be confidential and one party to the discussions should not reveal to any third party any technical, financial or other information relating to the discussions without the consent of the other party.[61]

Any comparison of the proposals should also consider their sustainability. The evaluation criteria for proposals of PFIPs are different from those of normal infrastructure projects. The contracting authority should not only rate the technical elements but also the financial elements of PFIP proposals. Evaluation criteria relating to the physical investment (i.e. the technical elements. for example, the construction works) are usually used in general infrastructure projects, but in proposals for PFIPs it is more important to show the the concessioner's capacity to deliver long-term stable operation and a high quality of service.[62] Therefore the contracting authority should not only focus on the price when comparing the proposals, as some bidders may offer an attractive but unrealistically low price with the intention of raising such prices once the concession is obtained.[63] Thus, the contracting authority should address the long-term needs and ensure the continuous delivery of the service at the required level of quality and safety, and at regulated prices.

The competition between proposals should be fair, which means each proposal should be evaluated under the same criteria and by the same procedure. The contracting authority should compare and evaluate each proposal in accordance with the evaluation criteria, with relative weight accorded to each criterion according

[59] The Legislative Guide, Chap. III on Selection of the concessioner, Section C on Procedures for requesting proposals, para 72.

[60] The Legislative Guide, Chap. III on Selection of the concessioner, Section H on Record of selection and award proceedings, paras 120–126.

[61] The Legislative Guide, Chap. III on Selection of the concessioner, Section C on Procedures for requesting proposals, paras 57.

[62] The Legislative Guide, Chap. III on Selection of the concessioner, Section C on Procedures for requesting proposals, para 73.

[63] The Legislative Guide, Chap. III on Selection of the concessioner, Section C on Procedures for requesting proposals, para 77.

to the evaluation process set forth in the request for proposals.[64] Therefore, it is recommended that the law should regulate the evaluation processes that contracting authorities may use to compare and evaluate proposals and the details of the application of these processes.[65] The Legislative Guide's Recommendation 24 and Model Provision 15(2) offer examples of an evaluation process:

> The contracting authority may establish thresholds with respect to quality, technical, financial and commercial aspects. Proposals that fail to achieve the thresholds shall be regarded as nonresponsive and rejected from the selection procedure.[66]

However, in the detailed notes to the Legislative Guide, it describes alternative evaluation processes, which require the contracting authority to evaluate nonfinancial criteria separately from financial criteria so as to avoid weighting financial criteria (such as the price) against nonfinancial criteria (such as the construction works). However, each country should select their evaluation process according to their specific situation.

5.3.2 Concession Award Without Competitive Procedures

Although competitive procedure is given priority, concession awards without competitive procedure may take place in exceptional circumstances. (Figure 5.1: black).

Concession awards without competitive procedure cannot be given priority because they have a number of disadvantages. They require highly skilled negotiators with sufficient experience in negotiating complex projects, and, since they also imply a higher level of discretion, those negotiations might carry with it a higher risk of abusive or corrupt practices.[67] However, the Legislative Guide and the Model Provisions made by UNCITRAL still list seven exceptional circumstances under which the contracting authority may be authorised to award a concession without using competitive procedures.[68] In cases pertaining to the listed exceptional

---

[64]The Model Provisions, Chap. II on Selection of the concessioner, Model provision 15(1).

[65]The Model Provisions, Chap. II on Selection of the concessioner, Model provision 15(2), Footnote 22.

[66]The Legislative Guide, Recommendation 24; The Model Provisions, Chap. II on Selection of the concessioner, Model provision 15(2).

[67]The Legislative Guide, Chap. III on Selection of the concessioner, Section D on Concession award without competitive procedures, para 88.

[68]The Legislative Guide, Recommendation 28; The Model Provisions, Chap. II on Selection of the concessioner, Model provision 18: (a) When there is an urgent need for ensuring continuity in the provision of the service and engaging in a competitive selection procedure would therefore be impractical; (b) In case of projects of short duration and with an anticipated initial investment value not exceeding a specified low amount; (c) Reasons of national defense or national security; (d) Cases where there is only one source capable of providing the required service (for example, because it requires the use of patented technology or unique know-how); (e) In case of unsolicited proposals of the type referred to intellectual property, trade secrets or other exclusive rights; (f)

circumstances, it is obvious that the competitive procedure is not applicable, whereas negotiations outside competitive procedures do apply. It is noteworthy that the last exceptional circumstance listed in Legislative Guide and the Model Provisions is a flexible option. If the country of the contracting authority desires to use negotiation procedures rather than competitive procedures, this subparagraph should be retained in law in order to offer enough flexibility to apply negotiation procedures. In contrast, if the country of the contracting authority wishes to limit exceptions to the competitive selection procedures, legislators may prefer not to include the subparagraph.[69]

Negotiation outside competitive procedures does not mean arbitrary choice. By contrast, the law is all the more necessary to ensure transparency and fairness in the conduct of the selection process.

Firstly, the law should require the approval of a higher authority to ensure that the award of concessions without competitive procedures is only possible in appropriate circumstances. A contracting authority must obtain the approval of a higher authority prior to engaging in a selection process through negotiation and outside competitive procedures. Therefore, the Model Provision suggests that the host country should appoint an authority that is competent to authorise negotiations.[70]

Secondly, the law should require the contracting authority to engage in negotiations with as many consortia judged capable of carrying out the project as circumstances permit.[71] Although the award is made without competitive procedures, proper competition is still bolstered by encouraging the participation of bidders. It is noteworthy that a host country wishing to enhance transparency in the use of negotiated procedures may establish, through specific regulations, qualification criteria to be met by consortia invited to negotiations.[72]

Thirdly, the law should require the contracting authority to establish evaluation criteria against which proposals will be evaluated and ranked.[73] The contracting authority should identify the proposals which meet those criteria and engage in discussions with each candidate in order to refine and improve the proposal to the point where it is satisfactory to the contracting authority and the candidate. Then

---

When an invitation to the pre-selection proceedings or a request for proposals has been issued but no applications or proposals were submitted or all proposals failed to meet the evaluation criteria set forth in the request for proposals, and if, in the judgment of the contracting authority, issuing a new request for proposals would be unlikely to result in a project award; (g) Other cases where the higher authority authorizes such an exception for compelling reasons of public interest.

[69]The Model Provisions, Chap. II on Selection of the concessioner, Model provision 18(g), Footnote 27.

[70]The Model Provisions, Chap. II on Selection of the concessioner, Model provision 18, Footnote 24.

[71]The Legislative Guide, Chap. III on Selection of the concessioner, Section D on Concession award without competitive procedures, paras 92–94; The Model Provisions, Chap. II on Selection of the concessioner, Model provision 19(b).

[72]The Model Provisions, Chap. II on Selection of the concessioner, Model provision 19(b), Footnote 29.

[73]The Model Provisions, Chap. II on Selection of the concessioner, Model provision 19(c); The Legislative Guide, Recommendation 29(b).

the project should be awarded to the party offering the "most economical" or "most advantageous" proposal amongst those amended through negotiation.[74] The establishment of evaluation criteria could curb the abusive and corrupt practices that may be brought by a high level of discretion in negotiation.

Fourthly, the law should require as much disclosure of information on the negotiation process as possible, with the exception of cases involving national security interests or business secrets. At the outset of the process, the contracting authority should publish a notice of its intention to commence negotiations for a concession contract. The notice should also disclose the specific circumstances and reasons for the decision to award the concession without competitive procedures.[75] Then the contracting authority should establish a record of the selection proceedings.[76] In order to further ensure transparency, the record of the selection proceedings and the project agreement should be open to public inspection.[77] Additionally, third parties such as banks, who offer a part of the finance for the project, should be notified in time as to the negotiation proceedings and the contractual terms.

Figure 5.1 shows that competitive procedures should be given priority, but that negotiation procedures may replace competitive procedures when concessions cannot be awarded through competitive procedure (Fig. 5.1: black). In China, concession awards have been granted without competitive procedures in case pertaining to PFIPs, but there are no relevant laws to regulate such awards. The recommendations of the Legislative Guide and Model Provisions indicate that the negotiation procedure of PFIPs in China should be regulated.

5.4 The Post-selection Stage Should Be Fair and Transparent

When the selection process is completed, bidders may disagree with the result. Bidders may claim to have suffered unfair treatment during the selection procedures. In this case, bidders should be entitled by law to appeal against the result. (Figure 5.1: red).

---

[74]The Legislative Guide, Chap. III on Selection of the concessioner, Section D on Concession award without competitive procedures, para 95.

[75]The Legislative Guide, Recommendation 29(c).

[76]The selection proceeding requires a record, but the record of the negotiation proceeding should be more strict and detailed. For instance, the Legislative Guide lists a general information required in the record (Chap. III on Selection of the concessioner, Section H on Record of selection and award proceedings, para 121), and then the additional information required in negotiation proceeding is listed afterwards (para 122).

[77]The Legislative Guide, Chap. III on Selection of the concessioner, Section D on Concession award without competitive procedures, para 96.

The bidder may claim to have suffered unfair treatment during the selection procedure because of a breach in duty imposed by the law on the contracting authority.[78] The Legislative Guide and the Model Provisions made by UNCITRAL advocate granting bidders the right to seek review of actions by the contracting authority, to determine whether these have been in violation of selection rules or of the rights of bidders. In this regard, the Legislative Guide and the Model provisions compare and discuss administrative review and judicial review. Although China currently has relevant laws on both administrative review and judicial review, the key problem is that the nature of concessioner selection of PFIPs has not been determined. If PFIP concessioner selection is regarded to be an administrative action,the bidders could seek administrative review. However, if PFIP concessioner selection is regarded to be a general contractual action, the bidders should seek judicial review.[79] At this stage, China must confirm the nature of concessioner selection pertaining to PFIPs.

However, two concepts suggested by the Legislative Guide and the Model Provisions are worthy of consultation. The first is a "pre-contract" recourse system. This system requires the review of the contracting authority's actions as early in the selection proceedings as is feasible. Before the concession is awarded, the contracting authority may be willing to correct any improper behaviour (of which it may even not have been aware). The contracting authority could then take corrective action before loss is caused, thus avoiding cases where monetary compensation is the only redress left for improper actions taken.[80] The second is a "post-contract" compensation system. If the concession award was declared to be invalid due to improper action by the contracting authority, both the Public Sector and the Private Sector may suffer greater losses, especially when public works have already been initiated. Therefore, when dealing with concession awards where there has been improper action by the contracting authority, due consideration must be paid to the integrity of the selection procedure, possible delays to the rendering of a public service, and the interests of the bidders. Excepting those cases where a concession award was the result of unlawful action, a good general solution is that the concession award should not be invalid, but that compensation is given to the injured party. Such compensation should not include loss of profits, but be limited to the costs incurred by the competitor in preparing for the competition.[81]

The bidder may claim to have suffered unfair treatment during the selection procedure because the other bidders have made some improper action in the competition. Neither the Legislative Guide nor the Model Provisions refers to the review procedures for this kind of matter. However, improper action by a bidder is not rare in a selection process, and includes unfair competition and collusion between bidders.

---

[78]The Legislative Guide, Recommendation 39; The Model Provisions, Chap. II on Selection of the concessioner, Model provision 27.

[79]Peng Tao, 'PPP' practice in China and Composition of PPP' Legal Framework', Zheng Fa Lun Cong(No. 6, Dec. 10, 2006) P84.

[80]The Legislative Guide, Chap. III on Selection of the concessioner, Section I on review procedures, para 127.

[81]The Legislative Guide, Chap. III on Selection of the concessioner, Section I on review procedures, para 131.

As a matter of fact, some countries have set up relevant laws to regulate the improper actions of bidders. In China, if the bidder's improper action arises during bidding procedures, it may be regulated by the Bidding Law of the People's Republic of China[82]; if the bidder's improper action arises in a selection procedure without competition, it may be regulated by the Anti-Unfair Competition Law of the People's Republic of China[83]; and if the bidder's improper action is serious, it may be punished by the Criminal Law of the People's Republic of China.[84]

To sum up, a review procedure is a basic requirement for attracting serious and competent bidders and for reducing the cost and the length of award proceedings. Therefore, it is essential to establish fair and efficient review procedures for concessioner selection of PFIPs in China.

As discussed above, if the concessioner selection is regarded to be a general contractual action, the bidders could seek judicial review. However, due to the specific character of concessioner selection in PFIPs, involving long-term negotiations and government actions, none of Biding Law, Government Procurement Law, Anti-unfair Competition Law or Administrative Reconsideration Law can be used to review selection procedure in PFIPs. There are even conflicts on how to deal with selection review within these statutes. Additionally, although China has not subscribed WTO Government Procurement Agreement (GPA) yet, it is worth mentioning the domestic review procedure[85] in WTO GPA as a possible model to improve Chinese laws on protecting bidder's review rights. The new legislation on concessioner selection of

[82]The Bidding Law of the People's Republic of China, adopted on August 30,1999; effect as of January 1, 2000:

Article 53: If a bidder colludes with one or more other bidders or with the bid inviting party in the submission of its bid, or if a bidder seeks to win the project by offering a bribe to the bid inviting party or one or more of the members of the bid evaluation committee, the acceptance of its bid shall be void, the bidder shall be imposed a fine of not less than 0.5% nor more than 1% of the amount of the project which it won and the persons in charge directly responsible and the other directly responsible persons of the unit shall be imposed a fine of not less than 5% nor more than 10% of the amount of the fine imposed upon the unit; if there are illegal earnings, such illegal earnings shall be confiscated; if the circumstances are serious, the bidder's bidding qualifications for projects which legally require the invitation of bids shall be suspended for one to two years and the same shall be publicly announced, or the administrative department for industry and commerce shall revoke its business license; if a crime is constituted, criminal liability shall be investigated according to law; if losses are caused to others, liability for compensation shall be assumed according to law.

[83]The Anti-Unfair Competition Law of the People's Republic of China, adopted on September 2nd, 1993; effect as of December 1st, 1993:

Article 27 If bidders act in collusion, raise or reduce the price of the bid; and bidder and invite tender ganged up in order to put the others out of the fair competition, its bid shall be invalid and the supervisor may fine amount from more than 10,000 to less than200, 000 RMB in accordance with the facts.

[84]The Criminal Law of the People's Republic of China, effect as of October 1st, 1997:

Article 223 Bidders who act in collusion with each other in offering bidding prices and thus jeopardize the interests of bid-inviters or of other bidders, if the circumstances are serious, shall be sentenced to fixed-term imprisonment of not more than three years or criminal detention and shall also, or shall only, be fined.

[85]WTO Government Procurement Agreement (GPA)

Article XVIII Domestic Review Procedures

PFIPs should offer bidder proper channels to review the selection procedure. Firstly, the bidder should be authorised to require the contracting authority to review selection procedure so that the contracting authority could take corrective action before loss is caused. Secondly, a procedure should be provided by law so that the bidder could look for fair review from independent third-parties. Finally, the bidder should have right to litigate if they dispute the result reached either by the contracting authority or through the review process.

5.5 Unsolicited Proposals Should Be Fair and Transparent

Apart from the concessioner selection procedures discussed above, there is a special selection procedure for PFIP concessioners regarding Unsolicited Proposals (Fig. 5.1: green). The Legislative Guide and the Model Provisions have described this kind of procedure and discussed at length how to regulate it. However, it is inconceivable that unsolicited proposals have never arisen in either Chinese practice or academic research concerning PFIPs.

When private investors identify an infrastructure need that may be met by a privately financed project, they may approach the public authority directly and submit an initial proposal for the development of a project in respect of which no selection procedure has been opened. The proposal is usually referred to as an "unsolicited proposal".[86]

Developed countries are very reluctant to accept unsolicited proposals because they consider the model of unsolicited proposal difficult to assess in its validity or seriousness, and because it weakens free competition.[87] By contrast, developing countries, especially countries which expect to develop PFIPs, find the unsolicited proposal model useful because this approach may be the only means by which these less experienced countries are exposed to PFIPs. Without the submission of an unsolicited proposal, the host government may never have entertained the notion of the PFIP as a viable development option.[88]

---

2. In the event of a complaint by a supplier, arising in the context of covered procurement in which the supplier has, or has had, an interest, that there has been a breach or a failure as referred to in para 1, the Party of the procuring entity conducting the procurement shall encourage the entity and the supplier to seek resolution of the complaint through consultations. The entity shall accord impartial and timely consideration to any such complaint in a manner that is not prejudicial to the supplier's participation in ongoing or future procurement or its right to seek corrective measures under the administrative or judicial review procedure.

[86] The Legislative Guide, Chap. III on Selection of the concessioner, Section E Unsolicited proposals, para 97.

[87] Lesguillons Henry, *'Selecting a project company'* (I.B.L.J. 1998, 6, 603–622) P614–615.

[88] Pertchik Jonathan M., *'The build, operate and transfer approach to infrastructure development in Mexico'* (P.P.L.R. 1995, 4, 168–200) P183.

If a country decides to use unsolicited proposal, relevant regulations should be issued. The regulations should safeguard the public interest, while protecting the rights of the promoter of the unsolicited proposal.[89]

The World Bank, UNIDO and some countries have issued some regulations about unsolicited proposal,[90] but the Legislative Guide and the Model Provisions give further suggestions for detailed procedures to deal with unsolicited proposal in accordance with the law (Fig. 5.1: green):

First of all, Public departments themselves which have the right and responsibility to entertain the unsolicited proposal should be authorised to do so by law. The Legislative Guide and the Model Provisions assume that the power to entertain unsolicited proposals lies with the contracting authority with the right to award the concession. However, some countries may consider a body separate from the contracting authority to have the power to entertain unsolicited proposals. In such a case, the body needs to be adequately coordinated with the contracting authority.[91]

Following the receipt of an unsolicited proposal, the next step is to determine the admissibility of the unsolicited proposal. The primary thing is to evaluate whether or not the project will be in the public interest. Evaluating whether a proposed project is in the public interest entails judgments regarding the potential benefits to the public offered by the project, and its relationship to existing government policies in the infrastructure sector concerned.[92] The further information that must be evaluated is the promoter's qualifications, the technical and economic feasibility of the project, and its environmental impact.[93] In order to ensure the integrity, transparency and predictability of the procedures for determining the admissibility of unsolicited proposals, the law should provide criteria for these evaluations.

After evaluating the unsolicited proposal, if the proposal is considered to be inadmissible and is then rejected, it should be returned to the promoter and its confidential content should be protected. If the proposal passes evaluation and the decision is to implement the project, selection procedures should be initiated. According to the Legislative Guide and the Model Provisions, there are two ways to implement this special selection process:

---

[89] Lesguillons Henry, *'Selecting a project company'* (I.B.L.J. 1998, 6, 603–622) P616.

[90] Ibid, P617–620.

[91] The Model Provisions, Chap. II on Selection of the concessioner, Model provision 20, Footnote 31.

[92] The Model Provisions, Chap. II on Selection of the concessioner, Model provision 21(1), Footnote 32.

[93] The Legislative Guide, Recommendation 31; The Model Provisions, Chap. II on Selection of the concessioner, Model provision 21(2).

5.5.1 *No Proprietary Concepts or Technology*

Procedures for handling unsolicited proposals without proprietary concepts or technology should consider rewarding the initial promoter.

When the evaluation is finished and the decision has been made to implement the project, unsolicited proposals which do not involve proprietary concepts or technology still have to participate in a normal competitive selection procedure (as in Section 5.3.1) against other participants to acquire the concession. However, the bidder who offered the unsolicited proposal should be given certain benefits to reward its initial submission, e.g. the initial bidder must be invited to participate in the competition unless it gives up this right, or the bidder may be given a premium.[94] This reward is necessary and significant. On the one hand, it provides incentive to encourage private investors to participate in the building of public infrastructure, whether they have proprietary concerns or not. On the other hand, unsolicited proposals submitted initially by private investors reflect a public voice and indicate public participation in the preliminary assessment of an infrastructure project, rather than government-initiated infrastructure project proposals (refer to Section 5.2.1). The difficulty in rewarding the initial bidder is determining its value, which should not be set too high or too low. The reward should not be so high as to discourage competing meritorious bids, which might result in the receipt of a project of lesser value simply in exchange for the preference given to the innovative bidder. The reward should not be so low as to frustrate the initiative of the author of the unsolicited proposal.[95]

5.5.2 *Proprietary Concepts or Technology*

There are two procedures for handling unsolicited proposals involving proprietary concepts or technology.

When the evaluation is finished and the decision has been made to implement a project, unsolicited proposals that involve irreplaceable proprietary concepts or technology may be awarded the concession directly (Fig. 5.1: green). The problem here is determining whether the proprietary concept or technology is irreplaceable or not. The Legislative Guide and the Model Provisions suggest obtaining elements of comparison from the unsolicited proposal. The essential output elements of the unsolicited proposal could be published, including for example, the capacity of the infrastructure facility, quality of the product or the service or price per unit. Then other interested parties may be invited to submit alternative or comparable proposals within

[94] The Legislative Guide, Recommendation 33; The Model Provisions, Chap. II on Selection of the concessioner, Model provision 22.

[95] The Legislative Guide, Chap. III on Selection of the concessioner, Section E Unsolicited proposals, para 113.

a certain period.[96] If no alternative proposals are received or the received proposals will not achieve the projected outputs, this would confirm that there is no reasonable alternative or substitute to the method or technology put forward in the unsolicited proposal. The unsolicited proposal could then be awarded the concession directly.[97] If other parties offer other alternatives or substitute the method or technology in a way that would meet the projected outputs, the unsolicited proposal should engage in competitive selection procedures against other participants but it should be given an incentive or a similar benefit.[98]

In China, it is impossible for private investors to submit unsolicited proposals for public infrastructure because only government has the right to decide whether to implement an infrastructure project or not. Even if private investors submit unsolicited proposals to relevant authorities, the unsolicited proposal may be ignored and the relevant authority may consider the private investor to be challenging their authority. However, it should be noted that unsolicited proposals are useful for facilitating the development of PFIPs. On the one hand, the China government, which may have not considered adopting a PFIP model at the beginning, may consider adopting a PFIP model through the submission of an unsolicited proposal. On the other hand, the private investor who initially submits the unsolicited proposal could gain some premium, which would encourage private investors to participate in PFIPs. In European countries which have experience in implementing PFIPs, unsolicited proposal is allowed and regulated by appropriate laws.[99] Those countries, such as China, which wish to facilitate PFIPs, may wish to establish legal procedures for dealing with unsolicited proposal.

5.6 Conclusion

This chapter answers the 4th research question, namely how the Chinese concessioner selection procedures of the PFIPs may be improved, based on the guidelines of the Legislative Guide and Model Provisions with supplementary reference to other countries' laws.

[96]The Legislative Guide, Chap. III on Selection of the concessioner, Section E Unsolicited proposals, para 115.

[97]The Legislative Guide, Chap. III on Selection of the concessioner, Section E Unsolicited proposals, para 116(a).

[98]The Legislative Guide, Chap. III on Selection of the concessioner, Section E Unsolicited proposals, para 116(b).

[99]EC Directive 96/92 concerning common rules for the internal market in electricity [1997] O.J. L27/20, Article 4, in Petros Vellas, *'Price regulation in energy project finance: the need for comprehensive state intervention'* (I.E.L.T.R. 2005, 3, 61–68) P63; French practice of the *contrats de partenariat* (Article L. 1411–11 of the CGCT) & Public Private Partnership Act 2005 (Poland) Article 10, in Maria Hauser and Jean-Baptiste Morel, *'New Polish law on public-private partnership'* (I.B.L.J. 2006, 1, 3–19) P10; European Bank for Reconstruction and Development, *'Public Private Partnerships'*, <http://www.ebrd.com/pages/sector/legal/concessions/ppp.shtml> accessed on 5th October, 2019.

This Chapter summarises the concessioner selection procedures of PFIPs (Fig. 5.1). The general concessioner selection procedure of PFIPs has three steps: pre-selection stage (Fig. 5.1: blue); selection stage (Fig. 5.1: black); post-selection stage (Fig. 5.1: red). Additionally, if the project is initiated by unsolicited proposal, a special selection procedure should be applied (Fig. 5.1: green). Countries such as China, which want to develop PFIPs, should establish laws that confirm concessioner selection procedures and support the implementation of each selection step, in order to offer fair and transparent competition to private investors, avoid corrupting contracting authorities, and ensure the successful accomplishment of PFIPs.

In the pre-selection phase, PFIPs should be launched in light of laws. Although PFIP launches are traditionally decided by government in China, it would be helpful to allow the public to participate in the preliminary assessment of the feasibility of a PFIP. Additionally, private finance's access to the infrastructure project market may be regulated in laws, so Chinese laws should guarantee market access to private finance insofar as this is possible, excepting areas of national security, if China wishes to facilitate the development of PFIPs. While due caution should be shown in the use of foreign finance, Chinese treatment of foreign finance should approach international standards to attract foreign private finance and high-level technology.

In the selection phase, Chinese laws should ensure the competitive selection procedure works as the primary model of selection, in order to select the most appropriate concessioner. Awards determined without competitive procedures through negotiation should be recognised only in exceptional cases. Moreover, in light of the features of PFIPs, regulations should be adjusted to fit the specific requirements of the concessioner selection procedure of PFIPs (for example, adding the pre-selection of bidders), to ensure the whole selection procedure is economical and efficient, and demonstrates integrity, confidence and transparency.

In the post-selection phase, the laws should offer competitors reasonable channels to query the selection result. On the one hand, the bidders should be able to review the contracting authority for improper action during the selection procedure. On the other hand, competitors should be protected from unfair action by fellow competitors. An important safeguard for the rules of the selection procedure is to offer the bidders the right to review actions by the contracting authority and other competitors. However, considering the public interest, an improperly awarded concession may be not invalid if the project has already been implemented. Nevertheless, injured competitors should be awarded due compensation in these instances.

Chinese laws have never referred to unsolicited proposal, but it is obvious that the model of unsolicited proposal is useful for developing PFIPs. Therefore, by referencing the recommendations in the Legislative Guide and the Model Provisions, relevant regulations on unsolicited proposal should be considered in the reform of Chinese laws on PFIPs.

To sum up, the concessioner selection procedures are very important in the successful accomplishment of PFIPs. The Legislative Guide and the Model Provisions made by UNCTRAL offer very detailed guidelines on establishing regulations regarding the selection procedures of PFIPs. Although the Legislative Guide and the Model Provisions have their own limitations in certain aspects, they are still useful for helping the reform of Chinese laws on PFIPs in this regard. The successful experience of other countries also offers valuable references for the reform of Chinese laws on concessioner selection procedures in PFIPs.

When the concession is awarded to the selected concessioner, the concessioner will face various relationships with other parties of PFIPs during the construction and operation of infrastructure. Countries such as China who wish to develop PFIPs need to establish laws regulating the rights and responsibilities of each party so that the project could be implemented smoothly. The issues arising when establishing laws to regulate the rights and responsibilities of each party of PFIPs will be discussed in Chap. 6.

Chapter 6
Construction and Operation of PFIPs: The Legal Framework and the Agreements

6.1 Introduction

After a concession is awarded to the selected concessioner, the concessioner will need to negotiate with the various participants of the PFIP concerning the construction and operation of the project.

The aim of this chapter is to discuss the content of various agreements of PFIPs and the potential impact of relevant laws on these agreements, with reference to the recommendations of the Legislative Guide and the Model Provisions. It also considers the impact of current Chinese laws and policies on these agreements, so that the Chinese laws and policies may be adjusted.

This chapter has six objectives. The first objective is to present the legal framework used in the construction and operation of PFIPs, which is formed through various agreements. The second objective is to analyse the relationships between the agreements. The third objective is to discuss the content of the project agreement, which is at the core of the legal framework, and the impact of relevant laws on this agreement to provide suggestions as to how China might improve these laws to facilitate PFIPs. The fourth objective is to discuss the content of the finance agreement and the impact of relevant laws on this agreement to provide suggestions as to how China might improve these laws to facilitate PFIPs. The fifth objective is to discuss the content of the subcontracting agreement and the impact of relevant laws on this agreement to provide suggestions as to how China might improve these laws to facilitate PFIPs. The sixth objective is to discuss the content of the user agreement and the impact of relevant laws on this agreement to provide suggestions as to how China might improve these laws to facilitate PFIPs.

This chapter consists of two sections.

Section 6.2 addresses the types of agreement that may be included in PFIPs (see Fig. 6.1), and the restrictions and impact of these agreements (see Fig. 6.2). PFIPs include five principal parties: the contracting authority, the concessioner, the financer, the user and the sub-contractor (Fig. 6.1: black). There are four kinds of agreement between these five parties, which clarify the rights and obligations of

S. Liang, *Legal Aspects of Privately Financed Infrastructure Projects (PFIPs) in China*,
https://doi.org/10.1007/978-981-15-6803-9_6

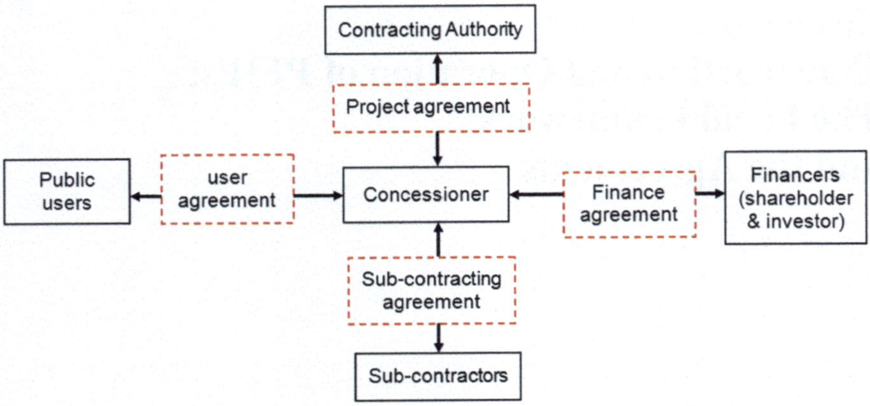

Fig. 6.1 The five main parties and four agreements in PFIPs

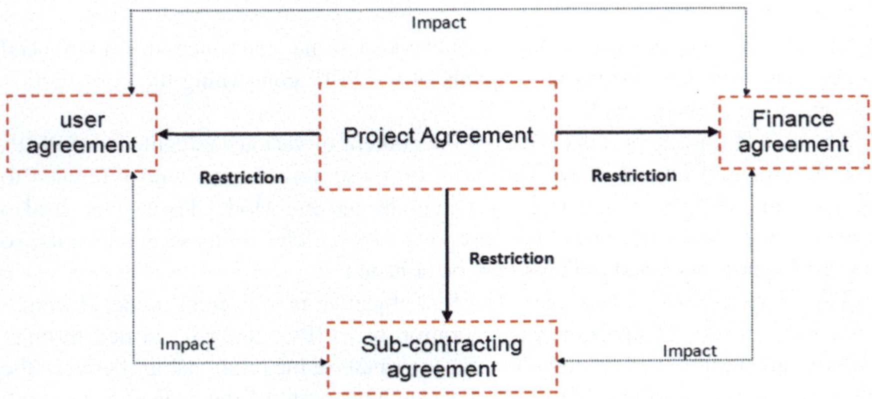

Fig. 6.2 The relationships among the four kinds of agreement

the parties: the project agreement, the finance agreement, the user agreement and the subcontracting agreement (Fig. 6.1: red). The project agreement is the core agreement of the PFIP and may restrict the other three kinds of agreement. At the same time, these three agreements may also affect each other. These agreements comprise the entire framework of PFIPs, and need to be addressed to ensure PFIPs are successful.

Section 6.3 discusses the contents of each agreement, with reference to some special issues and the possible impact of relevant laws.

The Legislative Guide and the Model Provisions[1] suggest that the content of a project agreement should be flexible enough to enable negotiation, but that there may be some mandatory requirements in the agreement based on the specific laws of the country in question. Six issues pertaining to the project agreement are discussed:

- Organisation of the project company
- Real estate (project assets, land, easements)
- Security interests
- Performance guarantee
- Protection of customers
- Duration, extension and termination

The Legislative Guide and Model Provisions[2] suggest that the finance agreement should address the issue of set-in right, which permits lenders to take over the concession when the concessioner cannot continue the project. This suggestion should be considered in Chinese law reform.

The Legislative Guide and Model Provisions[3] suggest that the subcontracting agreement should address the issue of a conflict in interests within the project company when its investors are also subcontractors. This suggestion should be considered in Chinese law reform.

The Legislative Guide and Model Provisions[4] suggest that the user agreement should address the issue of extra protection for special customers using the public service. This suggestion should be considered in Chinese law reform.

In countries such as China, which want to facilitate PFIPs, it is necessary to clarify the responsibilities and rights in agreements pertaining to PFIPs, and establish proper and relevant laws to regulate the contents of agreements and guarantee the efficacy of the agreements.

This chapter answers the fifth research question: How should the laws relating to the agreements involved in PFIPs be reformed in China, with reference to the guidelines of the Legislative Guide and the Model Provisions, and with supplementary reference to other countries?

---

[1] The Model Provisions, Model provision 28–48; the Legislative Guide, Chap. IV on Construction and operation of infrastructure: legislative framework and project agreement and Chap. V on Duration, extension and termination of the project agreement.

[2] The Model Provisions, Model provision 42; the Legislative Guide, Recommendation 60, Chap. IV on Construction and operation of infrastructure: legislative framework and project agreement, Section J. General contractual arrangements, para 148.

[3] The Model Provisions, Model provision 28(l); the Legislative Guide, Recommendation 56, Chap. IV on Construction and operation of infrastructure: legislative framework and project agreement, Section J. General contractual arrangements, para 99–101.

[4] The Model Provisions, Model provision 38,1(c); the Legislative Guide, Recommendation 53(c), Chap. IV on Construction and operation of infrastructure: legislative framework and project agreement, Section I. Operation of infrastructure, para 88–89.

6.2 The Legal Framework in Construction and Operation of PFIPs

The construction and operation of PFIPs includes five principal parties: the contracting authority, the concessioner, the financer, the user and the sub-contractor (Fig. 6.1: black). There are four kinds of agreements (Fig. 6.1: red) between the five parties, which regulate the rights and obligations of the parties.

6.2.1 The Agreements

The project agreement regulates the rights and obligations between the contracting authority and the concessioner. After the concessioner selection process, the selected concessioner makes a project agreement with the contracting authority concerning the construction and operation of PFIPs. The project agreement defines the scope and purpose of the project, provides details on the execution of the project, sets forth the conditions for the operation of the infrastructure or the delivery of the relevant services, and settles the project duration and the specific circumstances relating to extension or termination.[5]

The finance agreement regulates the rights and obligations between the financers and the concessioner. Due to the difficulties the concessioner of PFIPs might face, were it to raise the project finance by itself, the concessioner is likely to enter into a finance agreement with a finance lender. In large-scale infrastructure projects, different lenders are often involved at different phases of the project. More than one lender may be involved at the same phase of the project. In order to avoid disputes that might arise from conflicting actions taken by different lenders, lenders funding a large project sometimes do so under a common finance agreement, in which one or more financial institutions take a leading role in negotiating on behalf of the other participating financial institutions. The finance agreement generally includes the finance amount, the duration of the loan, the interest or other returns, the collateral requirements and the settlement of any breach in the agreement. If funding is provided by different lenders under separate finance agreements, the lenders may negotiate a so-called "inter-creditor agreement" between them, in case of conflict.[6]

The user agreement regulates the rights and obligations between the public users and the concessioner. After completing the construction of the infrastructure, the concessioner operates it as a service to public users, who may be individuals or groups. There should be an express or implied contract[7] between the public users

[5]The legislative Guide, Chap. IV on Construction and operation of infrastructure: legislative framework and project agreement, Section A General provisions of the project agreement, paras 1.

[6]The Legislative Guide, Introduction and Background information on PFIPs, Section B on Background information on privately financed infrastructure projects, paras 73.

[7]Implied contract means though it is not a written contract, the behaviors of purchase and service provision equals the contract has already concluded. For example, the regulations printed behind

and the concessioner, which constitutes the user agreement. The user agreement often describes the service scope, charge criteria, directions for use and compensation for breach.

The sub-contracting agreement regulates the rights and obligation between the sub-contractors and the concessioner. Given the complexity of infrastructure projects, the concessioner may contract the services of one or more construction companies to implement some or most of the construction work, and may also contract the services of companies with experience in the operation and maintenance of infrastructure during the operational phase of the project.[8] The concessioner may make various sub-contracting agreements with different sub-contractors. The sub-contracting agreement, as with any general commercial contract, includes the rights and obligations of each party, payment options, compensation for breach, and dispute settlement.

6.2.2 The Relationships Among the Agreements

The detailed content of the above four agreements may overlap with each other, since they support and limit each other (see Fig. 6.2). The "project agreement" between the contracting authority and the concessionaire is the central contractual document in a PFIP,[9] and therefore may restrict the other three agreements.

The project agreement may restrict the finance agreements. The principal advantage of PFIPs is that the contracting authority does not offer, or only partly offers, the project funds and the concessioner takes responsibility for the funds required to construct and operate the project. The total private funds for the project mainly come through three channels: a portion of the funds are contributed directly by the concessioner's shareholders; a portion is derived from loans extended to the concessioner by commercial banks and international financial institutions; and a portion is raised from the proceeds of the placement of bonds and other negotiable instruments in a capital market.[10] Generally, the law should not unnecessarily restrict the concessioner's ability to enter into financial arrangements as it sees fit for the purpose of financing the infrastructure. However, due to the specific requirements of PFIPs, in

---

the train ticket are regarded as the consent between the passenger and the train operator since the passenger uses it.

[8]The legislative Guide, Chap. IV on Construction and operation of infrastructure: legislative framework and project agreement, Section J General contractual arrangements, paras 99.

[9]The legislative Guide, Chap. IV on Construction and operation of infrastructure: legislative framework and project agreement, Section A General provisions of the project agreement, paras 1.

[10]The legislative Guide, Chap. IV on Construction and operation of infrastructure: legislative framework and project agreement, Section D on Financial arrangement, paras 35; The Legislative Guide, Introduction and Background information on PFIPs, Section B on Background information on privately financed infrastructure projects, paras 54–67.

order to accomplish the project successfully and consider the public interest, legislation usually allows or requires the project agreement to make certain restrictions on the finance agreements, used to raise funds for the project.

Firstly, the project agreement may require a limitation on the investment freedom of the project company's shareholders. This would mean the shareholders could not transfer their equity participation without obtaining the prior consent of the contracting authority. In PFIPs, concessioners are selected to carry out infrastructure projects at least partly on the basis of their experience and capability to undertake that sort of project. Therefore, if the concessioner's shareholders are entirely free to transfer their investment in a given project, contracting authorities may worry that there will be no assurance as to who will actually deliver the relevant services, which may negatively affect the success of the project or the service offered.[11] However, there are some arguments as to whether laws should allow the concessioner's shareholders to transfer their investment freely. Although the Legislative Guide intends to minimise limitations to the shareholders' rights to transfer their investment,[12] these rights have been strictly controlled in the previous PFIPs in China.[13] This issue will be discussed in detailed in Sect. 6.3.1.1.

Secondly, the project agreement may restrict guaranteed items in the finance agreement. Commercial banks and international financial institutions such as finance lenders may not want to finance the concessioners of PFIPs, considering the huge risks involved. One of the risks is that the new "project company"[14] lacks an established credit or financial record on which the lenders might rely, so lenders have to confirm the credit limit only on the basis of the project's cash flow and projected earnings. Lenders are afraid to offer large amounts in loan solely on the basis of a project's expected cash flow or assets. Another risk stems from the shareholders' lack of liability for the loan, which means that the lender cannot ask the project company's shareholders for the repayment of loan. The project's assets and revenue are strictly separated from the assets of the project company's shareholders, i.e. the project company's shareholders are not responsible for any finance over and above that which they have already invested in the project company. If a PFIP fails, the

[11] The legislative Guide, Chap. IV on Construction and operation of infrastructure: legislative framework and project agreement, Section G on Transfer of controlling interest in the project company, para 64; The legislative Guide, Chap. III on Selection of the concessionaire, paras 38–40.

[12] The legislative Guide, Chap. IV on Construction and operation of infrastructure: legislative framework and project agreement, Section G on Transfer of controlling interest in the project company, para 65–66.

[13] For example: The Company Law of the People's Republic of China, effect on January 1,2006:

Article 142: The shares of a company held by the initiators of this company shall not be transferred within 1 year as of the day of establishment of the company. The shares issued before the company publicly issues shares shall not be transferred within 1 year as of the day when the stocks of the company get listed and are traded in a stock exchange……

[14] A large-scale infrastructure project is often carried out by a new corporate entity specially established for that purpose by the project promoters. Such a new entity, often called a "project company", becomes the vehicle for raising funds for the project.

lender can only claim the project company's assets, not the shareholders'.[15] Thus, the lender may require some guarantee or other means of credit support from the contracting authority, users or other interested third parties to ensure repayment of loans. However, there are some restrictions on this guarantee in PFIPs, as written in the project agreement and to protect public interests. For example, the infrastructure or facility of the project may be public property, which may not be used as the project company's guarantee for the repayment of loans. This issue of financial guarantee will be discussed in detailed in Sect. 6.3.1.3.

The project agreement may also restrict the user agreement. Although the user agreement is an agreement between the concessioner and public users, the contracting authority has the responsibility to ensure that the public users are satisfied with the infrastructure's facilities and the service offered by the concessioner. Therefore, in the project agreement, the contracting authority often requires some restrictive items pertaining to the standard charge in the user agreement to keep charges affordable.[16] The concessioner, in turn, may be worried that its projected profits will become unrealistic because of a change in public policy. Therefore, the concessioners also expect to have an agreement concerning the possibility of adjusting the charge.[17] The issue of restricting standard charges will be discussed in Sect. 6.3.1.5.

The project agreement may impose restrictions on the sub-contracting agreements. In PFIPs, the concessioner may hire subcontractors to perform the construction or operation work agreed upon in the project agreement. Generally, the contracting authority should not restrict the concessioner's freedom to hire subcontractors because the investors in the Project Company may include construction or operation companies whose participation in the project is on the basis that they will be given sub-contracts for the execution of the construction or other work. If the contracting authority interferes excessively with the making of sub-contracts, it may discourage potential investors from investing in the PFIP. However, the concessioner should not enjoy an unlimited freedom to select its subcontractors. The contracting authority who awards the concession is responsible for monitoring the quality of the project, so the contracting authority needs to pay close attention to the subcontractor's technical capabilities and financial standing. If the subcontract lacks capacity, it will hinder the accomplishment of the project and harm the public interest. Therefore, the contracting authority often retains the right to review and approve the project company's subcontracts in the project agreement. In these cases, however, the project agreement should clearly define the procedures of review and approval and the circumstances under which the contracting authority's approval may be withheld. As a general rule, approval should not be withheld unless the subcontracts are found

[15]The Legislative Guide, Introduction and Background information on PFIPs, Section B on Background information on privately financed infrastructure projects, paras 54–55.

[16]The legislative Guide, Chap. IV on Construction and operation of infrastructure: legislative framework and project agreement, Section D on Financial arrangement, paras 37–46.

[17]The legislative Guide, Chap. IV on Construction and operation of infrastructure: legislative framework and project agreement, Section J on General contractual arrangement, paras 124.

to contain provisions manifestly contrary to the public interest or contrary to mandatory rules with the nature of public law that apply to the execution of PFIPs in the host country.[18]

Aside from the restrictions imposed by the project agreement on the other three kinds of agreement, the three kinds of agreements may affect each other (Fig. 6.2). The lenders may wish to ensure that the project company's subcontractors are not overpaid, to prevent repercussions on the project company's ability to repay loans. One particular instance may arise where the subcontractor is also one of the project company's shareholders, since there may be a potential conflict of interest between the project company and this shareholder. Therefore, it is possible for the lender to make certain restrictive items in the finance agreement, which may affect the subcontracting agreement.[19] The lender may even require a "direct payment" clause, enabling the contracting authority to pay sub-contractors directly to avoid this conflict of interest. A guarantee given in most PFIPs is the assignment to lenders of proceeds from the user agreement. The finance agreements may require that the proceeds of infrastructure projects be deposited in an escrow account managed by a trustee appointed by the lenders.[20] Therefore, the payments given in the user agreement may affect the loan repayments in the finance agreement. During the operation of the PFIP, subcontractors who operate the infrastructure directly offer services to public users in light of the user agreement, and the public users who pay for the service have the right to receive the same level of service detailed in the user agreement. Therefore, the service standard laid out in the user agreement should equal to the service quality requirements set forth in the subcontracting agreement, so that the operator offers a satisfactory level of service to the public users.

To sum up, there are five principal parties in the construction and operation of PFIPs: the contracting authority, the concessioner, the financer, the user and the subcontractor. Therefore, there are four kinds of agreements between the five parties, which regulate the rights and obligations of the parties: Project Agreement, Finance Agreement, User Agreement and Sub-contracting Agreement. The project agreement between the contracting authority and the concessioner is the central agreement. In order to protect the public interest, the project agreement may restrict the other three kinds of agreement. At the same time, the three kinds of agreements may affect each other.

[18]The legislative Guide, Chap. IV on Construction and operation of infrastructure: legislative framework and project agreement, Section J on General contractual arrangement, paras 99–101.

[19]The legislative Guide, Chap. IV on Construction and operation of infrastructure: legislative framework and project agreement, Section J on General contractual arrangement, paras 101.

[20]The legislative Guide, Chap. IV on Construction and operation of infrastructure: legislative framework and project agreement, Section E Security interests, paras 58.

6.3 Detailed Accounts of the Issues in the Agreements

The Legislative Guide and the Model Provisions have discussed the different approaches to certain issues in the 4 kinds of agreement. The section will compare these approaches with the methods used under Chinese law in similar circumstances.

6.3.1 *Project Agreement*

Both the Legislative Guide and the practice of various countries show that legislation concerning the project agreement of a PFIP should allow for the contracting authority and the concessioner to have the necessary flexibility to negotiate an agreement that takes into account the needs and particularities of a specific project. Legislation concerning the project agreement of PFIPs should only offer general legislative provisions on certain essential elements of the project agreement. If it is necessary, however, the legislation may make certain mandatory provisions concerning the content of clauses to be included in the agreement.[21] Some contentious issues in the project agreement will be discussed with regard to which solution may be applicable and suitable in the specific circumstances of Chinese law.

6.3.1.1 Organisation of the Project Company

The legislation may allow or require the project agreement between the contracting authority and the concessioner to affect the organisation of the project company.

As was discussed in Chap. 5, the private concessioner may be a project consortium which will establish a special purpose entity to be an independent legal entity with its own juridical personality under the project agreement after a successful bid. In this special purpose entity, the project's assets and revenue, and the rights and obligations relating to the project, are independently estimated and are strictly separated from the assets of the entity's shareholders. This special purpose entity is the project company. Although the project company is often required to be established as a legal entity under the Company Law of the host country,[22] according to the laws the project agreement may also be allowed or required to limit the organisation of the project company:

Company law often requires the company to formulate its articles of association to regulate its business scope and members such as shareholders, directors and managers. If the company wants to modify its articles of association, it has

[21]The legislative Guide, Chap. IV on Construction and operation of infrastructure: legislative framework and project agreement, Section A General provisions of the project agreement, paras 2–4.

[22]The legislative Guide, Chap. IV on Construction and operation of infrastructure: legislative framework and project agreement, Section B on the organization of the concessioner, paras 14.

to go through certain process and obtain a certain level of shareholder agreement. However, as PFIPs are closely related to the public interest, the laws that regulate project agreements may also provide that the entry into force of changes in the article of association of the project company should be effective upon approval by the contracting authority.[23]

Company law often requires that shares should be transferred under certain conditions. For example, the transfer of shares should require the prior approval of a certain percentage of the other shareholders, or the original shareholders have to undertake to keep their shares for a certain period. However, due to the close relationship between PFIPs and public interest, the laws may require the project agreement to give some limitations on the transfer of shares in the project company. One such limitation is the requirement that the contracting authority approve the transfer. Project agreements according this kind of right to the contracting authority must consider two primary aspects. Firstly, the contracting authority may be satisfied with the experience that the selected bidding consortium demonstrated in the pre-selection phase or satisfied with the guarantees provided by the parent organisations of the original consortium and its subcontractors. Therefore, the contracting authorities may be worried that, if the project company's shareholders are entirely free to transfer their shares, the project may be not completed by the consortium who satisfied the contracting authority at the outset.[24] Secondly, the contracting authority may want to prevent transfer of shares to particular investors because of protecting public interest. For example, the contracting authority may wish to control the acquisition of controlling shares in public service providers to avoid monopolies through liberalised shares transfer. At the same time, it may not be appropriate for a company that has defrauded one part of Government to be employed by another through a newly acquired subsidiary.[25]

The Legislative Guide expects the host country to have adequate company law in place to support the organisation of project companies. In China, the organisation of project companies is also required to follow the Chinese Company Law, which has general provisions on how to regulate articles of association[26] and the transfer of

---

[23]The legislative Guide, Chap. IV on Construction and operation of infrastructure: legislative framework and project agreement, Section B on the organization of the concessioner, paras 18.

[24]The legislative Guide, Chap. IV on Construction and operation of infrastructure: legislative framework and project agreement, Section G on Transfer of controlling interest in the project company, para 64.

[25]The legislative Guide, Chap. IV on Construction and operation of infrastructure: legislative framework and project agreement, Section G on Transfer of controlling interest in the project company, para 67.

[26]The Company Law of the People's Republic of China, effect on January 1,2006:

Article 11: The Company established according to this law shall formulate its articles of association which are binding on the company, its shareholders, directors, supervisors and senior managers.

Article 44: The discussion methods and voting procedures of the shareholders' meeting shall be prescribed in the articles of association, unless it is otherwise provided for by this Law. A resolution made at a shareholders' meeting on amending the articles of association, increasing or reducing the registered capital, merger, split-up, dissolution or change of the company form shall be adopted by the shareholders representing 2/3 or more of the voting rights.

shares.[27] Moreover, although there is no specific law on PFIPs in China, the provincial regulations, such as the Beijing Urban Infrastructure Concession Regulation of 2005, includes provisions that allow the project agreement to give the contracting authority the right to restrict the transfer of shares in the project company.[28] Therefore, in Chinese PFIPs, if the project agreement includes items that limit the organisation of the project company, this could be supported by relevant laws.

6.3.1.2 Real Estate

Provisions relating to the real estate of the project are an essential part of the project agreement. There are three issues relating to real estate in PFIPs, which need appropriate laws to regulate. These are the ownership of project assets; land required for execution of the project; and easements.

6.3.1.2.1 Project Assets

The ownership of project assets refers to the ownership of the physical infrastructure and affixes required for the provision of the public service in the project, whether it is the infrastructure offered by the contracting authority at the beginning of the

---

Article 104: When a shareholder attends the shareholders' meeting, he shall have one voting right for each share he holds……when the shareholders' meeting makes a decision to modify the articles of association or to increase or reduce the registered capital, or a resolution about the merger, split-up, dissolution or change of the company form, the resolution shall be adopted by shareholders representing 2/3 or more of the voting rights of the shareholders in presence.

[27]The Company Law of the People's Republic of China, effect on January 1, 2006:

Article 72: All or some of the stock rights of the shareholders of a limited liability company may be transferred between the shareholders. Where a shareholder intends to transfer his/its stock rights to any non-shareholder, he/it shall be subject to the approval of more than half of the other shareholders. The shareholder shall notify the other shareholders in written form of the matters on the transfer of stock rights for their approval. If any of the other shareholders fails to give it a reply within 30 days after the receipt of the written notice, it shall be deemed to have agreed to the transfer. If half or more of the other shareholders disagree to the transfer, the shareholders who disagree to the transfer shall purchase the stock rights to be transferred. If they refuse to purchase these stock rights, they shall be deemed to have agreed to the transfer. Under the same conditions, the other shareholders have a prior right to purchase the stock rights to be transferred upon their approval. If two or more shareholders claim the prior rights, they shall determine their respective percentage of purchase through negotiation. If they fail to reach an agreement during the negotiation, they shall exercise the prior rights on the basis of their respective percentage of capital contributions. Unless it is otherwise provided for of the transfer of stock rights in the articles of association, the articles of association shall be followed.

Article 142: The shares of a company held by the initiators of this company shall not be transferred within 1 year as of the day of establishment of the company. The shares issued before the company publicly issues shares shall not be transferred within 1 year as of the day when the stocks of the company get listed and are traded in a stock exchange.

[28]Beijing Urban Infrastructure Concession Regulation 2005, Provision 14: "The concession agreement could agree on limitation of the transfer of shares".

project, new infrastructure constructed by the concessioner, or improvements or additions to the original infrastructure.[29] The Legislative Guide considers it advisable for the project agreement to specify which assets will be public property and which will become the private property of the concessioner, with the exception of host countries which have laws that clearly state that physical infrastructure and its affixes required for the provision of public services must be regarded as public property.[30] The project agreement could identify which assets the concessioner must transfer to the contracting authority without any charge once the project has been completed; which assets the contracting authority could purchase from the concessioner if this is necessary; and which assets the concessioner may freely remove or dispose of once the project is completed.[31]

However, most Chinese PFIPs adopt a BOT or BT format, which means that project assets are transferred to the contracting authority without charge after the completion of the project. Although Chinese laws have not determined that physical infrastructure for the provision of public service is to be considered public property, and have allowed project agreements to approach other kinds of consensus,[32] there are rarely cases in practice in which the infrastructure is purchased by the contracting authority or owned by the private concessioner. As a matter of fact, Chinese legal scholars have been suggesting that laws should facilitate private investors to own public infrastructure for a long time,[33] but with insubstantial effect.

6.3.1.2.2 Land

Land may be required for execution of the project. The issues related to this land are very complicated. Infrastructure is often large-scale, such as roads, power stations or hospitals, and requires a large piece of land (e.g. power stations) or large cross of land (e.g. roads). The land required may belong to a large number of individual owners. Therefore, acquiring the land may involve a long and complex process of negotiation with numerous property transfers. The Legislative Guide anticipates that the contracting authority would take responsibility for providing the land required for the implementation of the project, adopting the most efficient process of acquisition

[29] The legislative Guide, Chap. IV on Construction and operation of infrastructure: legislative framework and project agreement, Section C The project site, assets and easements, paras 21.

[30] The legislative Guide, Chap. IV on Construction and operation of infrastructure: legislative framework and project agreement, Section C The project site, assets and easements, paras 22.

[31] The legislative Guide, Chap. IV on Construction and operation of infrastructure: legislative framework and project agreement, Section C The project site, assets and easements, paras 26.

[32] For example, Beijing Urban Infrastructure Concession Regulation 2005, Provision 4(3): "...or other ways agreed by the local government.".

[33] Liang Huixing, *"Nationalization, it is dangerous!"* (2006) <http://article.chinalawinfo.com/Article_Detail.asp?ArticleId=35983> access on 19/01/2013.

(e.g. "expropriation"),[34] so as to avoid unnecessary delays or costs.[35] The Legislative Guide also suggests the laws authorise the concessioner to perform certain actions to facilitate the expropriation and share the ownership of land with the contracting authority.[36]

This issue is particularly tough and complicated in China, since land ownership in China is a fraught issue. The Chinese land ownership regime is different from other countries' land regimes, where parties are free to trade in land. In China, urban land belongs to the state. Rural land also belongs to the state, unless it has been allocated to a rural collective.[37] Although Chinese laws on the registration of land ownership and the categories of land use are messy,[38] both Chinese Constitution Law[39] and the subsequent laws[40] passed under this constitution framework all assert one basic principle: socialist public ownership over all land rather than the ownership of land by any individual or organisation.[41] In other words, no individuals or organisations (with the exception of the rural collectives) who occupy the land have ownership of the land although they enjoy the right to use it. They only have the ownership and trade use of the buildings or facilities attached to the land rather than the land itself.

---

[34]"Expropriation" means the procedure whereby private property is compulsorily acquired by the Government against the payment of appropriate compensation to the owners. The Legislative Guide calls it as "compulsory acquisition". However, in order to consist with the Chinese domestic legal system, "expropriation" is used in this book.

[35]The legislative Guide, Chap. IV on Construction and operation of infrastructure: legislative framework and project agreement, Section C The project site, assets and easements, paras 27.

[36]The legislative Guide, Chap. IV on Construction and operation of infrastructure: legislative framework and project agreement, Section C The project site, assets and easements, paras 29.

[37]The definition of "collective ownership" (see Chapter 4 of this book footnote94); Xiaojing Qin, *'The impact of political forces on urban land ownership reform in transitional China'* (I.J.L.B.E. 2010, 2(3), 206–217)P207.

[38]Riley Mary L., *'People's Republic of China: land rights - enforcement of regulations'* (I.C.C.L.R. 1997, 8(3), C45-46).

[39]The Constitution of the People's Republic of China, adopted on March 14, 2004: Article 10 (See Chapter 4 of this book footnote 95).

[40]E.g. the Land Administration Law of the People's Republic of China (2004 Amendment)

Article 2: The People's Republic of China resorts to a socialist public ownership i.e. an ownership by the whole people and ownerships by collectives, of land. In ownership by the whole people, the State Council is empowered to be on behalf of the State to administer the land owned by the State. No unit or individual is allowed to occupy, trade or illegally transfer land by other means. Land use right may be transferred by law. The state may make expropriation or requisition on land according to law for public interests, but shall give compensations accordingly. The State introduces the system of compensated use of land owned by the State except the land has been allocated for use by the State according to law.

Article 8: Land in urban districts shall be owned by the State. Land in the rural areas and suburban areas, except otherwise provided for by the State, shall be collectively owned by peasants including land for building houses, land and hills allowed to be retained by peasants.

[41]Lo T. Augustine, *'Debate surrounding the new property law in China'* (C.S.L.R. 2008, 4(2), 182–200) P188; K. Wilhelm, *'Rethinking Property Rights in Urban China'* (2004, 9 UCLA J. Int'l Law & For. Aff) P243.

It is not permitted to transfer absolute land ownership but land-use rights may be transferred subject to certain conditions.[42] Two levels of urban land transaction are permitted in Chinese law. The first level is the assignment of a right to use the land, in which the state, as the owner of the land, assigns the right to use the land for a specified time period to land users, who in turn pay fees for the assignment thereof to the State (except allocated land,[43] which is assigned without charge but is taxed).[44] The state can assign land use rights through auction, tender or negotiation.[45] The time period assigned for the right depends on the purpose of the proposed development. 70 years are assigned for residential use, 50 years for industrial, educational, scientific, technological, cultural, health, athletic, or multiple uses, and 40 years for business, tourism, and recreational use.[46] The second level of urban land transaction is the transfer of land-use rights, in which land users re-assign their land use right to other users through sale, exchange, and donation. However, if the land has not been developed and utilised in accordance with the requirements of first level land transaction, the land use right may not be transferred.[47] In other words, the first level of the land market is monopolised by the state while the second level is where private land transactions are conducted.[48] By way of a simple example, the estate developers buy the land use right from state in the first level (residential use is 70 years) and then sell the apartments in the second level after building residential buildings. When people buy an apartment, the payment includes the cost of the apartment and the land-transfer fee. Due to the 70 year time limitation of the land use right, the owner of an apartment still has to pay the land-transfer fee every seventy years. Meanwhile, the apartment owner cannot dispute expropriation by the state because the state retains ownership of the land.

Large-scale infrastructure in PFIPs may need a large amount of urban land and occupy the land for a long time. It would be prohibitive to ask private investors to purchase so many land use rights and the private investor could not afford to pay so many land-transfer fees. Moreover, if the land required for a PFIP includes rural land belonging to collectives, the state must expropriate the land from the collectives before the land can be assigned to the project conductors. Although the collective

---

[42]Qin Xiaojing, *'The impact of political forces on urban land ownership reform in transitional China'* (I.J.L.B.E. 2010, 2(3), 206–217) P213.

[43]In PFIPs, the land required for the project should be allocated land according to the Land Administration Law of the People's Republic of China (2004 Amendment),

Article 54: A paid leasing should be go through in use of land owned by the State by a construction unit. But the following land may be obtained through government allocation with the approval of the people's governments at and above the county level according to law: 1……; 2. Land for building urban infrastructure and for public welfare undertakings; 3……; 4…….

[44]Interim Regulations of the People's Republic of China Concerning the Assignment and Transfer of the Right to the Use of the State-owned Land in the Urban Areas 1990, Article 8.

[45]Ibid., Article 13.

[46]Ibid., Article 12.

[47]Ibid., Article 19.

[48](n 42).

owns their land, the land can only be transferred to the state from the collective.[49] Therefore, there is no way that a private investor could buy the land directly from the collective.

Even though the land policy hinders the development of welfare, the market and the economy in China, and despite the many arguments for reform put forward by academics,[50] information from the Chinese Communist Party and government shows that it will not be changed for the foreseeable future.[51] Therefore, it would be impossible to change domestic laws to comply with the expectation of the Legislative Guide made by UNCITRAL in a short amount of time. In this case, only the contracting authority can take responsibility for allocating the land required for the implementation of the project in Chinese PFIPs. It would be impossible for the Chinese contracting authority to authorise the concessioner to expropriate land or share the ownership of land as suggested in the Legislative Guide. However, it is more noteworthy that, in China, as individuals and organisations own the buildings or facilities attached the land, it is essential to compensate the owners during an expropriation process. This kind of compensation has requirements in the form of criteria and procedure in Chinese domestic law.[52] However, the private concessioner should be warned that cases of expropriation in the past few years indicate that the execution of expropriation in China is not always smooth. There is fierce conflict between the contracting authority and the property owners concerning compensation, which results in serious delays and a large increase in the project's costs. For example, in a famous case in Zhejiang province of China, the contracted road had to be built around a house as the occupants refused to move (shown as Fig. 6.3).[53] Therefore, during the negotiation and drafting of the project agreement, the contracting authority and the concessioner should have an agreement on project delays or increased costs in response to failed expropriation.

6.3.1.2.3 Easement

Easement is the right to use another person's property for a specific purpose.[54] Common examples of such rights are the private right of way, the right to light

---

[49] Land Administration Law of the People's Republic of China (2004 Amendment), Article 43, 44.

[50] Xu Cheng Gang, *'State monopoly of land ownership brings social problems'*, Chinese Reform (2011.4). The Chinese University of Hong Kong website, <http://www.usc.cuhk.edu.hk/PaperCollection/Details.aspx?id=8098> accessed on 27th May, 2019.

[51] Zheng Yong Nian, *'Land ownership reform'*, News of the communist party of China Website, <http://theory.people.com.cn/n/2013/0427/c83865-21309832-2.html> accessed on 27th May, 2019.

[52] Regulation on the Expropriation of Buildings on State-owned Land and Compensation (2011); Regulation on the Dismantlement of Urban Houses (2001); Land Administration Law of the People's Republic of China (2004 Amendment).

[53] BBC news on 23 November 2012, *'Road built around house as Chinese couple refuse to move'*, <http://www.bbc.co.uk/news/world-asia-20463192> accessed on 20th January 2020.

[54] The legislative Guide, Chap. IV on Construction and operation of infrastructure: legislative framework and project agreement, Section C The project site, assets and easements, paras 31. The case

Fig. 6.3 Expropriation failed. *Source:* China news, photo from http://www.chinanews.com/tp/hd2011/2012/11-22/150035.shtml accessed on 20th January 2020

and the right of support. In PFIPs, the concessioner often needs to use the property of third parties to access the project site or to perform or maintain any work required for the provision of the public service (for example, to install poles or electric transmission lines above third parties' property or to lay oil, gas or water pipes).[55] The Legislative Guide and the Model Provisions indicates that there are two ways to acquire this easement[56]: One is that the law itself to authorises the concessioner to enter, pass through or do work or affix installations upon the property of third parties, as required for the construction, operation and maintenance of public infrastructure. If the behaviour of the concessioner substantially hinders the property owner's rights and interests when they use this owner's property, the owner may be entitled to compensation under law.[57] The other is that the concessioner makes use of the property with the owner's consent. As it is neither expeditious nor cost effective to leave the direct acquisition of easements from owners to the concessioner, the Legislative Guide advises that those easements be acquired compulsorily by the contracting authority at the same time as the project site is acquired.[58]

---

of *Re Ellenborough Park* [1956] Ch 131 is the leading English case on easement, which also show the easement is separated from the land ownership.

[55]The legislative Guide, Chap. IV on Construction and operation of infrastructure: legislative framework and project agreement, Section C The project site, assets and easements, paras 30.

[56]The Model Provisions, Chap. III on Contents and implementation of the concession contract, Model provision 33 Easements, Variant A & B; The legislative Guide, Chap. IV on Construction and operation of infrastructure: legislative framework and project agreement, Section C The project site, assets and easements, paras 30–32.

[57]The legislative Guide, Chap. IV on Construction and operation of infrastructure: legislative framework and project agreement, Section C The project site, assets and easements, paras 32.

[58]The legislative Guide, Chap. IV on Construction and operation of infrastructure: legislative framework and project agreement, Section C The project site, assets and easements, paras 31.

At present, there is a big gap in easement in Chinese law. China passed the first Property Law to refer to easements in 2007, but this only regulates the creation of an easement between equal parties in civil law through contract, rather than easements acquired for public infrastructure and the provision of public service.[59] Specific regulations on the infrastructure construction in specific sectors may include articles on easements. The Oil and Natural Gas Pipeline Protection Law of the People's Republic of China (2010) clearly states that the pipeline enterprise is entitled to easement when it patrols, inspects or maintains the pipes.[60] The Highway Law of the People's Republic of China (2004) indicates that construction units are entitled easement when they construct or maintain the road.[61] However, these regulations in these specific sectors are only applied to the specific areas, rather than to general public infrastructure, so some constructors or operators are not entitled to easements by law. As a matter of fact, legally authorised easements for public service providers have been discussed by Chinese scholars for a long time. A number of Chinese scholars strongly agree that "legal easements" should be confirmed in law.[62] "Legal easements" mean that the public service provider is automatically empowered through easements by law to transit through the property of third parties to access the project site or do work or affix installations upon the property of third parties. Legal easements could convenience the performance of public infrastructure projects and avoid the risk of corruption present in expropriation. In Chinese PFIPs, when the private concessioner makes a project agreement with the contracting authority, it is better to ask the contracting authority to acquire the easements from third party property owners, no matter the sector of the public infrastructure, to avoid project process delays or cost increases.

---

[59]The Property Law of the People's Republic of China (2007), Chapter XIV Easement Rights, Article 156–169.

Article 157: "For the creation of an easement, the parties concerned shall conclude an easement contract in written form….".

[60]Oil and Natural Gas Pipeline Protection Law of the People's Republic of China (2010)

Article 27: "The relevant entities and individuals along a pipeline route shall provide necessary convenience for such operations as the patrol, inspection and maintenance of pipeline by the pipeline enterprise. ….".

[61]The Highway Law of the People's Republic of China (2004)

Article 28: "No unit or individual is allowed to intrude or collect fees illegally for the use of State owned waste hills, wasteland or for the digging of sand, stone or earth from the State owned waste hills, wasteland, river beds and polders for highway construction only if necessary procedures as provided for by related laws and administrative decrees have been undertaken for the respective actions."

Article 38: "People's governments at the county and township levels should organize free services of rural residents on both sides of roads for highway construction and maintenance according to the related regulations of the State.".

[62]Li yan-rong, *"Research on the Legal Easement in the Context of Land Administration"* (2012), China Land sciences (Vol. 26 No.6. Jun., 2012); Chen, shujuan, *"The Application of easements under Public Ownership"* (2012), Science of Law (Vol. 03, 2012); Cai wu, *"Preliminary analysis of nature of servitude administrative"* (2004), Journal of Guangxi Administrative Cadre Institute of Politics and Law (Vol. 19. No. 2. Mar. 2004).

6.3.1.3 Security Interests

Security arrangements[63] are crucial for financing infrastructure projects, particularly where the financing is structured under the modality of the PFIP. In PFIPs, the project company established by the private concessioner takes responsibility for raising finance, and constructing and operating the infrastructure project. The project company, as the main entity implementing the project, is often required by the other parties of the project to provide security, so that the sale of assets or contributions by the third party guarantor will first go towards repaying their outstanding debts. However, the project company cannot create this security without restrictions. Firstly, as the most important agreement in the PFIP, the project agreement may involve some items on security interests, which may affect the security arrangements between the project company and other parties in the PFIP. The security arrangements created by Project Company should be subject to any restrictions contained in the project agreement.[64] Secondly, the project agreement is not simply free to create security interests either. Some security arrangements often derive from general principles of law or from statutory provisions and cannot be waived by the contracting authority through contractual arrangements in the project agreement.[65] Besides the above two restrictions, the Legislative Guide and the Model Provisions also suggest that the concessioner should have the right to create security interests over any of its assets, rights or interests, including those relating to the infrastructure project, as required to secure any financing needed for the project.[66] The following sections will analyse and discuss how security arrangements may be created by the project company in the project agreement.

6.3.1.3.1 Guarantee by the Contracting Authority or Other Governmental Sectors

The project company may ask the contracting authority or other governmental sectors to provide certain loan guarantees when they conclude the project agreement. The Legislative Guide points out that some countries' domestic laws authorise the contracting authority or other agencies in the host government to provide loan

---

[63]Security arrangements in project finance generally play a defensive or preventive role by ensuring that, if a third party acquires the debtor's operations, all of the proceeds resulting from the sale of those assets will go first to repayment of outstanding loans.

[64]The Model Provisions, Chap. III on Contents and implementation of the concession contract, Model provision 35 Security interests; The legislative Guide, Chap. IV on Construction and operation of infrastructure: legislative framework and project agreement, Section E Security interests, paras 52.

[65]The legislative Guide, Chap. IV on Construction and operation of infrastructure: legislative framework and project agreement, Section E Security interests, paras 53.

[66]The Model Provisions, Chap. III on Contents and implementation of the concession contract, Model provision 35 Security interests.

guarantees for the repayment of loans taken by the project company of a PFIP.[67] In other words, it means the contracting authority or the governmental sector has to take responsibility for the repayment of the loan when the private concessioner cannot repay the financer or the project fails. In countries where governments are powerful and reliable, this kind of guarantee is often welcomed by creditors. However, this model is not applied in China. The Guarantee Law of the People's Republic of China strictly prohibits the state organs from providing any guarantees for commercial entities.[68] The Bank of China has notified all its subsidiary finance institutes that state organs are not accepted as guarantors for loans.[69] The Legislative Guide concurs that the contracting authority should not make any guarantees on the debts incurred by the concessioner to the sub-contractors.

6.3.1.3.2 Guarantee by Physical Assets

The project agreement could allow the project company to create security interests through its physical assets. It means the project company could create security interests if it had the ownership of the project assets or the relevant land. The reason why there is a discussion on the ownership of the project assets and its relevant land in Sect. 6.3.1.2 about Real Estate is that the confirmation of the ownership decides what physical property could be used by the project company to create security interests.

If project assets are public property or have to be transferred to the public body at the end of the project, there may be legal obstacles to negotiating the security arrangements required to obtain financing for the project. As the project company lacks the title deeds to the property, in many legal systems it has no (or only limited) power to encumber the property. Therefore, the project agreement should facilitate the negotiation of security arrangements by indicating the types of asset which may are permitted as collateral for such security interests. In China, where most PFIPs are formed according to the BOT or BT model, the project assets cannot be used as security interests because they have to be transferred to the contracting authority at the end of the project. Moreover, even if the PFIP adopted another model, which did not need to be transferred at the end of the project, the Guarantee Law of the People's Republic of China forbids the creation of mortgages on public facilities.[70] If the project assets of PFIPs are to be allowed to be owned by the project company

---

[67] The legislative Guide, Chap. II on Project risks and government support, Section C Government support, paras 38.

[68] The Guarantee Law of the People's Republic of China (1995)

Article 8: "No State organs may act as a surety, except in the case of securing loans, for on lending, from a foreign government or an international economic organization as is approved by the State Council.".

[69] Notice of Bank of China on the state organ cannot be guarantor after take effective of The Guarantee Law (1995).

[70] The Guarantee Law of the People's Republic of China (1995)

Article 37 The following property may not be mortgaged:

in China, the Guarantee Law of the People's Republic of China should be amended to correspond with this principle.

In some legal systems, if the project company owns the land used in the project or owns the adjacent land or the leasehold interest or the right to use the land, the project company could use these to create security interests.[71] However, this kind of security arrangement would be impossible in China because all Chinese land belongs either to the state or to collectives. Moreover, in Chinese PFIPs, the land offered by the contracting authority may only be used for the purpose of constructing the project, so the leasehold interest or right to use the land could not to be used to create security interest.

6.3.1.3.3 Guarantee by Intangible Assets

The project agreement could allow the project company to create security interests on its intangible assets. The main intangible asset in an infrastructure project is the concession itself, which is the concessioner's right to conduct and operate the infrastructure and to charge users who use the service provided by the project. The concession provides its holder with the authority to control the entire project and entitles the concessioner to earn revenue generated by the project and to acquire reasonable profits. Sometimes the value of the concession is much greater than the combined value of all of the physical assets involved in a project. Therefore, the lender may regard the concession to be an important part of the security arrangements negotiated with the concessioner.[72] If there is a security interest in the concession, failure to repay the loan would entitle the lender to take over the concession and make arrangements for the continuation of the project under another concessioner. It should be noted that, in many legal systems, the security interest created on the concession must be made with the consent of the contracting authority.[73] The contracting authority must consider the capability of the new concessioner. Moreover, the contracting authority needs to follow the same procedures that applied to the selection of the original concessioner. It is impossible for the contracting authority to accept a new concessionaire that has not been selected according to those procedures and has been chosen by the lender directly.[74] In China, the law also regulates the concessioner's obligation not to dispose of the concession or related assets without the prior consent

(3) educational facilities, medical and health facilities of schools, kindergartens, hospitals and other institutions or public organizations established in the interest of the public and other facilities in the service of public welfare;

[71] The legislative Guide, Chap. IV on Construction and operation of infrastructure: legislative framework and project agreement, Section E Security interests, paras 52.

[72] The legislative Guide, Chap. IV on Construction and operation of infrastructure: legislative framework and project agreement, Section E Security interests, paras 56.

[73] The legislative Guide, Chap. IV on Construction and operation of infrastructure: legislative framework and project agreement, Section E Security interests, paras 57.

[74] The legislative Guide, Chap. IV on Construction and operation of infrastructure: legislative framework and project agreement, Section J General contractual arrangements, paras 149.

of the contracting authority, regardless of whether this disposal is in the form of assignment, lease, security or any other form.[75]

The project agreement may allow the project company to create security interests on its trade receivables. A form of security interest often used in PFIPs is the assignment to lenders of proceeds from contracts with future customers of the concessioner. This kind of security arrangement is a typical element in the financing arrangements negotiated with the lenders, by which the proceeds of infrastructure projects are deposited in an escrow account managed by a trustee appointed by the lenders. This way is also accepted in China.

6.3.1.4 Performance Guarantee

The concept of security interest put forward in Sect. 6.3.1.3 is a guarantee to ensure repayments by the project company to the lender. This section discusses the guarantee to ensure the performance by the project company of the PFIP to the contracting authority. In some countries, the law generally requires adequate guarantees of performance to be provided by the concessioner and these performance guarantees are concluded in the project agreement.[76] The Legislative Guide gives two types of performance guarantee: the first is a monetary performance guarantee, i.e. the guarantor pays the contracting authority funds up to a stated limit to satisfy the liabilities of the concessioner in the event of non-performance. The second is a performance bond, i.e. the guarantor rectifies defective structures or finishes incomplete structures, and the guarantor compensates the contracting authority for losses caused by the concessioner's failure to perform.[77] In Chinese law, a performance guarantee is also required for project agreements, but the level of performance guaranteed is not regulated.[78]

6.3.1.5 Protection to Customers

The contracting authority may require the project company to provide services to the general public with the specific obligation to ensure the availability of the service under the same conditions for all users and customers of the same category, excepting where the objective criteria are different (e.g. the difference between normal consumers and business or industrial consumers; the difference between the

---

[75]Beijing Urban Infrastructure Concession Regulation 2005, Article 25.

[76]The legislative Guide, Chap. IV on Construction and operation of infrastructure: legislative framework and project agreement, Section J on General contractual arrangements, paras 108.

[77]The legislative Guide, Chap. IV on Construction and operation of infrastructure: legislative framework and project agreement, Section J on General contractual arrangements, paras 109.

[78]Beijing Regulation 2005, Chapter 2 Award procedures, Article 12(9):

Article 12: The concession agreement should include:

……(9) performance guarantee.

hours of low-level and peak consumption).[79] Moreover, the different treatment of certain users or customers may be the result of legislative action (e.g. discounted transport for schoolchildren or senior citizens).[80] In China, the project company undertakes to comply with the price formulated by the competent price authority in the form of a fixed or guided price when delivering the product or service to the public.[81]

However, the Legislative Guide agrees that if the defective construction or operation of an infrastructure facility results in the death of or personal injury to employees of the concessioner, users of the facility or any other third parties, or it results in damage to their property, the project company alone should bear the responsibility in that regard and that the contracting authority should not be part of any guarantee as regards such third-party claims, except where the damage was caused by a serious breach by or the recklessness of the contracting authority.[82]

6.3.1.6 Duration, Extension and Termination

The project agreement must specify a period for the concession. This period may be decided through negotiations between the contracting authority and the concessioner, with consideration to the length of time necessary to allow the concessionaire to repay its debts in full and to enjoy reasonable profits.[83] Although the period is generally negotiated by both the contracting authority and the concessioner, some unexpected impediments or other changes of circumstances may arise during the life of the concession. Thus, extension should be applied in certain exceptional situations. These situations may be specified in the project agreement through negotiation between the contracting authority and the concessioner, or they may be listed in laws.[84] In China, the duration of the concession is to be provided in the project agreement, depending on the nature of the sector, the scope of project, the form of the concession and other relevant factors, but in no case shall it last for more than 30 years.[85] The project company may request an extension of the concession period subject to the evaluation and approval of the municipal government.[86] The municipal government has exclusive power in this decision and is often also the contracting authority. There

[79]The legislative Guide, Chap. IV on Construction and operation of infrastructure: legislative framework and project agreement, Section I on Operation of infrastructure, paras 88.

[80]The legislative Guide, Chap. IV on Construction and operation of infrastructure: legislative framework and project agreement, Section I on Operation of infrastructure, paras 89.

[81]Beijing Urban Infrastructure Concession Regulation 2005, Article 23.

[82]The legislative Guide, Chap. IV on Construction and operation of infrastructure: legislative framework and project agreement, Section J General contractual arrangements, paras 105–106.

[83]The legislative Guide, Chap. V on Duration, extension and termination of the project agreement, Section B on Duration of the project agreement, paras 3.

[84]The legislative Guide, Chap. V on Duration, extension and termination of the project agreement, Section C on Extension of the project agreement, paras 8.

[85]Beijing Urban Infrastructure Concession Regulation 2005, Article 13.

[86]Beijing Urban Infrastructure Concession Regulation 2005, Article 22.

is no Chinese law that restricts the exclusive power of the municipal government if it rejects a project extension.

Although the project agreement may include items on the termination of the project, the grounds for terminating the project agreement before the expiry of its term and the consequences of any such termination are often dealt with in domestic legislation.[87] However, there is no Chinese law that deals with the consequences of the decision by one of the parties to terminate the project. Though the Contract Law could be applied, it is not appropriate to PFIPs because it need more strict restrictions on terminating the project.

6.3.2 Finance Agreement

The concessioner may negotiate with the lender on all aspects of the loan, but the finance agreement cannot contravene the relevant laws and the project agreement.

The Legislative Guide and the Model Provisions[88] emphasise the step-in rights for the lender in those instances when the concessioner is unable to complete the project. In PFIPs, the lenders' main security is the profits accrued by operating the project, so they are particularly concerned with risks of interruption or termination prior to any repayment of their loans. If the concessioner is unable to complete the project, the lenders would be interested in looking for a new concessioner to complete the project and operate it profitably.

Although it may be in the interest of all the parties involved in a PFIP to avert the termination of the project by allowing the project to continue under the responsibility of a new concessioner chosen by the lender, the appointment of the new concessioner should be subject to the approval of the contracting authority. Therefore, a number of recent agreements for large infrastructure projects have included clauses allowing the lenders to select, with the consent of the contracting authority, a new concessioner to perform under the existing project agreement.[89]

6.3.3 Sub-contracting Agreement

The concessioner has the freedom to make contracts with subcontractors, but the sub-contracting agreement cannot contravene the relevant laws and the project agreement.

---

[87] The legislative Guide, Chap. V on Duration, extension and termination of the project agreement, Section D on Termination, paras 9.

[88] The Model Provisions, Model provision 42; the Legislative Guide, Recommendation 60, Chap. IV on Construction and operation of infrastructure: legislative framework and project agreement, Section J. General contractual arrangements, para 147–150.

[89] The Legislative Guide, Chap. IV on Construction and operation of infrastructure: legislative framework and project agreement, Section J. General contractual arrangements, para 150.

The Legislative Guide and the Model Provisions particularly point out that laws intended to prevent conflicts of interest in corporate management may be more important in PFIPs because the project company may engage its own shareholders to perform work or provide services.[90] However, PFIPs have a special feature in that private investors may join the project company simply because it expects to be given the principal sub-contracts for the construction of the project or for other work. If legal limitations to this behaviour are too strict, they may discourage the participation of potential investors and raise the financial burden of the concessioner.[91]

Modern company laws should contain specific provisions regulating the conduct of managers so as to prevent conflicts of interest. Provisions of this type require that managers act in good faith in the best interest of the company and do not use their positions to foster their own or any other person's financial interests to the detriment of the company. This issue should also be regulated in the project agreement. The contracting authority may disallow subcontracts which harm the company's interests.[92]

Although the Chinese Company Law does not particularly deal with issues pertaining to the project company in PFIPs, it sets out the general tenet that the company shareholders should not injure the company's interests.[93] The interests of the project company in a PFIP are protected by the Chinese Company Law. However, if China expects to protect the project company better through a specific law on PFIPs, it should give the contracting authority the power to monitor any subcontracts made between the project company and its shareholders so that subcontracts which may harm the project company's interest could be prohibited from the outset.

6.3.4 User Agreement

The concessioner and the users are free to negotiate responsibilities and rights, but the user agreement cannot contravene the relevant laws and the project agreement.

---

[90]The Model Provisions, Model provision 28(l); the Legislative Guide, Recommendation 56, Chap. IV on Construction and operation of infrastructure: legislative framework and project agreement, Section J. General contractual arrangements, para 99–101.

[91]The Legislative Guide, Chap. IV on Construction and operation of infrastructure: legislative framework and project agreement, Section J. General contractual arrangements, para 100.

[92]The legislative Guide, Chap. VII on Other relevant areas of law, para 32.

[93]The Company Law of the People's Republic of China, effect on 1st January, 2006

Article 20: The shareholders of a company shall comply with the laws, administrative regulations and articles of association, and shall exercise the shareholder's rights according to law. None of them may injure any of the interests of the company or of other shareholders by abusing the shareholder's rights, or injure the interests of any creditor of the company by abusing the independent status of juridical person or the shareholder's limited liabilities......

Article 21: Neither the controlling shareholder, nor the actual controller, any of the directors, supervisors or senior managers of the company may injure the interests of the company by taking advantage of its connection relationship.......

The Legislative Guide and the Model Provisions require the concessioner to offer service under the same conditions to all users and customers of the same category.[94] In China, universal service obligation[95,96] is not common, but the Chinese Customer Law[97] does require the concessioner to offer a quality of the service consistent with the price.

The Legislative Guide and Model Provisions also point out that the user agreement may follow some special laws concerning special customers using the public service. For example, reduced water or electricity rates may apply to lower-income or rural users.[98]

6.4 Conclusion

This chapter answers the 5th research question, namely how the Chinese legal framework and agreements in PFIPs may be improved, based on the guidelines from the Legislative Guide and Model Provisions and with supplementary reference to other countries.

This chapter summarises all the agreements that may form part of PFIPs clarifying the responsibilities and rights of each party. These agreements compose a framework to ensure the project's success, so they are very important. According to the aims of the Legislative Guide and the Model Provisions, the agreements should be concluded with the consent of the two parties, but the content of the agreements should not breach any mandatory rules in law. Moreover, the agreements on finance, user and subcontract should be subordinate to the project agreement, which is the core of the framework. Therefore, countries as China, which want to facilitate PFIPs, may find it necessary to establish relevant laws to regulate these agreements and remove unreasonable barriers in the legislation.

According to Figs. 2.6, 5.1, the five parties (contracting authority, concessioner, financer, user and sub-contractor) can make four kinds of agreements (project agreement between the concessioner and the contracting authority, finance agreement

[94] The Model Provisions, Model provision 38,1(c); the Legislative Guide, Recommendation 53(c), Chap. IV on Construction and operation of infrastructure: legislative framework and project agreement, Section I. Operation of infrastructure, para 88–89.

[95] Universal service obligation means that the basic fixed line services are available at an affordable price to all citizen-customers across the country.

[96] Prosser Tony, 'The Regulatory Enterprise: Government, Regulation, and Legitimacy' (Oxford Unversity Press, 2010).

[97] The Consumer protection Law of the People's Republic of China 1993, adopted on 31st October, 1993:

Article 10 Consumers shall enjoy the right of fair deal. Consumers shall, in their purchasing commodities or receiving services, have the right to obtain fair deal prerequisites such as guarantee of quality, reasonable prices and correct measurement, and have the right to refuse any compulsory transaction of business operators.

[98] The Legislative Guide, Chap. IV on Construction and operation of infrastructure: legislative framework and project agreement, Section I. Operation of infrastructure, para 89.

between the concessioner and the financer, user agreement between the concessioner and the users and subcontracting agreement between the concessioner and the subcontractor), which form the legal framework of PFIPs. Furthermore, the concessioner is the core party of the PFIPs, since it makes agreements with other parties. The project agreement between the concessioner and the contracting authority is the core agreement of the PFIP's legal framework, and restricts the other three agreements. Meanwhile, the other three agreements (finance agreement, user agreement, and subcontracting agreement) may impact each other as well.

This chapter discussed each agreement in a PFIP. The Legislative Guide and the Model Provisions aim to grant the agreements enough freedom to regulate responsibilities and rights of the parties by the parties themselves. However, the project agreement cannot contravene mandatory laws in the host country. The other three agreements cannot contravene the project agreement, in addition to mandatory laws in the host country. Therefore, the Legislative Guide and the Model Provisions suggest that countries which expect to establish legislation on PFIPs may need to review any unreasonable mandatory rules in their domestic laws.

The law should not set up too many restrictions to the contents of project agreements. It should grant the concessioner and the contracting authority enough flexibility to negotiate an agreement that is satisfactory to both parties. However, there may be some mandatory rules in the domestic laws of the host country that significantly affect this negotiation. Here are the six issues discussed in this chapter, arising from mandatory rules in domestic law.

- Organisation of the project company: The Legislative Guide and the Model Provisions suggest that the project agreement gives the contracting authority rights to monitor the modification of articles of association and any transfer of in the project company.
- Real estate: The Legislative Guide and the Model Provisions suggest that the project agreement identify the ownership of the project's assets because the domestic law of the host country may forbid the private investor from owning the infrastructure (as does China). They suggest that the project agreement should ensure the contracting authority offers the land and easements required in the project, if there are mandatory rules on land ownership.
- Security interests: The Legislative Guide and the Model Provisions suggest that the project agreement confirm those physical assets and intangible assets of the project company which may be used as security interests. In China, certain assets may not be used as security interests due to mandatory rules.
- Performance guarantee: The Legislative Guide and the Model Provisions suggest that the project agreement should request the project company to offer guarantees to ensure the performance of the project.
- Protection of customers: The Legislative Guide and the Model Provisions suggest that the project agreement ensures the project company provides proper service to customers.
- Duration, extension and termination: The Legislative Guide and the Model Provisions suggest that the project agreement fixes the duration of the project with

concessioner, and clarifies the exceptions which could extend or terminate the project.

Regarding finance agreements, the Legislative Guide and the Model Provisions suggest that domestic laws should not restrict the lender from looking for a new concessioner when the previous concessioner is proved incapable of completing the project. However, the appointment of the new concessioner needs the approval of the contracting authority.

Regarding subcontracting agreements, the Legislative Guide and the Model Provisions suggest that the domestic laws of the host country restrict possible conflicts of interest, such as a situation where the subcontractor is also one of the shareholders of the project company. However, the subcontracting agreement should be allowed if it obtains the approval of the contracting authority.

Regarding user agreements, the Legislative Guide and the Model Provisions suggest the domestic laws of host country should protect the customers so that the customers may receive satisfactory service.

These agreements form the legal framework of PFIPs and ensure the project's success. However, disputes may arise between the parties. The fair, proper and timeous resolution of these disputes would increase the confidence of participants in PFIPs. Host countries which offer proper dispute settlements would attract more private investors. Chapter 7 will discuss how to establish proper dispute settlement.

Chapter 7
Dispute Settlement

7.1 Introduction

Chapter 6 analysed the various agreements among the participant parties in PFIPs. However, it is inevitable that disputes concerning these agreements will arise. The resolutions of these disputes, if made fairly, properly and timeously, could enhance the confidence of the parties participating in PFIPs. A host country which can offer proper dispute settlement would attract more private investors. In other words, the investors, lenders, subcontractors and users would be encouraged to participate in projects, if they have confidence that any disputes arising from contracts forming part of the project will be resolved fairly and efficiently. The contracting authority could also execute its monitoring function more effectively and reduce its administrative costs through an efficient procedure of dispute settlement.[1] As the recent, popular theory on the relationship between global justice and international economic law[2] shows, an efficient dispute settlement system in international economic law can promote global justice as well.

The aim of this chapter is to discuss what dispute settlements of PFIPs could be used in China and how to remove undesirable restrictions to these settlements in Chinese law, according to the recommendations of the Legislative Guide and the Model Provisions.

There are three objectives in this chapter. The first objective is to present a method for solving disputes on project agreements between the contracting authority and the private concessioner (Project Company). The second objective is to present a method for solving disputes on sub-contracting agreements or finance agreements or other normal agreements, which may arise between equal parties (between the Project Company and the financers, or between the Project Company and the sub-contractors, or between the investors, or between the subcontractors and their suppliers). The third

[1] The legislative Guide, Chap. VI on Settlement of disputes, Section A General remarks, para 1.

[2] Carmody Chios, Garcia Frank J., and Linarelli John, *'Global justice and international economic law: opportunities and prospects'* (Cambridge, 2013), p 287.

S. Liang, *Legal Aspects of Privately Financed Infrastructure Projects (PFIPs) in China*,
https://doi.org/10.1007/978-981-15-6803-9_7

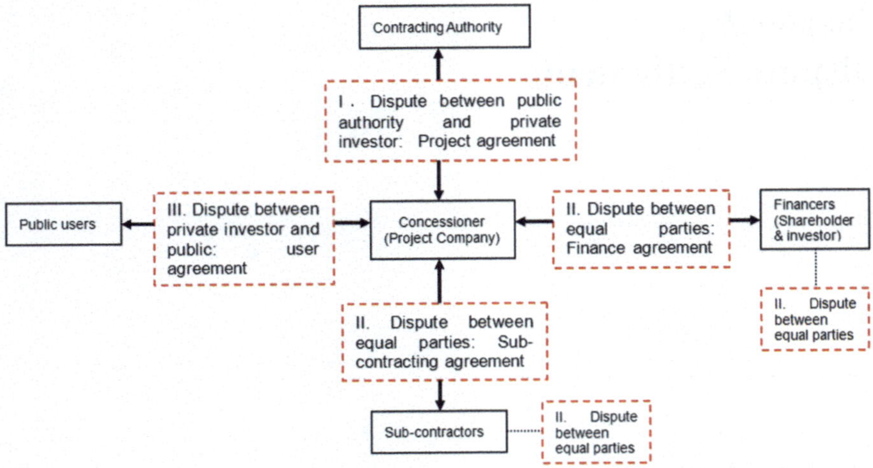

Fig. 7.1 The disputes between the parties in PFIPs

objective is to present a method for solving disputes on user agreement between the user and the private concessioner (Project Company).

This chapter consists of four sections.

Based on the framework of agreements in PFIPs presented in the last chapter, the disputes that might arise in PFIPs may be divided into three types (Fig. 7.1: red parts).

Section 7.2 addresses the disputes that might arise between the contracting authority and the private concessioner (Project Company), i.e. the disputes on project agreement (Fig. 7.1: red I).

Before considering how to settle the disputes in light of the project agreement of PFIPs, the first step would be to consider the nature of the project agreement in PFIPs. Academics have argued intensely whether the project agreement should be defined as a "public" contract or as a "private" contract. In certain countries, the "public" contract and the "private" contract are treated separately by public law and private law. The result of this argument is very important because it determines what settlements or relief may be offered to the disputants. This issue will be discussed in terms of the nature of project agreement in Sect. 7.2.1.

The Legislative Guide and the Model Provisions recommend a series of methods for preventing or settling disputes concerning project agreements in PFIPs, from conciliatory methods such as early warning, to antagonistic methods such as arbitration and judicial proceedings.[3] In Chinese legal practice, the definition of the nature of the project agreement in PFIPs is vague, so the public authority often intervenes in this kind of agreement and a lot disputes are solved by administrative act or Administrative Law. However, if China expects to facilitate PFIPs and attract more

[3]The Model Provisions, Chap. V on Settlement of disputes, Model provision 49; The legislative Guide, Chap. VI on Settlement of disputes, Section B Disputes between the contracting authority and the concessionaire, paras 10–41.

foreign private investors, it is necessary to improve and reform its current laws. It is important to remove possible legal obstacles, so that the contracting authority and the project company are free to agree on non-judicial methods, including arbitration, for the settlement of disputes arising in connection with PFIPs. These issues will be discussed in Sects. 7.2.2, 7.2.3, 7.2.4.

Section 7.3 addresses disputes that might arise between equal parties, such as between the Project Company and the financers, or between the Project Company and the sub-contractors, or between the investors, or between the subcontractors and their suppliers, i.e. the disputes on common contracts (Fig. 7.1: red II).

These kinds of contracts are common contracts between two commercial entities about which there is no argument on its nature as a "public" or "private".

The Legislative Guide and the Model Provisions recommend that equal parties to commercial contracts within an infrastructure project should be free to agree on a method to settle the dispute, whether litigation or arbitration, and a forum which will settle any dispute in a binding decision. Host countries wishing to facilitate PFIPs should review their laws so as to eliminate any uncertainty in this regard.[4] Chinese laws on such commercial contracts will be analysed for obstacles to the freedom of the parties to agree to dispute settlement mechanisms, and suggestions will be made as to improvements on these laws.

Section 7.4 addresses the disputes that might arise between the public user and the private concessioner (Project Company), i.e. the disputes on user agreement (Fig. 7.1: red III).

The user agreement is generally considered to be a common contract, but the user agreement in PFIPs often has direct consequences for the public users, in which the public interest is reflected. Since this kind of contract involves a public element, the methods to deal with the disputes concerning the user agreement are necessarily different from common contracts.

The Legislative Guide and the Model Provisions recommend that host countries should establish special mechanisms for handling claims brought by their customers, apart from the settlement methods of litigation and arbitration. Certain host countries may allow regulatory agencies to make administrative interventions on occasion. Irrespective of the settlement method applied in the host country, it is important to remove possible legal obstacles and to provide a clear authorisation for those entities.[5] Chinese laws concerning user agreements should be reviewed, and then improved or reformed if legal obstacles exist.

Section 7.5 proposes a hypothesis. Through the discussion of the above three kinds of disputes, it may be concluded that arbitration can settle disputes in most circumstances, if the law allows the freedom of the parties to choose the method of dispute settlement in the agreements of PFIPs. Therefore, it is worth noting that the

[4]The Model Provisions, Chap. V on Settlement of disputes, Model provision 50; The legislative Guide, Chap. VI on Settlement of disputes, Section C Disputes between project promoters and between the concessionaire and its lenders, contractors and suppliers, para 42.

[5]The Model Provisions, Chap. V on Settlement of disputes, Model provision 51; The legislative Guide, Chap. VI on Settlement of disputes, Section D disputes involving customers or users of the infrastructure facility, paras 43–45.

parties in PFIPs would have to establish consistency across the arbitration provisions in the various contracts.[6] While arbitration could establish a consistent procedure of dispute settlements, the differing goals and preferences of the parties of PFIPs make this theory unachievable.

The three kinds of dispute settlement recommended by the Legislative Guide and the Model Provisions will be discussed in the following sections. These settlements will be connected with the current situation in China, to consider which methods would work and which methods would not. Combined with the methods summarised in Chinese PFIP practice, the analysis and discussion will integrate an appropriate model to solve the disputes in Chinese PFIPs.

This chapter answers the sixth research question. With reference to the guidelines of the Legislative Guide and Model Provisions, and with supplementary references to other countries, how should the laws on dispute settlement in PFIPs be reformed in China?

7.2 The Disputes Between the Contracting Authority and the Private Concessioner (Project Company)

In PFIPs, disputes may arise between the contracting authority and the private concessioner (Project Company), i.e. the disputes on the project agreement (Fig. 7.1: red I).

This kind of dispute is different from the disputes outlined in Chap. 5, which addressed the fairness and transparency of the selection procedure used by the contracting authority (Sect. 5.4 argued that the post-selection stage should be fair and transparent). The disputes currently under review are those disputes which arise in the various phases of implementation of PFIPs after a concession has been awarded and where the selected bidder is already considered the concessioner. Disputes in connection with the project agreement are often special because they may involve problems that do not frequently arise in common contracts. One reason is that complex infrastructure projects involve a number of participant parties and a lot of technical problems. The other reason is that one of the parties is the contracting authority so these disputes may refer to governmental functions and public interests.[7] Therefore, the methods for preventing and settling this kind of dispute may be different to the general dispute methods used in common contracts.

[6] Hoffman Scott L., 'the law and business of international project finance' (2008),Cambridge, P408.

[7] The legislative Guide, Chap. VI on Settlement of disputes, Section B Disputes between the contracting authority and the concessionaire, para 3.

7.2.1 The Nature of the Project Agreement

Scholars from different countries debate the nature of the project agreement in PFIPs.[8] Most Chinese scholars consider it to be a contract with public and private characteristics, which should be managed by both public law and private law.[9] Vincent-Jones defines it as a new public contract in which powers and responsibilities are devolved to public agencies in various contracting arrangements, while preserving central government controls and powers of intervention. It is a distinctive mode of governance and appears to require a new legal system to regulate it.[10] British legislation has given a broad definition to public contracts to include public services contracts, public supply contracts or public works contracts.[11] To sum up, most scholars consider the project agreement of PFIPs to be neither a purely "private" contract nor a purely "public" contract.

The nature of the project agreement in PFIPs is difficult to define because it involves characteristics of both "private" and "public" contracts. It could be considered to be a "private" contract because it requires an agreement between the parties to decide their rights and obligations, rather than insisting on absolute obedience by one side.[12] However, it could also be considered to be a "public" contract because one party of the agreement is the public authority and the content of the agreement offers an infrastructure facility or service which the public requires. The most important to this distinction is that some of concessioner's rights need a concession to be awarded by the public authority, for example, the concessioner's authority to collect tariffs.[13]

There has been no definitive decision in the discussion on the nature of the project agreement in PFIPs and the debate may continue for a long time. However, irrespective of the definition given, the legal reliefs and settlements applied to disputes on project agreements in PFIPs always mixes methods of private law and public law in practice. In China, the nature of the project agreement of PFIPs is not defined either, but it is doubtless that public powers inevitably intervene. Therefore, it would be better to review and improve current Chinese laws so that the public power could be used under reasonable limitation by law to avoid cases where the concessioner suffers loss because of an abuse of public power.

---

[8]Public Contracts in Legal Globalization (PCLG), website: <http://www.public-contracts.net/inhalte/home.asp>.

[9]Deng Xiaopeng, Shen Liyin, 'Research on Attributes of PPP Contract from an Administrative Law View' (Construction Economy, 2007. 01); Zhan zhongle, Liu Shuran, 'Clarification of the Legal Issues of PPP Agreement' (Legal Science, 2007.03).

[10]Vincent-Jones Peter, 'The new public contracting: regulation, responsiveness, relationality' (Oxford university press, 2006), Preface.

[11]Public Contracts Regulations 2006/5 2.—Interpretation (This version in force from: October 1, 2011 to present).

[12]Deng Xiaopeng, Shen Liyin, 'Research on Attributes of PPP Contract from an Administrative Law View' (Construction Economy, 2007. 01).

[13]The legislative Guide, Chap. IV on Construction and operation of infrastructure: legislative framework and project agreement, Section D Financial arrangement, para 37.

The nature of the project agreement (whether a "public" contract or a "private" contract) determines the judicial relief or dispute settlement applied in connection with the project agreement in the host countries. The so-called "private" contract occurs between two equal parties who freely negotiate their rights and obligations to make a consistent agreement,[14] which is often controlled by the private law.[15] According to the general principle of contract law, the equal parties are free to make an agreement on the method of dispute settlement, with due consideration for the mandatory provisions of the host country.[16] Traditional "public" contracts are quasi-contracts made by the public government to administer and to develop public affairs,[17] and are often controlled by the public law.[18] This means that the public authority may intervene in this kind of contract. The reason for the particular emphasis on public contracts here is that exclusively public contracts restrict the freedom of the two parties to arrange dispute settlement.

7.2.2 Conciliatory Dispute Settlement

The Legislative Guide and the Model Provisions recommend some conciliatory methods to settle disputes between the contracting authority and the concessioner on the project agreement in PFIPs, in addition to those antagonistic methods such as arbitration and judicial proceedings. The advantages of these conciliatory methods are that it could prevent disputes from arising in advance so as to preserve the business relationship between the parties and that conciliatory methods are flexible enough to allow for a choice of competent experts to assist in the settlement of disputes. However, the disadvantage of these conciliatory methods is that they are not as strong as antagonistic methods. The settlements are often launched and organised by the parties themselves so they are difficult to recognise and enforce, even if the final decision is made through a conciliatory dispute settlement.

The project agreement could involve an early warning provision. Under this provision, if one of the parties feels that events that have occurred, or claims that the party

[14] O'Sullivan & Hilliard, *'The law of contract'* (Oxford University Press, 2008), P2.

[15] Private law means the laws manage the interactions among individuals, organizations or states worked as civil subjects without the intervention of the state or government, such as Contract Law, Tort Law, Civil Law and so on.

[16] The mandatory provisions would not invalid due to the agreement in the contract between two parties. For example, some prohibitions to protect the public interests could be agreed to execute in contract. O'Sullivan & Hilliard, *'The law of contract'* (Oxford University Press, 2008).

[17] Vincent-Jones Peter, *'The new public contracting: regulation, responsiveness, relationality'* (Oxford university press, 2006), P11–18.

[18] Public law means the laws govern the relationship between the state and the general population, such as Administrative Law, Constitution, Criminal Law and so on.

intends to make actions, which have the potential to cause disputes, the party who finds these events or has claims should warn the other party as soon as possible.[19]

A "partnering charter" could be set up alongside the project agreement to design a resolution procedure to determine claims and resolve other problems, beginning at the lowest possible level of management and at the earliest possible opportunity. This could be drafted and signed in workshops attended by the key parties in the project. The aim of this charter would be to create an environment of trust, focusing on teamwork and cooperation for all key parties involved in the project.[20]

The parties of the project agreement could appoint a facilitator who would assist the parties in resolving any disputes. This facilitator does not give subjective opinions on the dispute, but rather facilitate the parties in analysing the merits of their cases.[21]

The parties of project agreement could arrange conciliation and mediation before adopting antagonistic methods to dispute settlement. Conciliation and mediation require third-person assistance whereby a person or a panel assists the parties in an independent and impartial manner to reach a harmonic settlement of their dispute. This kind of dispute settlement is generally non-binding and does not enforce settlement. The conciliator's responsibility is to facilitate settlement by directing the parties' attention to the core issues and possible solutions, rather than by giving a judgment. If this conciliation and mediation ends unsuccessfully, it is not an obstacle to the parties choosing to apply litigation or arbitration.[22] In EU procurement law, the European Commission can propose a conciliator drawn from a list of independent people, who then organises a panel to conciliate the dispute.[23] The Legislative Guide also gives suggestions on how to use conciliation and mediation,[24] and it even gives a sample provision[25] of a project agreement that agreed to use conciliation and mediation to settle a dispute.

The parties of the project agreement could employ a neutral third party to give a non-binding expert estimate on the merits of the dispute and a suggested outcome. The neutral expert third party attends to the possible outcome of the more expensive

[19]The legislative Guide, Chap. VI on Settlement of disputes, Section B Disputes between the contracting authority and the concessionaire, para 11; Trepte Peter, *'Public procurement in the EU: a practitioner's Guide'* (2nd ed, Oxford university press, 2007), p 552.

[20]Ibid., para 12.

[21]Ibid., para 13.

[22]Ibid., para 14–16.

[23]Bovis Christopher, *'EC public procurement: case law and regulation'* (Oxford university press, 2006), p 597.

[24]UNCITRAL Conciliation Rules, Official Records of the General Assembly, Thirty-fifth Session, Supplement No. 17 (A/35/17).

[25]Accompanying UNCITRAL Conciliation Rules, a model conciliation clause could be: "Where, in the event of a dispute arising out of or relating to this contract, the parties wish to seek an amicable settlement of that dispute by conciliation, the conciliation shall take place in accordance with the UNCITRAL Conciliation Rules as at present in force".

and usually slower binding procedures such as arbitration or court proceedings, rather than the issue of the dispute.[26]

The senior executives of the parties of the project agreement could stage a mini-trial with a "tribunal" composed of a senior executive of each party and a third neutral person. The purpose of this mock trial is to demonstrate how the senior executives of the parties understand the issues of the dispute and to predict what the outcome of a real trial might be.[27]

The parties of project agreement could arrange for an estimate of an expected settlement to be made by senior executives from both parties.[28]

The project agreement could appoint an independent expert to review disputes about technical aspects of the construction of the infrastructure facility, but the powers of the independent expert, and the circumstances under which the independent expert's advice or decision may be sought by the parties, should be set forth in the project agreement.[29]

The project agreement could establish a permanent board composed of experts appointed by both parties to assist in the settlement of disputes that may arise during the construction and the operational phases (hereafter referred to as "dispute review board"). The dispute review board may prevent misunderstandings between the parties from developing into formal disputes that would require settlement in arbitral or judicial proceedings. Generally, when potential conflicts are detected, the board would propose solutions. As the solutions are given by experts with standing and prestige, the parties are likely to accept them. Then, even if the arbitral or judicial proceedings are used, the court or arbitral tribunal may regard the decision made by the dispute review board as a powerful recommendation made by independent experts familiar with the project from the outset and based on contemporaneous observation of the project prior to, and at the time of, the dispute having first arisen.[30]

The parties of project agreement could arrange non-binding arbitration before commencing with judicial proceedings. Non-binding arbitration is conducted in a similar manner to binding arbitration and the same rules may be used, but the procedure ends with a recommendation rather than an enforceable decision. Therefore, if the dispute is still unresolved under non-binding arbitration, it is unnecessary to have a second arbitration and litigation may be pursued instead.[31]

The use of conciliatory methods to settle disputes on the project agreements of PFIPs have not been forbidden in relevant Chinese laws. Therefore, these dispute settlements may be arranged freely between the contracting authority and concessioner. The methods of conciliation and mediation are especially popular in practice

---

[26]The legislative Guide, Chap. VI on Settlement of disputes, Section B Disputes between the contracting authority and the concessionaire, para 17.

[27]Ibid., para 18.

[28]Ibid., para 19.

[29]Ibid., para 20–22; Trepte Peter, *'Public procurement in the EU: a practitioner's Guide'* (2nd ed, Oxford university press, 2007), p 566.

[30]Ibid., para 23–28.

[31]Ibid., para 29.

in Chinese PFIPs.[32] However, there are two issues that arise: firstly, current Chinese laws need to be improved to protect the private concessioner from abuse by the public authority, for example accepting the recommendations of conciliation and mediation under pressure from the government. Secondly, these conciliatory methods should not be mandatory for project agreements. Although these conciliatory methods are helpful in resolving disputes, safeguards must be created so that they are not used as merely a delaying tactic before the result is appealed according to an antagonistic method such as litigation or arbitration. The time allowed for attempts to resolve disputes through these methods should be limited.[33] The Legislative Guide points out that the project agreement should avoid excessively complex procedures or to impose too many different procedures, which may also delay the settlement of disputes.[34]

7.2.3 *Litigation*

Judicial proceedings may be used to settle disputes about the project agreement between the contracting authority and the concessioner, unless the parties have agreed to exclude judicial proceedings excepting arbitration, and this agreement is not prohibited by the mandatory laws of the host country.

Litigation is used to settle disputes about the project agreement with the following advantages. Unlike arbitration, whose essence is compromise, litigation bases decisions on fact and law. Even after Arbitratio, judicial proceeding may still be used to compel arbitration or enforce an arbitration award. Judicial proceedings developed over time are more mature, and provide more readily available measures such as interim relief.[35] Generally, the contracting authority, lenders and insurers prefer litigation. The contracting authority prefers litigation because the contracting authority is familiar with the local judicial proceedings and language, and the local court is more likely to protect public policy and public interest.[36] Lenders and insurers prefer litigation because judicial proceedings offer them strict and legally enforceable claim to the loan and collateral documents.[37]

On the other hand, litigation is sometimes excluded from dispute settlements on project agreements for the following disadvantages: The judicial proceeding often

[32] Deng Xiaopeng, Shen Liyin, 'Research on Attributes of PPP Contract from an Administrative Law View' (Construction Economy, 2007. 01); Song Biao, 'The research on the PPP legal framework in China' (Adult Higher Education Journal, 2010.02).

[33] Hoffman Scott L., 'the law and business of international project finance' (2008),Cambridge, P406.

[34] The legislative Guide, Chap. VI on Settlement of disputes, Section B Disputes between the contracting authority and the concessionaire, para 10.

[35] Hoffman Scott L., 'the law and business of international project finance' (2008),Cambridge, P405.

[36] The legislative Guide, Chap. VI on Settlement of disputes, Section B Disputes between the contracting authority and the concessionaire, para 39.

[37] Sandrock Otto, 'Is international arbitration inept to solve disputes arising out of international loan agreement?', 11 J.INT'L ARB.33(1994).

takes more time; the court may lack experience in the highly technical and complex issues involved in infrastructure projects; the local court may have unjust intentions with regard to the contracting authority.[38] Generally, the concessioner, project investors and subcontractors dislike litigation. The private investors, especially foreign investors, may be unwilling to engage in judicial proceedings, especially when the rules are unfamiliar.[39] In China, where judicial corruption is considered an issue, most foreign private investors are very reluctant to litigate.

7.2.3.1 Jurisdiction

Although the project company established by the concessioner may be registered in a foreign country, and the members of the consortia comprising the concessioner may be foreign investors, the court of the host country retains territorial jurisdiction on the disputes relating to the project agreement between the contracting authority and the concessioner in PFIPs. There are four reasons for this territorial jurisdiction: firstly, the infrastructure is generally considered to be immovable property. According to the general rule of private international law, the title claims to immovable property are governed by the *lex situs*, i.e. the law of immovable property where the immovable property is situated governs disputes.[40] Secondly, there is a sufficient connection between the substance of the claim and the court of the host country.[41] The claim relates to a dispute about a PFIP project agreement for an infrastructure project mainly to be performed in the host country, and in which both of the parties may be domiciled in the host country. Therefore, the host country has the closest connection with the claim. Thirdly, the court of the host country is the most convenient forum in which the case can most suitably be tried in the interests of the parties and the ends of justice.[42] Fourthly, the decision made by the court of the host country is most easily recognised and enforced. The project assets are under the control of the country where it is located, and the law of that country may refuse to recognise a foreign judgment relating to these assets.[43] The principal account of the project is generally located in a bank of the host country, from which it is easy to adopt interim relief proceeding and enforcement after the proceedings. In light of the above four

---

[38]Hoffman Scott L., *'the law and business of international project finance'* (2008),Cambridge, P407; The legislative Guide, Chap. VI on Settlement of disputes, Section B Disputes between the contracting authority and the concessionaire, para 41.

[39]The legislative Guide, Chap. VI on Settlement of disputes, Section B Disputes between the contracting authority and the concessionaire, para 40.

[40]French Duncan, Matthew Saul and White Nigel D., *'International law and dispute settlement: new problems and techniques'* (Oxford: Hart, 2010); Counsil Regulation (EC) No 44/2001 on jurisdiction and the recognition and enforcement of judgments in civil and commercial matters, Article 22(1).

[41]Clarkson C. M. V. and others, *'The conflict of laws'* (3rd ed, Oxford: Oxford University Press 2006), P52.

[42]Ibid., P91; Spiliada Maritime Corpn vs Cansulex Ltd [1987] AC 460.

[43]Ibid., P118.

reasons, the court of the host country should have territorial jurisdiction, although there may be courts in other countries that have jurisdiction because of particular factors.

7.2.3.2 Choice of Laws

Although the court of the host country has territorial jurisdiction, the law applied to the dispute may be controversial. If the dispute about the project contract is considered to be an administrative dispute (See Sect. 7.2.1 on the nature of the project agreement), it should exclusively apply Administrative Law protocols, rather than the choice of law agreed upon by the parties. With regards to public contracts, the public interests are prioritised over the arrangement of private interests. On the other hand, if the dispute is considered to be a general dispute between two equal parties (See Sect. 7.2.1 on the nature of the project agreement), the contracting authority and the concessioner[44] are permitted to agree to an appropriate law to be applied to their dispute.[45] If the law applied to this dispute is not chosen expressly by the parties, the governing law should be the law of the country with which the contract is most closely connected.[46] In PFIPs, the law which is the most possible to govern the project agreement is the law of the host country to which the project is undoubtedly regarded as most closely connected. Firstly, the infrastructure, as an immovable property, is situated in the host country. Secondly, the performance of the project, which is at the heart of the contract, is implemented in the host country.[47] It is also worth noticing that an agreement about the choice of law may be invalid, if the agreement is in conflict with the public interest or the mandatory rules of the host country.[48] As a matter of fact, the Legislative Guide gives tacit consent to applying the law of the host country.[49] This avoids trouble because it keeps the laws regulating the nature of the project agreement and its application consistent.

---

[44]Generally, the concessioner in PFIPs includes the foreign elements that it may be registered in a foreign country or its all or primary investors are foreign person or entities. Otherwise, it is unnecessary to discuss the choice of the law that the laws of the host country should be applied because both parties of the contract are in the host country and the project is implemented in the host country.

[45]Clarkson C. M. V. and others, *'The conflict of laws'* (3rd ed, Oxford: Oxford University Press 2006), P170.

[46]Ibid.

[47]Contracts (applicable law) act 1990 (1990 c 36), Article 4(2)(3).

[48]Clarkson C. M. V. and others, *'The conflict of laws'* (3rd ed, Oxford: Oxford University Press 2006), P195; Contracts (applicable law) act 1990 (1990 c 36), P326, Article 7.

[49]The legislative Guide, Chap. VI on Settlement of disputes, Section B General provisions of the project agreement, paras 5–8.

7.2.3.3 Application to China

China has also adopted the international principles on jurisdiction discussed above. Therefore, when PFIPs are implemented in China, Chinese courts have territorial jurisdiction on disputes relating to the project agreement. With regard to the choice of law, when the dispute refers to an administrative award, litigation is administrative and should exclusively apply Chinese administration law. If disputes about the project contract only refer to general business matters, in which it could be considered to be a private contract, it has to apply Chinese Contract Law as well because the Contract Law of the People's Republic of China involves mandatory rules to the effect that the law of the People's Republic of China must be applied to the project agreement,[50] even though Chinese laws allow parties to choose the law under agreement.[51] To sum up, under the current Chinese laws, if disputes about the project agreement of PFIPs in China are to be settled through litigation, they may be sued in Chinese courts to which only Chinese laws may be applied.

7.2.4 Arbitration

The countries which wish to facilitate PFIPs and attract foreign investment should review their current laws and remove possible legal obstacles to provide clear authorisation for the domestic contracting authority and the concessioner to agree on arbitration to settle disputes. Arbitration is different from litigation. It requires the parties themselves to set up the machinery to handle a dispute, or series of disputes, involving forums and laws.[52]

Arbitration has the following advantages, when it is selected to settle disputes about the project agreement: the arbitration forum offers more neutrality, which could result in a more transparent and unbiased decision. The concessioner may be reluctant to resolve disputes in the host country where the government is likely to

[50]The Contract Law of the People's Republic of China,

Article 126(2): "For a Chinese-foreign equity joint venture contract, Chinese-foreign contractual joint venture contract, or a contract for Chinese-foreign joint exploration and development of natural resources which is performed within the territory of the People's Republic of China, the law of the People's Republic of China shall be applied.".

[51]General Principles of the civil law of the People's Republic of China (1987)

Article 145: "The parties to a contract involving foreign interests may choose the law applicable to settlement of their contractual disputes, except as otherwise stipulated by law. If the parties to a contract involving foreign interests have not made a choice, the law of the country to which the contract is most closely connected shall be applied."

The Contract Law of the People's Republic of China(1999)

Article 126(1): "Parties to a foreign-related contract may select the applicable law for resolution of a contractual dispute, except as otherwise provided by law. Where parties to the foreign-related contract fail to select the applicable law, the contract shall be governed by the law of the country with the closest connection thereto.".

[52]Merrills J.G., *'International dispute settlement'* (5th ed, Cambridge University Press), p 83.

meddle or otherwise interfere in court proceedings. The parties can choose arbitrators who have expert knowledge in the particular type of project to ensure a quick and efficient resolution.[53] Arbitral proceedings are flexible and informal, which may be less disruptive of business relations between the parties than judicial proceedings. The proceedings and arbitral awards can be kept confidential, while judicial proceedings and decisions are required to be open to public scrutiny.[54] The concessioner, in particular the foreign concessioner, generally prefers arbitration because of the neutral decision-making of the arbitration forum, its speed and efficiency.[55]

Arbitration does also have some disadvantages when it comes to settling disputes about the project agreement. Arbitration has a limited or complete lack of discovery proceedings, such as the presentation of evidence. Arbitration may not be able to provide any meaningful interim relief to allow the project to stay in construction or operation while the dispute is resolved.[56] The legal doctrine of *Pacta Sunt Servanda*[57] is difficult to apply to the project agreement of a PFIP by an arbitrator because of considerations of the public interest. The arbitrator may also be tempted to allow the host government to change the project agreement, even if it will affect the rights of the concessioner.[58]

7.2.4.1 Choice of Forum

The parties of a project agreement in a PFIP could make an agreement to choose to resolve their disputes in an arbitration forum. It is different from the litigation proceedings where the court of the host country has territorial jurisdiction based on certain principles. The jurisdiction of the arbitration forum is only authorised by the agreement of the contract parties. Therefore, arbitration only has the jurisdiction to solve the dispute when the parties consent to the arbitration forum before the disputes or after. In light of disputes about the project agreement in PFIPs, it is essential to consider some issues when choosing an arbitration forum:

Firstly, it is uncertain whether these commercial arbitration centres and institutions may rule on disputes about project agreements, since they are difficult to define as public or private. This uncertainty also impacts on sovereign immunity. If the type of dispute is regarded to be a commercial dispute between equal parties, most national and international arbitration centres could arbitrate the disputes. If this type of dispute is regarded to be an administrative dispute, these disputes would be not

[53] Hoffman Scott L., 'the law and business of international project finance' (2008),Cambridge, P406.

[54] The legislative Guide, Chap. VI on Settlement of disputes, Section B Disputes between the contracting authority and the concessionaire, para 30.

[55] Hoffman Scott L., 'the law and business of international project finance' (2008),Cambridge, P407.

[56] Ibid.

[57] It is a doctrine that every international agreement binds the parties and requires that it be performed in good faith. No government should have the right to change an existing contract to further its own political, social, or economic goals.

[58] Hoffman Scott L., 'the law and business of international project finance' (2008),Cambridge, P413–414.

in the regulatory scope of commercial arbitration. Even if arbitration has already been agreed upon between the parties to the project agreement, it may be frustrated or hindered if the contracting authority is able to plead sovereign immunity, either as a bar to the commencement of arbitral proceedings or as a defence against the recognition and enforcement of the arbitration award.[59]

A second issue relates to which arbitration forum should be chosen, between an ad hoc model[60] and an institutional model. While some arbitration forums take place in international or national institutions, the parties of the contract could also choose arbitrators who would organise their own temporary arbitration forum. However, temporary arbitration forums convened on an ad hoc basis have many disadvantages: the complexity of PFIPs combined with the number of parties and interests may make it difficult to approach a comfortable decision for all concerned. Also, the decision made by the temporary arbitration forum is not easily recognised or enforced after the process is completed.[61]

Moreover, when the parties to a PFIP project agreement choose an arbitration forum, the selection must consider whether the government will be likely to meddle in that forum, and whether the concessioner will be confident that an unbiased, transparent decision may be reached in that place.[62] Therefore, it is better for the arbitration forum to take place outside the host country, to ensure that the decision is not biased because of governmental pressure. China has its own arbitral tribunal—CIETAC, which has been developing and extending its influence in the world, but the parties, may choose another forum outside of China. The parties may sense the possibility of unfairness in the arbitration procedure when the powerful Chinese government is one party to the dispute.

It is worth noting a well-known arbitration forum—the International Centre for Settlement of Investment Dispute (ICSID). This arbitration forum is fit specifically to solve disputes about project agreements in PFIPs. The ICSID, which was established under the Convention on the Settlement of Investment Disputes between States and Nationals of Other States (hereafter referred to as "Washington Convention") provides facilities for the conciliation and arbitration of disputes between member countries and investors who qualify as nationals of other member countries. The parties to the dispute must voluntarily consent in writing to submit to decisions of the centre. Investors who qualify as nationals of other member countries include natural persons and juridical persons. Consent by an agency of a State requires the approval of that State unless the State notifies the Centre that no such approval is required. Once the parties have given their consent to arbitration under the ICSID Convention, neither may withdraw its consent unilaterally. All ICSID members are

---

[59]The legislative Guide, Chap. VI on Settlement of disputes, Section B Disputes between the contracting authority and the concessionaire, para 33.

[60]It means the contracting parties can decide to administer the arbitration themselves rather than pursuant to an institutional model. The parties can select their own arbitrators to organize a temporary arbitration forum, thereby ensuring maximum autonomy.

[61]Hoffman Scott L., *'the law and business of international project finance'* (Cambridge University Press, 2008), P412.

[62]Ibid., P417.

required to recognise and enforce ICSID arbitral awards.[63] The Legislative Guide also suggests that disputes about project agreements in PFIPs are suitable for submission to the ICSID, which solves disputes on genera; investment issues between states and foreign investors.[64]

7.2.4.2 Choice of Laws

In addition to their choice of arbitration forum, the parties of the project agreement may also freely choose the laws to be applied by the arbitration forum to solve their disputes. However, the law applied to the arbitration agreement may be different from the law applied to the substantive disputes between the parties. Therefore, laws applied to the arbitration include three aspects:

Firstly, laws decide the validity of the arbitration agreement made between the contracting authority and the concessioner.

(1) The parties' capability to make an arbitration agreement affects the validity of the arbitration agreement. The law about the capability of the parties to make arbitration agreement may not be chosen generally. The capability of the host country to make an arbitration agreement is authorised by the law of the host country, while the legal status of the concessioner to make an arbitration agreement is generally authorised by the law of the country where it is registered. On the one hand, if the host country wishes to solve disputes about the project agreement through arbitration, its domestic laws should remove legal obstacles to this and clearly authorise the contracting authority to do so, to prevent the contracting authority from rejecting arbitration agreements based on limited capacity. On the other hand, the project company may reject the arbitration agreement, based on a lack of legal status such as its failure in legal register. However, in practice, in order to stabilise the investment relationship, the arbitration agreement should be treated as valid, if the capacity of the parties may be authorised by the law under which the parties choose to solve the substantive dispute, or the law of the seat of the arbitral forum or the convention compiled by the international arbitral institution, when there is no choice is made by the parties.[65]

(2) Whether the disputes on the project agreement of PFIPs are allowed to submit to arbitration affects the validity of the arbitration. The parties may consent to laws about the validity of the arbitration subject, which are generally the same as laws that are chosen to apply the substantive project agreement. Only when disputes about the project agreement of PFIPs are allowed to be settled through arbitration in light of the law chosen by the parties, is the arbitration agreement valid. If the law chosen

[63]Schreuer Christoph H., *'The ICSID convention: a commentary'* (Cambridge University Press, 2005), P82–344; the Convention on the Settlement of Investment Disputes between States and Nationals of Other States (hereafter refer to "1965 Washington Convention"), Article 25(1)(2)(3)(4).

[64]The legislative Guide, Chap. VI on Settlement of disputes, Section B Disputes between the contracting authority and the concessionaire, para 31.

[65]Clarkson C. M. V. and others, *'The conflict of laws'* (3rd ed, Oxford: Oxford University Press 2006), P252.

by the parties regards disputes about the project agreement to be administrative, the arbitration agreement may be invalid since these disputes may not be arbitrated. If the parties fail to make a choice, the decision could be made in light of the convention with which the international arbitral institution complies or the law of the place where the arbitral forum is located. However, the arbitration agreement still may be invalid if there are mandatory rules in the convention with which the international arbitral institution complies, or in the law of the place where the arbitral forum is located, or in the law of the place where the arbitration award will be enforced (i.e. these mandatory rules regard the disputes on the project agreement of PFIPs to be administrative disputes which may not be arbitrated), even if the law chosen by the parties considers disputes possible to arbitrate.[66]

Secondly, laws regulate the procedure of the arbitration, i.e. the procedural law which governs the arbitration proceedings (such as the proceedings of the arbitration forum in accepting arbitration applications and in granting an award). The parties may consent to the law used in the arbitration proceedings. If the parties fail to make a choice, the arbitration forum generally applies the convention with which the international arbitral institution complies or the law of the seat of the arbitral forum. However, the procedural law chosen by the parties may not be applied if there are mandatory rules in the convention with which the international arbitral institution complies, or in the law of the place where the arbitral forum is located. For example, the arbitration forum may require that the arbitration submitted to this forum must apply its own procedure rules or the procedure law of the seat of the arbitration forum.[67]

Thirdly, the law should apply to the disputes about the project agreement, i.e. a substantive law to solve the disputes. The parties may consent to the law to be applied to the substance of the disputes. The doctrine of *renvoi*[68] is generally excluded.[69] If the parties fail to make a choice, the arbitration forum generally applies the law determined by rules governing a conflict of laws. Arbitrators first decide which law rule is applicable (for example the principle with the closest connection to the dispute), and then apply the rule to identify the substantive law of that country. This means arbitrators have a lot of discretionary power over which law to use to solve the dispute, when there is an absence of consensus between the parties.[70] However, when arbitrators consider which rule is applicable to the particular conflict of law, they also have to consider the substantive law identified by the rules to assess whether it includes provisions that conflict with the mandatory rules of the seat of the arbitration

---

[66] Ibid., P257.

[67] Ibid., P252–254.

[68] It means, in the conflict of law, a reference to a foreign law involves applying that country's conflicts rules as opposed to its domestic laws.

[69] Hoffman Scott L., '*the law and business of international project finance*' (Cambridge University Press, 2008), P408.

[70] Clarkson C. M. V. and others, '*The conflict of laws*' (3rd ed, Oxford: Oxford University Press 2006), P256.

forum, the place of enforcement, and international laws (for example the substantive laws applied may include provisions against public policy in other relevant places).

7.2.4.3 ICSID

It is important to note how laws are applied if a request for arbitration is submitted to the ICSID. Laws are much more conveniently applied if the request for arbitration is submitted to the ICSID.

Since the Washington Convention[71] confirms both the capability of the parties to apply the arbitration and the arbitration subject, arguments about the validity of the arbitration agreement are rare. The capacity of the contracting authority to make an arbitration agreement is confirmed by all host countries who are signatories to the ICSID. Member states can notify the ICSID of the class or classes of disputes which it would consider submitting to the jurisdiction of the Centre.[72] It also has precedents to confirm whether the action is on behalf of the state or the commercial entities themselves. In the case of *Consortium L.E.S.I. v. Algeria*, ANB was a representing the Algeria government, so its behaviour was treated as the behaviour of the state.[73] In the case of *Joy v. Egypt*, Egypt's actions in this case followed the protocols of business behaviour, so ICSID had no jurisdiction.[74]

The capabilities of the project company are also confirmed in the Washington Convention.[75] In the case of *Société v. Senegal*, a company registered in the host country was treated as a foreign private investor because its primary shareholders were foreign private investors.[76]

The jurisdiction of ICSID, as defined by the Washington Convention, includes disputes about the project agreement on the investments made by the contracting authority and the project company.[77] Investment dispute is defined in the case of *Salini v. Morocco*, which gives five criteria to confirm whether a dispute is controlled by ICSID, although in practice these criteria are quite flexible.[78] Arbitration proceedings are therefore already offered by the Washington Convention.[79] Variation in

[71]The Washington Convention 1965 relates to settlement of investment disputes between nation states and citizens of other countries. The Convention created the International Centre for Settlement of Investment Disputes (or ICSID).

[72]Convention on the Settlement of Investment Disputes between States and Nationals of Other States (hereafter refer to "1965 Washington Convention"), Article 25(4).

[73]*Consortium Groupement L.E.S.I.—DIPENTA v. People's Democratic Republic of Algeria* (ICSID Case No. ARB/03/8).

[74]*Joy Mining Machinery Limited v. Arab Republic of Egypt* (ICSID Case No. ARB/03/11).

[75]1965 Washington Convention, Article 25(2).

[76]*Société Ouest Africaine des Bétons Industriels v. Senegal* (ICSID Case No. ARB/82/1).

[77]1965 Washington Convention, Article 25(1).

[78]*Salini Costruttori S.p.A. and Italstrade S.p.A. v. Kingdom of Morocco* (ICSID Case No. ARB/00/4).

[79]1965 Washington Convention, Chapter IV, Section 3.

these proceedings is possible through the parties' agreement, excepting when the mandatory rules disallow it.[80]

The ICSID decide on disputes in light of the law chosen by the parties. If the parties fail to make a choice, the ICSID clearly states that the law of the host country should be applied, although international law may also be applicable.[81]

7.2.4.4 Recognition and Enforcement

Irrespective of the arbitration forum or the decision, a dispute settlement may only be considered a success if the award is recognised and enforced.

The Convention on the Recognition and Enforcement of Foreign Arbitral Awards (hereafter refer to "New York Convention"), which has 148 contracting countries,[82] deals recognising and enforcing foreign arbitral awards, and the grounds on which a court may refuse to recognise or enforce the award. Irrespective of the arbitral forum that makes the arbitral award, whether a national, international or provisional arbitral forum, if the country required to recognise and to enforce the award is a contracting member of the convention, to some extent there is some assurance of a binding commitment and of the reliability of the arbitration. However, the contracting members of the convention are also allowed to have reservation clauses to refuse the recognition and enforcement of certain foreign arbitral awards.[83]

Arbitral award made by the ICSID should be recognised and enforced by the contracting states of the 1965 Washington Convention.[84] Enforcement of the award shall be governed by laws concerning the enforcement of judgments in the state in whose territories such enforcement is sought.[85]

Additionally, if there are other bilateral treaties or multilateral treaties concerning the recognition and enforcement of arbitral award made by the country where the enforcement is claimed, the country also needs to follow those treaties.

7.2.4.5 Application to China

In China, there have been no disputes about the project agreement in a PFIP settled by arbitration thus far.[86] However, there is intense controversy as to whether disputes

[80] 1965 Washington Convention, Article 37–40&56; Christoph H.Schreuer, *'The ICSID convention: a commentary'* (Cambridge University Press, 2005), P672.

[81] 1965 Washington Convention, Article 42(1).

[82] 1958 New York Arbitration Convention, website: <http://www.newyorkconvention.org/>.

[83] The Convention on the Recognition and Enforcement of Foreign Arbitral Awards (hereafter refer to "New York Convention"), Article 1(3).

[84] 1965 Washington Convention, Article 54(1).

[85] 1965 Washington Convention, Article 54(3).

[86] Huang Teng and others, *'the comparison analysis on the government management of PPP'*, Project Management Technology (2009.01), P9.

about the project agreement are to be considered administrative disputes or not. If it is considered to be an administrative dispute, it may not be arbitrated by the Arbitration Law of the People's Republic of China.[87] Even if this dispute is arbitrated in a foreign arbitral forum, it would not be recognised or enforced in China because the arbitration would contravene the mandatory rules of China. However, if China wants to facilitate and develop PFIPs, it should reform and improve its current laws to allow arbitration to settle disputes about project agreements in PFIPs. In light of the experience of other countries, arbitration would be of benefit to the Chinese situation.

The primary work of Chinese legislators is now to ensure that disputes about the project agreements in PFIPs, or parts thereof, may be settled through arbitration, i.e. these disputes are no longer regarded to be administrative disputes. The Legislative Guide suggests that the legislator should clarify the areas where contracting authorities may or may not plead sovereign immunity.[88]

The secondary work of Chinese legislators is to remove unnecessary mandatory rules from the relevant Chinese laws, in case they trouble the jurisdiction of the national or international forums, and the choice of laws applied to arbitration.

Finally, China should clarify its reservation clauses in international conventions. China is the member of the New York Convention but it has two reservation clauses: in the first, China only recognises and enforces foreign arbitral awards made in the territory of another contracting state; in the second, China only applies the convention to legal relationships considered to be commercial under Chinese laws. If the disputes are regarded as commercial under Chinese law, the foreign arbitral awards would be recognised and enforced in China.[89] However, the Chinese Supreme Court issued a notice stressing that the definition of a commercial legal relationship does not include investment relationships between foreign private investors and the host state.[90] Therefore, it is means the arbitration awards on project agreements in PFIPs would not be recognised or enforced in China.

The Chinese reservation clause to the 1965 Washington Convention is similarly important. Although China joined the 1965 Washington Convention and accepts arbitral awards made by the ICSID, it retains a reservation clause by which it only considers submitting 'disputes over compensation resulting from expropriation and

---

[87]The Arbitration Law of the People's Republic of China(1994),

Article 3 The following disputes shall not be submitted to arbitration:

(1) ……; and

(2) administrative disputes falling within the jurisdiction of the relevant administrative organs according to law.

[88]The legislative Guide, Chap. VI on Settlement of disputes, Section B Disputes between the contracting authority and the concessionaire, para 33.

[89]Tao Jingzhou, *'Arbitration law and practice in China'* (2nd ed, Kluwer Law International BV, 2008), P188.

[90]Notice of the Supreme People's Court on Implementing the Convention on the Recognition and Enforcement of Foreign Arbitral Awards Acceded to by China(No. 5 [1987] of the Supreme People's Court, April 10, 1987), Article 2.

nationalisation'.[91] Therefore, not all disputes about the project agreements in PFIPs could be submitted to the ICSID. As a result of this reservation, China has only participated in ICSID arbitration twice so far.[92] If China expects to use arbitration as a dispute settlement, it should consider amending this reservation to the 1965 Washington Convention.

There is still a long way to go before disputes about the project agreements of Chinese PFIPs may be settled through arbitration. However, if China is intent on developing PFIPs, Chinese legislators should start to review and reform Chinese laws.

7.3 The Disputes May Arise Between the Equal Parties

In PFIPs, disputes may arise between the concessioner (Project Company) and other parties as equal subjects of law or among equal parties, i.e. the disputes about general agreements (Fig. 7.1: red II). These disputes include disputes between the project financers, or disputes between the concessioner (Project Company) and its shareholders, lenders, subcontractors, suppliers and other business partners.

The Legislative Guide and the Model Provisions recommend that the parties to this type of dispute shall be free to choose the appropriate mechanisms for settling the dispute.[93] Therefore, all the dispute settlement methods discussed in Sects. 7.2.2, 7.2.3, 7.2.4 could be applied, on the basis of a free agreement between the parties, and without doubts as to the nature of the agreement. However, due to the different preferences of the participants in PFIPs (lenders may prefer litigation while the subcontractors may prefer arbitration) the dispute settlement may be a compromise through negotiation. The law should give the maximum freedom to parties to choose a method of dispute settlement congenial to all parties.

Third parties are regulated differently in different countries. In the US, agreements on dispute settlements may apply to the project participant who is not party to the contract in dispute. Some parties in PFIPs may benefit from the contracts, even though they are not one of the direct contractual parties. For example, the project company is not a party to a subcontract between its construction contractor and the contractor's supplier, but the project company benefits from the performance of the subcontract as it helps to accomplish the whole project. In this case, if the project company wants to sue the supplier for a failed performance that results in the delay of the whole project, the project company could act as a third-party beneficiary of

[91] Yang Shu-dong, *'Investment Arbitration and China: Investor or Host State?'*, Op. J., Vol. 2/2011, Paper n. 6, pp 1–19, <http://lider-lab.sssup.it/opinio> accessed on 9th March, 2020.

[92] Both of them are pending now. Ekran Berhad v. People's Republic of China (ICSID Case No. ARB/11/15); Ping An Life Insurance Company of China, Limited and Ping An Insurance (Group) Company of China, Limited v. Kingdom of Belgium (ICSID Case No. ARB/12/29).

[93] The Model Provisions, Chap. V on Settlement of disputes, Model provision 51; The legislative Guide, Chap. VI on Settlement of disputes, Section C Disputes between project promoters and between the concessionaire and its lenders, contractors and suppliers, para 42.

the subcontract. It would still have to adhere to the arbitration provisions in the subcontract made by the construction contractor and the supplier.[94] In the UK, the third party could be treated as a party to the arbitration agreement as regards disputes between itself and the promisor, relating to the enforcement of a substantive term by the third party.[95] In China, there are no provisions relating to the effect of an arbitration agreement on a third party.

In Chinese PFIPs, these disputes are settled as disputes in general agreement in which the dispute settlement is freely agreed upon by the parties. It follows a similar pattern to the requirements set out in the Legislative Guide and the Model Provisions.

7.4 Disputes Between the User and the Private Concessioner (Project Company)

In PFIPs, disputes may arise between the user and the private concessioner (Project Company), i.e. the disputes about the user agreement (Fig. 7.1: red III).

The Legislative Guide and the Model Provisions recommend that simplified and efficient mechanisms should be established for handling claims submitted by the individual persons acting in their non-commercial capacity. These mechanisms could be either a special facility or department set up within the project company for receiving and handling claims expeditiously, or a regulatory agency set up by the public authority.[96]

The Legislative Guide and the Model Provisions recommend that, for the entities or enterprises, disputes could be settled by the usual methods used in general contracts, including litigation and arbitration. However, it is important to note whether the user agreement is regarded as a "public" contract, which would make the disputes administrative disputes, since the buyer is a state-owned enterprises or the public authority. If the host country expects to settle this type of dispute by free agreement, the law of the host country should clarify that this user agreement is a general agreement.[97]

In Chinese PFIPs, claims from individual persons that lead to the use of dispute settlement mechanisms involve either a department set up within the project company or a public regulatory agency. The customers may also opt to go to court. For the entities or enterprises, the dispute is considered to be a normal dispute between equal

---

[94] Hoffman Scott L., 'the law and business of international project finance' (2008), Cambridge, P412.

[95] UK Contract and Third Party Act 1999, Section 8.

[96] The Model Provisions, Chap. V on Settlement of disputes, Model provision 50; The legislative Guide, Chap. VI on Settlement of disputes, Section D Disputes involving customers or users of the infrastructure facility, para 44.

[97] The legislative Guide, Chap. VI on Settlement of disputes, Section D Disputes involving customers or users of the infrastructure facility, para 45.

parties and is settled by the method agreed upon by the parties, regardless it is the public authority, a state-owned enterprise or a normal enterprise.

7.5 Hypothesis

The following is an idealised hypothesis that all disputes arising in PFIPs could be settled by one method.[98] According to the dispute settlement of arbitration, all the disputes in the same PFIP could submit to the same arbitration forum and apply the same laws.

The advantages would be consistent results, efficient resolution without project delays, less expense and so on. However, this hypothesis is impossible, since the differing goals and preferences of the parties involved in PFIPs cannot make a single settlement procedure achievable.

7.6 Conclusion

This chapter responds to the 6th research question, namely how Chinese dispute settlements in PFIPs may be improved, based on the guidelines from the Legislative Guide and Model Provisions, and with supplementary reference to other countries.

The principle of dispute settlement in PFIPs is to solve the dispute in an efficient and fair way. The resolution proceedings should be quick and professional, ensure fair and transparent treatment, and protect the project's continuance during the resolution process.

The disputes in PFIPs may be divided into three types, in light of the different agreements:

The first involves disputes between the contracting authority and the concessioner. The Legislative Guide and the Model Provisions recommend two types of dispute settlement: one uses conciliatory methods such as conciliation and mediation; the other uses antagonistic method, i.e. litigation and arbitration.[99] The conciliatory settlements to dispute may be optional according to the law of the host country. Considering that one of the parties of any project agreement is the public authority and the subject of the agreement refers to an infrastructure with close connection to the public interest, the nature of the project agreement (whether public contract or private contract) may be identified differently in different countries. If the project agreement is identified as a public contract, disputes about the project agreement would be administrative disputes that the host country has exclusive jurisdiction

[98]Scott L. Hoffman, 'the law and business of international project finance' (2008), Cambridge, P407–408.

[99]The Model Provisions, Chap. V on Settlement of disputes, Model provision 49; The legislative Guide, Chap. VI on Settlement of disputes, Section B General provisions of the project agreement.

over and the only law that might be applied is its administrative law. Arbitration may not be used. If the project agreement is identified as a private contract, the dispute would be a dispute of general commercial contract, which means that the dispute settlement could be decided upon by agreement of the parties as long as it obeyed certain mandatory rules in the host country. In Chinese PFIPs, the nature of the project agreement is vague. Therefore, in practice, no arbitration has been applied to disputes about project agreements thus far, and most of these disputes have been solved by mediation or litigation in China. To sum up, if China is intent on facilitating PFIPs and gaining the confidence of foreign investors, Chinese law should clarify the nature of project agreements and remove improper restrictions to related settlements of disputes. Private investors often prefer settle disputes through methods such as arbitration since this would be less affected by the host government.

The second type of dispute occurs between the concessioner and other parties as equal subjects of law or among equal parties. The Legislative Guide and the Model Provisions recommend that this type of dispute shall be solved by the settlement method agreed by the parties.[100] In Chinese PFIPs, the way to solve this type of dispute is consistent with the recommendations of the Legislative Guide and the Model Provisions.

The third type of dispute occurs between the concessioner and the users. The Legislative Guide and the Model Provisions recommend that simple and efficient mechanisms should be offered to individual persons, while the general dispute settlement to normal commercial contracts should be offered to entities, excepting when the entity is the public authority or a state-owned enterprise when the contract may be considered to be an administrative contract.[101] In Chinese PFIPs, all user agreements are considered to be normal purchase agreements no matter the nature of the entity.

Although it would be ideal if all the disputes could be solved according to the same settlement procedure to prevent a conflict in the decisions, this would be impossible in practice.

The previous seven chapters (include this one—Chapter 7) have analysed and discussed all the aspect issues of PFIPs, the next Chapter which is the last chapter—Chap. 8 will summarise all these discussions and present the conclusions of this book.

[100]The Model Provisions, Chap. V on Settlement of disputes, Model provision 51; The legislative Guide, Chap. VI on Settlement of disputes, Section C Disputes between project promoters and between the concessionaire and its lenders, contractors and suppliers.

[101]The Model Provisions, Chap. V on Settlement of disputes, Model provision 50; The legislative Guide, Chap. VI on Settlement of disputes, Section D Disputes involving customers or users of the infrastructure facility.

Chapter 8
Conclusion

8.1 Introduction

This book has great significance for both the study and the practice of infrastructure development in China. Its subject matter will continue to be of relevance for the foreseeable future.

The Legislative Guide on Privately Financed Infrastructure Projects made by UNCITRAL[1] was published in 2000 and the Model Legislative Provisions on Privately Financed Infrastructure Projects was published in 2003. They were published over ten years ago. However, when compared with other well-known model laws[2] made by UNCITRAL, it seems that the Legislative Guide and Model Provisions have not been paid enough attention, since they have rarely appeared in the domestic laws of countries and have not been the subject of extensive academic discussion. However, with increased development in developing and developed countries, there has been an increase in attention on financial models channelling private investment into public infrastructure, and the relevant legislation to facilitate them. It is no doubt that the Legislative Guide and Model Provisions made by UNCITRAL will become more and more important as an international standard for national legislations on Privately Financed Infrastructure Projects.

The more exact word "PFIPs" replaces the old word "BOT". According to the suggestion of the Legislative Guide and the Model Provisions, this would unify the term used for infrastructure projects financed by private investors. In the past decades, private investors financed public infrastructure through various models such as BOT, BOO, PFIP, M&Q, etc. The name PFIPs could invoke all these models. An

[1] It stands for United Nations Commission on International Trade Law. It is the core legal body of the United Nations system in the field of international trade law. In order to increase these opportunities worldwide, it is formulating modern, fair, and harmonized rules on commercial transactions.

[2] Such as UNCITRAL Arbitration Rules (2010); Model Law on International Commercial Arbitration (2006); Model Law on Public Procurement (2011); United Nations Convention on Contracts for the International Sale of Goods (CISG) (1980).

S. Liang, *Legal Aspects of Privately Financed Infrastructure Projects (PFIPs) in China*,
https://doi.org/10.1007/978-981-15-6803-9_8

exact and unified name could avoid misunderstanding and facilitate international harmonisation.

According to the current data, Chinese plans for developing infrastructure in China are forecasted to 2030.[3] UK plans for developing its infrastructure in the UK are also forecasted to 2030.[4] However, according to their fiscal data, neither China as a developing country nor the UK as a developed country could accomplish these plans if they only rely on their national finance. The Chinese Ministry of Finance has received many reports from various provinces to claim the national deficit to develop infrastructure.[5,6] Meanwhile, the report of the UK HM Treasury has claimed that:

> Estimates suggest that demand for infrastructure investment could remain high until 2030, and possibly beyond. The majority of investment in economic infrastructure in the UK is already provided by the Private Sector and this additional investment will also need to be met primarily from Private Sector sources.[7,8]

PFIPs would provide a remedy to this fiscal gap, given their success in various countries. PFIPs have also been used in China, with varying degrees of success and failure.

The significance of this book is that it establishes the defects of the current Chinese laws on PFIPs, and suggests ways of improving and reforming Chinese laws to achieve international standards in order to facilitate the development of PFIPs in China, since PFIPs need fair, efficient and transparent laws. As PFIPs provide a possible way to remedy fiscal insufficiencies in the development of infrastructure, the topic of improving and reforming laws on PFIPs will undoubtedly be popular in the next decades in both Chinese academia and legislative practice.

The book suggests that the Legislative Guide and the Model Provisions made by UNCITRAL can be used to guide the improvement and reform of Chinese laws on PFIPs, attracting more foreign private investors and facilitating the development

---

[3]Notice of the State Council on the long-term planning of major national scientific and technological infrastructure construction (2012–2030); Ministry of Transport of PRC, *'National Expressway Network Plan'* (Jan, 2005); State Council Standing Committee, 'long-term railway network plan (to 2020)' (Jan, 2004).

[4]HM Treasury and Infrastructure UK, 'National Infrastructure Plan: update 2012' (December, 2012), <http://www.hm-treasury.gov.uk/d/national_infrastructure_plan_051212.pdf> accessed on 20th March, 2020.

[5]Ministry of Finance of People's Republic of China, <http://www.mof.gov.cn/> accessed on 6th June, 2020.

[6]There are some doubt voices that China should be rich enough to fund its infrastructure developing because it spent much money to buy a large number of US government bonds. However, as a matter of fact, Chinese government buying the plenty of US government bonds is not conflict with the Chinese deficit to develop infrastructure but it has no better choice. See the detail explanation in 1.2.1 in Chapter 1.

[7]HM Treasury and Infrastructure UK, 'Strategy for national infrastructure' (March, 2010), P9 <http://www.direct.gov.uk/prod_consum_dg/groups/dg_digitalassets/@dg/@en/documents/digitalasset/dg_186451.pdf> accessed on 20th March, 2020.

[8]Though there are doubt voice that the PFIPs in the UK is to make the profits private and the risk public, this result is not caused by the model of PFIPs itself but the shortcoming of relevant laws and policies.

of PFIPs. The law of other countries are used as model where the content of the Legislative Guide and Model Provisions are not appropriate for the specific situation of China. There are six primary research questions answered in this book.

8.2 The Answer for the First Research Question

Do Chinese laws on PFIPs need to be reformed to facilitate the development of PFIPs?

This question was addressed in Chap. 2, which concludes that Chinese laws on PFIPs must be reformed, otherwise they would remain an obstacle to the development of PFIPs in China.

Section 2.2 of Chap. 2 gives evidence of how the PFIP model has already been applied in the construction of Chinese infrastructure and how it would be used more and more in the next few decades. It details five exemplary cases: the first successful infrastructure built according to the PFIP model in China, Shajiao B Power Plant in 1984; the largest-scale Chinese infrastructure construction involving the PFIP model to date, China's Western Development; the most famous Chinese PFIP, Beijing Olympic Stadium; the most concerning current infrastructure construction in China, Low-rent housing; the longest-term Chinese infrastructure development plan, the "long-term railway network plan" to 2020.

Section 2.2 of Chap. 2 points out that PFIPs are worthy of further development because they can bring enormous benefits to China. PFIPs were proposed to resolve a conflict between government funding shortages and the public demand for infrastructure. PFIPs were shown to promote initiatives by the Private Sector to assist public services. PFIPs were also proposed to break government or State-owned enterprise monopolies in the Chinese infrastructure market. PFIPs thus promote value for money and might limit corruption in Chinese infrastructure constructions.

Section 2.3 of Chap. 2 claimed that the defects of current Chinese laws on PFIPs may hinder or risk the development of PFIPs. The deficiencies in Chinese current laws are listed as follows:

- The current Chinese laws on PFIPs are unstable. There is no stable national law on PFIPs in China, but certain provinces of China have issued provincial regulations on PIPs, which are only valid in that province.
- The current Chinese laws on PFIPs are contradictory. Provincial regulations from different provinces contradict each other.
- The provincial regulations on PFIPs in China are not comprehensive and not specific to all aspects of PFIPs. Even if these provincial regulations were compiled together, they would not be comprehensive and specific to all aspects of PFIPs. Neither the selection procedure for private concessioners nor the definition of rights and obligations of the Public and Private Sector are clear.
- The private investors in PFIPs do not have adequate legal protection in China.
- The public interest in PFIPs does not have enough legal protection in China either.

Section 2.4 of Chap. 2 showed that the objective conditions in China are now ready for a legal reform on PFIPs. China has almost abandoned governmental monopoly in the public service market and is encouraging private finance to invest in public infrastructure through the issue of a series of policies, while the Chinese market economy has matured. Additionally, provincial regulations on PFIPs offer a basic foundation to establish a national legislation on PFIPs although this needs further support from the Legislative Guide and Model Provisions issued by UNCITRAL.

Section 2.5 of Chap. 2 proposed the aims for the reform of Chinese legislation on PFIPs. Such legislation should establish a nationally comprehensive legislation on PFIPs which could achieve international standards so that the law of China could balance private and public interests to facilitate the development of PFIPs.

To sum up, from the development of PFIPs in China and the review of Chinese current laws on PFIPs, it concluded that the defects of Chinese laws hinder the development of PFIPs in China. Therefore, it is urgent to improve and reform the Chinese laws on PFIPs.

8.3 The Answer for the Second Research Question

Why use the Legislative Guide and Model Provisions[9] made by UNCITRAL as guidelines to improve the Chinese laws on PFIPs? Why use other countries' laws[10] on PFIPs as supplementary reference?

This question is analysed and discussed in Chap. 3, which concludes that the Legislative Guide and Model Provisions made by UNCITRAL provide the best guide for the reform of Chinese laws on PFIPs. Moreover, it is necessary to use other countries' laws as a supplementary reference.

In addition to the Legislative Guide and Model Provisions made by UNCITRAL, Chap. 3 lists four international conventions and treaties which refer to PFIPs. Although each has their own advantages, their disadvantages indicate they are not proper to guide the reform of Chinese laws on PFIPs.

The working group on Trade and Investment made by the WTO was quickly dismissed since the Agreement on Trade Related Aspect of Investment Measures (hereafter referred to as "TRIMs") is the only multi-agreement on investment issued by the WTO. It is not applied to general international investment but only to investment-related trade, and does not refer to the question of PFIPs. Therefore, neither the working group nor the TRIMs could offer guidance on the reform of Chinese laws on PFIPs.

The OECD has made some measures and institutes that refer to PFIPs, but these efforts do not form a systematic guide specific on PFIPs. The Multilateral Agreement on Investment (hereafter referred to as "MAI") made by the OECD has been seen

[9]The Legislative Guide, Introduction and Background information on PFIPs; and the Model Provisions, Chap. I on General provisions.

[10]Such as British law, EU law and so on.

as a great attempt to harmonise the fragmented BITs on investment but it quickly collapsed because it could not balance the interests of the various parties involved. Although the substantive provisions issued by the OECD are too few to be useful to guide the reform of Chinese Laws on PFIPs, institutions established by the OECD such as the Istanbul Center, and the Public-Private Partnership Units, could support the reform in China.

The World Bank has not issued any substantive provisions about PFIPs, but it set up a famous dispute settlement centre—ICSID—which could greatly affect the arbitration system in the reform of Chinese law on PFIPs.

After analysing the disadvantages of the various international agreements on investment issued by the three international institutes—the WTO, the OECD, the World Bank—Chap. 2 lists the exclusive advantages of the Legislative Guide and Model Provisions made by the UNCITRAL. The Legislative Guide and Model Provisions made by the UNCITRAL provide an international standard to guide all aspects of laws on PFIPs in order to facilitate the development of PFIPs worldwide. China, as a member of UNCITRAL, has adopted other guidance made by UNCITRAL, so it will be easy for China to accept the Legislative Guide and Model Provisions in its reform of laws on PFIPs.

Some countries' laws on PFIPs may be used as a supplementary reference because of their rich experience in using PFIPs. Although the focus on their own situation in some countries' laws on PFIPs means they could not become the primary guideline for Chinese law reform, these examples could be used to remedy gaps in the guidelines from the Legislative Guide and Model Provisions.

Through these comparisons, this chapter concludes that the Legislative Guide and Model Provisions made by UNCITRAL provide the best guide to reform Chinese laws on PFIPs. Nevertheless, it is necessary to use other countries law as a supplementary reference.

8.4 The Answer for the Third Research Question

With reference to the Legislative Guide and Model Provisions[11] and with supplementary references from other countries,[12] how should the general legislative and institutional framework on PFIPs in China be improved?

This question is analysed and discussed in Chap. 4, which concludes that the reform of Chinese laws on PFIPs should be based on the principles of transparency, fairness, long-term sustainability and elimination of undesirable restrictions, as suggested by the Legislative Guide and Model Provisions.

[11]The Legislative Guide, Recommendation 1–11, Chap. I on general legislative and institutional framework; the Model Provisions, Chap. I on General provisions, Model Provision 1–4.

[12]The British regulations about the regulatory institutions; The British special regulations about the customer protection by Consumer Council for Water (CCWater).

The structure of the Legislative Guide and the Model Provisions is appropriate for use in the new Chinese legislation on PFIPs. The structure first gives the general legislative and institutional framework, and then follows this with the specific areas of concessioner selection, contracts in PFIPs and dispute settlement. It is considered the most proper structure for the new Chinese legislation on PFIPs. Additionally, the law reform in China can adopt and modify the recommendations in the Legislative Guide and the Model Provisions rather than copy them.

To achieve the goal of transparency, the Chinese laws on PFIPs should offer clear and readily accessible laws, and efficient procedures so that the potential private investors may predict and estimate the costs and risks involved in their investments, and may thus offer their most advantageous terms. Additionally, the Chinese laws on PFIPs should involve mandatory rules on disclosing administrative information.

To achieve the goal of fairness, the reform of legal framework on PFIPs in China should attempt to balance more the public interest and the private interest. Additionally, the protection of the customer's interests is necessary as one of the primary objectives in further Chinese legislation on PFIPs.

To achieve the goal of long-term sustainability, the Chinese legislation on PFIPs should ensure the institutional capacity to undertake the various tasks entrusted to public authorities involved in infrastructure projects, throughout the phases of implementation. It should identify the authorised sectors empowered to award concessions and to enter into agreements for the implementation of PFIPs; it should identify the regulatory sectors that are empowered to regulate the implementation of PFIPs; and it should ensure the administrative coordination. Additionally, in order to ensure the long-term sustainability of PFIPs, Chinese legislation on PFIPs not only needs to ensure its institutional capability, but also to ensure the Chinese marketisation to achieve a proper balance between competitive and monopolistic provision of public services.

To achieve the goal of the elimination of undesirable restriction, the reform of Chinese laws on PFIPs should review all the laws on PFIPs and eliminate any undesirable restrictions. Although China is a communist country, the Chinese Constitution should confirm the legality of private investment into public services. Although Chinese land may only be owned by the state, the laws should ensure that private concessioners can obtain the land use rights required for projects (as allocated land without charge). Although foreign exchange has long-standing restrictions in China to protect the Chinese monetary market, the laws should offer essential exemptions to foreign private investors in PFIPs. Therefore, all the Chinese laws on PFIPs should be reviewed and improved.

8.5 The Answer for the Fourth Research Question

With reference to the guidelines of the Legislative Guide and Model Provisions[13] and with supplementary reference to other countries,[14] how should the selection procedures of the concessioner of PFIPs be improved to make the process more fair and transparent in China?

This question is analysed and discussed in Chap. 5, which concludes that the selection procedure of the concessioner of PFIPs in China has defects and should be reformed.

In the pre-selection phase, the Chinese laws should encourage the public to participate into the infrastructure contracting plan as much as is possible. Although Chinese PFIPs are traditionally decided by government, it would be helpful if the laws allow the public to participate in the preliminary assessment of the feasibility of PFIPs. Additionally, the Chinese laws should allow as much private investment into the public infrastructure market as possible. With the exception of areas related to national security, undesirable restrictions should be removed from Chinese laws so that other areas could open market access to private investment. With due caution in treating foreign finance, the Chinese criteria would do better to approach international standards so that the foreign private finance and high technology would participate in Chinese PFIPs.

In the selection phase, in order to select the most appropriate concessioner, Chinese laws should ensure the competitive selection procedure is used as the primary model, while awards without competitive procedure through negotiation are recognised only in exceptional cases. Moreover, in light of the features of PFIPs, the laws should adjust their regulations to fit to the specific requirements of the PFIP concessioner selection procedure (for example, including the pre-selection of bidders), ensuring that the whole selection procedure is economical and efficient, and performed with integrity, confidence and transparency.

In the post-selection phase, Chinese laws should offer competitors reasonable channels through which they might complain about the selection result. On the one hand, the bidders could review the decision of the contracting authority for improper action during the selection procedure. On the other hand, it is useful to protect the bidders from unfair competition with their competitors. An important safeguard of complying with the rules of selection is that the laws offer the bidders the right to review actions by the contracting authority and other competitors. However, these rights should be subject to the public interest, since the concession award may be not invalid if the project has already been implemented. In these instances, there should be compensation for the injured competitor.

Chinese laws have never referred to unsolicited proposal, but it is obvious that the model of unsolicited proposal could help the Public Sector in implementing the PFIP

[13]The Legislative Guide, Recommendation 14–39, Chap. III on Selection of the concessioner; and the Model Provisions accompanied therein, Chap. II on Selection of the concessioner, Model Provision 5–27.

[14]EU regulations on market access are used as supplemental reference.

model. Referencing the recommendations in the Legislative Guide and the Model Provisions, relevant regulations on unsolicited proposal could be considered in the reform of Chinese laws on PFIPs.

To sum up, the concessioner selection procedures are very important in their impact on the successful completion of PFIPs. The Legislative Guide and the Model Provisions made by UNCITRAL offer very detailed guidelines on establishing laws regarding the selection procedures of PFIPs. Although the Legislative Guide and the Model Provisions have their own limitations, they are still useful in the reform of Chinese laws on PFIPs. The successful experience of other countries, and unions such as the EU, can also offer valuable guidance in the reform of Chinese laws on PFIPs.

8.6 The Answer for the Fifth Research Question

With reference to the guidelines of the Legislative Guide and Model Provisions[15] and with supplementary reference to other countries, how should the laws relating to the agreements involved in PFIPs be reformed in China?

This question is analysed and discussed in Chap. 6, which concludes that the relevant laws referring to the agreements involved in PFIPs in China involve some undesirable restrictions that it is necessary to review and reform.

In project agreements, the law should give the concessioner and the contracting authority enough flexibility to negotiate a fair contract. However, some mandatory rules or some special policies of specific national circumstance are necessary so that the contracting authority may not fail in their duty to protect public interests. There are six issues discussed in this chapter.

- The Company Law of China should remove undesirable restrictions. The legislation should allow the project agreement to restrict the organisation of the project company to some extent, so that the changes to the project company can be monitored by the contracting authority. This concept is already included in Chinese current provincial regulations, and should be retained and improved during the reform of Chinese law on PFIPs.
- The Land Law of China should remove its undesirable restrictions. The legislation should resolve the problem of land requirements in the project. Since land in China is only owned by the state rather than by private owners, the project agreement should ensure that the contracting authority offers the land and the easement of the land required for the project.

[15] The Legislative Guide, Chap. IV on Construction and Operation of infrastructure: Legislative framework and Project agreement, Chap. V on Duration, Extension and Termination of the Project Agreement; and the Model Provisions accompanied therein, Chap. III on Contents and Implementation of the Concession contract, Chap. IV on Duration, Extension and Termination of the Concession Contract.

- The Guarantee Law of China should remove its undesirable restrictions. The Guarantee Law of China strictly prohibits state organs from providing any guarantee to commercial entities. However, it should be kept consistent with the project agreement. Additionally, the project agreement should clarify what physical property or intangible assets may be used by the project company to provide security, and what conflict this may have with the Chinese Guarantee Law.
- In Chinese law, a performance guarantee is also required to confirm the project agreement, but the guaranteed level of performance is not regulated.
- The Consumer Law of China should offer more appropriate rules. Although the Consumer Law requires the project company to provide equal service to all customers, some difference in the treatment of certain customers and the price formulated by the competent price authority also needs to be clarified in the laws on PFIPs.
- There is no Chinese law that restricts the exclusive power of the municipal government if it rejects a project extension. Also, there is no proper Chinese law that deals with the consequences of the decision by one of the parties to terminate the project in PFIPs.

Although concluding the finance agreement should aim to make raising finance convenient, its content could not be against the relevant law and some finance arrangements need the approval of the contracting authority.

Although the Consumer Law could be used to protect the users of PFIPs, the provider of public service should be restricted by a user agreement that grants more protection to customers in Chinese laws on PFIPs.

Aside from the approval of the contracting authority, subcontracting agreements should also be controlled by the conflict of interest provisions in Company Law.

8.7 The Answer for the Sixth Research Question

With reference to the guidelines of the Legislative Guide and Model Provisions[16] and with supplementary reference to other countries,[17] how should the laws relating to the settlement of disputes in PFIPs be reformed in China?

This question is analysed and discussed in Chap. 7, which concludes that the current Chinese laws on investment dispute settlement are not satisfactory to solve the disputes that may arise in PFIPs and therefore an improvement is necessary.

The principle of dispute settlement in PFIPs is to solve the dispute in an efficient and fair way. The solution proceedings should be quick and professional, ensure a fair and transparent decision, and allow the project to continue during the dispute settlement process.

[16] The Legislative Guide, Chap. VI on Settlement of Disputes; and the Model Provisions accompanied therein, Chap. V on Settlement of Disputes.

[17] The definition of public contract in Britain is broad.

For disputes between the contracting authority and the concessioner, the Legislative Guide and the Model Provisions recommend two types of dispute settlement: one uses conciliatory methods such as conciliation and mediation; the other uses antagonistic method, i.e. litigation and arbitration. The conciliatory settlements to dispute would be optional, according to the law of the host country. Considering one of the parties of a project agreement is the public authority and the subject of the agreement refers to infrastructure with close connection to the public interest, whether the project agreement is considered a public contract or a private contract may differ in different countries. In China, the nature of project agreement defined as "public" or "private" will affect the option of the dispute settlements. If the project agreement is identified as a public contract, the dispute on the project agreement would be an administrative dispute over which the host country has exclusive jurisdiction and only its administrative law applies. This means that arbitration cannot be used. If the project agreement is identified as a private contract, the dispute on project agreement would be a dispute of a general commercial contract. The dispute settlement will be confirmed by the agreement of the parties, but obey certain mandatory rules. In Chinese PFIPs practice, due to the vague nature of the project agreement, no arbitration has been applied to resolve disputes on the project agreement of PFIPs so far. Most of these disputes are solved by mediation or litigation. To sum up, if China intends to facilitate PFIPs and enhance the confidence of the foreign investors, Chinese law should clarify the nature of the project agreement and remove improper mandatory rules.

For disputes between the concessioner and other parties who are equal subjects in law, or among equal parties, the Legislative Guide and the Model Provisions recommends a solution by a settlement agreed between the parties. In Chinese PFIPs, the way to solve this type of dispute is consistent with the recommendations of the Legislative Guide and the Model Provisions.

For disputes between the concessioner and the users, the Legislative Guide and the Model Provisions recommend that simple and efficient mechanisms should be offered to individual persons while the general dispute settlement for normal commercial contracts should be offered to entities, excepting when the entity is the public authority or a state-owned enterprise when the contract may be considered to be an administrative contract. In Chinese PFIPs, all user agreements are considered to be normal purchase agreements no matter the nature of the entity.

Although it is expected that all the disputes could be solved with the same settlement in case of a conflict of decision, it is impossible in practice.

8.8 Conclusion

This book is the most detailed and systemic response to the reform of Chinese laws on PFIPs to date. It analyses and discusses how the Legislative Guide and the Model Provisions made by UNCITRAL may be adopted in the reform of Chinese laws on PFIPs, including responses to aspects of the general legislative and institutional framework, the selection of the concessioner, the various agreements in PFIPs and the settlement of disputes. In those moments where the Legislative Guide and the Model Provisions have not referred to some special issues that pertain to China, this book uses other countries or international organisations as a precedent to supplement its discussion of PFIP reform in China.

This book offers a strong theoretical basis for the development of PFIPs in China, and suggestions to aid the reform of Chinese laws on PFIPs. It also offers itself as a general reference for any other country expecting to reform its law on PFIPs.

Bibliography

Article

1. J. Avina, Public-Private Partnerships in the fight against crime: an emerging frontier in corporate social responsibility. J. Finan. Crime (2011)
2. R. Broomhill, Neoliberal globalismand the local state: a regulation approach. J. Aust. Polit. Econ (No 48)
3. C'M'S Cameron McKenna LLP, China revised the guideline catalogue of industries for foreign investment. Law-now China on 31/01/2012
4. W. Cai, Preliminary analysis of nature of servitude administrative. J Guangxi Adm. Cadre Inst. Polit. Law **19**(2) (2004)
5. F. Cao, Regulating procurement of privately financed infrastructure in China: a review of the recent legislative initiatives and the emerging regulatory framework (2007). Pub Procurement Law Rev **3**, 147–173 (2007)
6. F. Cao, The emerging legal framework for private finance in infrastructure in China: a preliminary review of the Beijing Concession Regulation. Pub Procurement Law Rev **62** (2006)
7. A.P.C. Chan, D.W.M. Chan, J.F.Y. Yeung, Y.L. Xu, S.Q. Wang, Y.J. Ke, Critical risk factors affecting the success of PPP projects in CHINA: a delphi study. J. Manage. Eng. ASCE **136**(5), 484–494 (2010)
8. S. Chen, The application of easements under public ownership. Sci. Law **03** (2012)
9. X. Deng, L. Shen, Research on attributes of PPP contract from an administrative law view. Constr. Econ. **01** (2007)
10. P. Green, Efficiency review by Sir Philip Green: key findings and recommendations. (11 October 2010)
11. R.P. Guo, J-J. Guo, PPP model for the supply of China's western rural infrastructure. J. Chang'an Univ. (Soc. Sci. Edn.) **11**(3) (2009)
12. R.P. Guo, J-J. Guo, The application and perfection of the PPP Mode in China's western rural infrastructure supply. Res West. Dev. 19–23 (2009)
13. Hauser Maria and Morel Jean-Baptiste, *'New Polish law on public-private partnership'*(I.B.L.J. 2006, 1, 3-19)
14. J. Holloway, Infrastructure projects in mainland China. Const. L.J. **20**(5), 278–279 (2004)
15. T. Huang, others, the comparison analysis on the government management of PPP. Project Manage Technol (2009.01)
16. S. Jarvin, The role of international commercial arbitration in the modern world. Arbitration **75**(1), 65–70 (2009)
17. Jiang li-li, *'Analysis the inevitability and appropriate radio of China holding US Treasury securities'* (Special Zone Economy,2010, No12)

S. Liang, *Legal Aspects of Privately Financed Infrastructure Projects (PFIPs) in China*,
https://doi.org/10.1007/978-981-15-6803-9

18. Y.J. Ke, S.Q. Wang, P.C.C. Albert, Public-private partnerships in China's infrastructure development: lessons learnt
19. Y.J. Ke, S.Q. Wang, A.P.C. Chan, Risk allocation in public-private partnership infrastructure projects: comparative study. J. Infrast. Syst. **16**(4), 343–351
20. Y.J. Ke, S.Q. Wang, etc., Changes of political risks in China's PPP Projects. (The 6th National Civil Engineering Forum for Graduate Students, Tsinghua University, 2008)
21. E. Laryea, (2011) Why Ghana should implement certain international legal instruments relating to international sale of goods transactions. A.J.I.C.L. **19**(1), 1–37 (2011)
22. H. Lesguillons, Selecting a project company. I.B.L.J. **6**, 603–622 (1998)
23. Y-R. Li. Research on the legal easement in the context of land administration. Chin. Land Sci. **26**(6) (2012)
24. H. Liang, Nationalization, it is dangerous! (2006)
25. J. Linarelli, The limited case for permitting SME procurement preferences in the agreement on government procurement, ed. by S. Arrowsmith, D. Anderson Robert D. *The WTO Regime on Government Procurement: Challenge and Reform* (Cambridge, 2011)
26. T.A. Lo, Debate surrounding the new property law in China. C.S.L.R. 4(2), 182–200 (2008)
27. Magazine Mlex, *'Bar tenders from abroad'* (Issue 10-Europe, July-September 2012)
28. B. Martor, Public-Private Partnerships. IBLJ (2008)
29. C. McLachlan, Investment treaties and general international law. I.C.L.Q. **57**(2), 361–401 (2008)
30. R.M. Nelson, others, Greece's debt crisis: overview, policy responses, and *implications*. Congressional Res. Ser. (14, May, 2010)
31. T. Peng, 'PPP' practice in China and Composition of PPP' legal framework. Zheng Fa Lun Cong **6** (2006)
32. J.M. Pertchik, The build, operate and transfer approach to infrastructure development in Mexico. P.P.L.R. **4**, 168–200 (1995)
33. X. Qi, Y. Ke, S. Wang, Analysis of critical risk factors causing the failures of China's PPP projects. Chin. Soft Sci (5)107–113 (2009)
34. X. Qin, The impact of political forces on urban land ownership reform in transitional China I.J.L.B.E. **2**(3), 206–217 (2010)
35. M.L. Riley, People's Republic of China: land rights - enforcement of regulations. I.C.C.L.R. **8**(3), C45–46 (1997)
36. O. Sandrock, Is international arbitration inept to solve disputes arising out of international loan agreement?. 11 J.INT'L ARB.33 (1994)
37. J. Shen, S.Q. Wang, M. Qiang (2005) The political risks in China's BOT/PPP project: a case study. Chin. Bus. Invest. Finan. 50–56(1) 2005
38. J. Shen, S.Q. Wang, M. Qiang, The political risks in China's BOT/PPP project: a case study. Chin. Bus. Invest. Finan. 50–56(1) (2005)
39. A. Sims, The public interest defense in copyright law: myth or reality? Eur. Intellect. Property Rev. E.I.P.R. **28**(6), 335–343 (2006)
40. A.J. Smith, Privatized Infrastructure: the role of government. Thomas Telford (1999)
41. S. Son, Legal analysis on public-private partnerships regarding model PPP rules. (June 2012, UNCITRAL Visiting Scholar (2011.7.26—2012.7.25.), Faculty of Law at the Dankook University in Republic of Korea)
42. B. Song, The research on the PPP legal framework in China. Adult Hig. Edu. J. (2010.02)
43. G-Y. Song, China's purchase of american treasury securities: source, prof it and impact. Fudan J. (Soc. Sci. Edn.) (4) (2008)
44. J-Y. Tao, The advantages and disadvantages of China holding of US treasury securities. Commercial Times (12) (2010)
45. J. Tao, Arbitration law and practice in China. (2nd ed, Kluwer Law International BV, 2008)
46. S. Tully, The 2000 Review of the OECD guidelines for multinational enterprise. 50 I.C.L.Q (2001)
47. A. Veditz Leslie, *The Channel Tunnel: A Case Study* (National Defense University, Washington, D.C., 1993)

48. P. Vellas, Price regulation in energy project finance: the need for comprehensive state intervention. I.E.L.T.R. **3**, 61–68 (2005)
49. C. Wadlow, The great pharmaceutical patent robbery, and the curious case of the chemical foundation. Intellect. Proper. Q. I.P.Q. **3**, 256–292 (2010)
50. Q.K. Wang, S.Q. Wang, Application of PPP pattern in low-rent housing. Constr. Econ. **10**(300) 27 (2007)
51. R.N. Wang, Practice and legal perfection of BOT investment in China. J. Jinling Inst. Technol. **19**(4) 42 (2005)
52. S.Q. Wang, Lessons learnt from the PPP practices in China (keynote speech). Asian Infrastructure Congress 2006, organized by Terrapinn and sponsored by IAPF, Hong Kong, 29–30th Nov, 2006
53. T.S. Wang, Comparative research on PFI project between Britain and Japan. IEC (1)49 (2008)
54. X. Wang Zhou, Y. Zhang, Feasibility analysis of PPP financing pattern on infrastructure construction in the west part of China. J. Northwest Sci-Tech Univ. Agric. For. (Soc. Sci. Edn)
55. Wilhelm K., *'Rethinking Property Rights in Urban China'* (2004, 9 UCLA J. Int'l Law & For. Aff)
56. A. Xia, J. Li, Innovation in infrastructure financing in western area: a PPP pattern. J. ChongQing Technol. Bus. Univ. (West Econ. Forum) 75–78 (2004)
57. C.G. Xu, State monopoly of land ownership brings social problems. Chin. Reform (2011.4)
58. S-D. Yang, Investment arbitration and china: investor or host state. Op. J., **2**(6), 1–19 (2011)
59. D-M. Yuan, J-J. Liu, The reasons why China hold so much US treasury securities. Contemp. Econ. Res (No 12), 28–32 (2012)
60. L. Zhu, Structure research of PFI contract based on <Standardization of PFI Contracts>. Optim. Capital Constr. **28**(6) (2007)

Book

61. S. Arrowsmith, R.D. Anderson, *The WTO Regime on Government Procurement: Challenge and Reform* (Cambridge, 2011)
62. H. Asif, Qureshi, R.Z. Andreas, *International Economic Law* (2nd edn Thomson: Sweet & Maxwell, 2007)
63. C. Bovis, *EC Public Procurement: Case Law and Regulation* (Oxford University Press, 2006)
64. C. Carmody, J. Garcia Frank, J. Linarelli, *Global Justice and International Economic Law: Opportunities and Prospects* (Cambridge, 2013)
65. C.M.V. Clarkson, others, *The Conflict of Laws*, 3rd ed (Oxford University Press, Oxford, 2006)
66. D.G. Cracknell, *Conflict of Laws*, 3rd ed (Old bailey press)
67. M. Dixon, R. McCorquodale, S. Williams, *Cases and Materials on International Law*, 5th edn (Oxford University Press, 2011)
68. R. Dolzer, C. Schreuer, *Principles of International Investment Law* (Oxford University Press, 2008)
69. K. Hartley, *Problems of using partnering and similar private sector practice in the public sector environment: the example of PPPs/PF. Public Procurement: The Continuing Revolution*, ed by A. Arrowswith, T. Martin (Kluwer law international, 2003)
70. J. Hill, A. Chong, *International Commercial Disputes: Commercial Conflict of Laws in English Courts*, 4th edn. (Hart Publishing, Oxford and Portland, Oregon, 2010)
71. S.L. Hoffman, *The Law and Business of International Project Finance* (Cambridge, 2008)
72. M. Matsushita, T.J. Schoenbaum, P.C. Mavroidis, *The World Trade Organization: Law, Practice, and Policy*, 2nd ed (Oxford University Press, 2006)

73. G. McCormack, *Secured Credit and the Harmonisation of Law, the UNCITRAL Experience* (Edward Elgar, USA, 2011)
74. J.G. Merrills, *International Dispute Settlement,* 5th ed (Cambridge University Press)
75. L. Mistelis, Is harmonisation a necessary evil? The future of harmonisation and new sources of international trade law, in *Foundations of International Trade Law*, ed. by I. Fletcher, L. Mistelis, M. Cremona (London, Sweet & Maxwell, 2001)
76. J. O'Sullivan, J. Hilliard, *The Law of Contract* (Oxford University Press, 2008)
77. OECD, *Dedicated Public-Private Partnership Units: A Survey of Institutional and Governance Structures* (2010)
78. OECD, Multilateral Centre for Private Sector Development Istanbul, *Basic Elements of a Law on Concession Agreement* (19/09/2002)
79. T. Prosser, *The Regulatory Enterprise: Government, Regulation, and Legitimacy* (Oxford Unversity Press, 2010)
80. P. Reeves, *An Introduction to Social Housing,* 2nd ed. (Elsevier Butterworth-Heinemann, 2005)
81. J.E. Salzman, *Decentralized Administrative Law in the Organization for Economic Cooperation and Development.* 68 Law & Contemporary Problems (2005)
82. H. Schreuer Christoph, *The ICSID Convention: A Commentary* (Cambridge University Press, 2005)
83. I. Shihata, *Towards a Greater Depoliticization of Investment Disputes: The Roles of ICSID and MIGA.* (The Wold Bank in a Changing World, 1991)
84. A.J. Smith, *Privatized Infrastructure: The Role of Government* (Thomas Telford, 1999)
85. M. Sornarajah, *The International Law on Foreign Investment*, 3rd ed. (Cambridge University Press, 2010)
86. P. Subedi Surya, *International Investment Law*, 2nd edn. (Oxford and Portland, Oregon, 2012)
87. P. Trepte, *Public Procurement in the EU: A Practitioner's Guide,* 2nd ed. (Oxford University Press, 2007)
88. P. Trepte, *Regulating Procurement* (Oxford University Press, 2004)
89. P. Vincent-Jones, *The New Public Contracting: Regulation, Responsiveness, Relationality* (Oxford University Press, 2006)
90. G.D. Vinter, *Project Finance*, 3rd edn. (Sweet & Maxwell, London, 2006)
91. E.R. Yescombe, *Public-Private Partnerships: Principles of Policy and Finance* (Elsevier, 2007)

Legislation and Legal Documents: China

92. Administrative Measures for the Information Disclosure of Commercial Franchise 2007
93. Administrative Measures on the Concession of Municipal Public Utilities 2004
94. Central and western regions of infrastructure project loan interest subsidy management 2010
95. China news, photo from <http://www.chinanews.com/tp/hd2011/2012/11-22/150035.shtml> accessed on 20th January 2020
96. Circular Concerning the Issues of Absorbing Foreign Investment through BOT was issued in 1995
97. Circular Concerning the Issues of the Approval and Administration of Experimental Foreign-invested Concession Projects was issued in 1995
98. Decision of the State Council on Reforming the Investment System 2004
99. General Principles of the civil law of the People's Republic of China 1987
100. Interim Regulations of the People's Republic of China Concerning the Assignment and Transfer of the Right to the Use of the State-owned Land in the Urban Areas 1990
101. Measures for the Administration on the Franchise of Municipal Public Utilities 2004

102. Notice of the General Office of the State Council on the Relevant Issues concerning the Appropriate Handling of the Existing Projects Guaranteeing the Fixed Return from Investments by Foreign Parties 2002
103. Notice of the Supreme People's Court on Implementing the Convention on the Recognition and Enforcement of Foreign Arbitral Awards Acceded to by China (No. 5 [1987] of the Supreme People's Court, April 10, 1987)
104. Opinions of the Ministry of Construction on Accelerating the Marketization of Urban Utilities 2002
105. Regulation on the Administration of Commercial Franchises 2007
106. Regulation on the Dismantlement of Urban Houses 2001
107. Regulation on the Expropriation of Buildings on State-owned Land and Compensation 2011
108. Regulations on the Foreign Exchange System of The People's Republic of China 2008
109. Research Reports of PPP Legislation in Infrastructure Development 2008
110. Several Opinions of the State Council on Encouraging, Supporting and Guiding the Development of Individual and Private Economy and Other Non-Public Sector of the Economy 2005
111. Several Opinions of the State Council on Further Doing a Good Job in the Utilization of Foreign Investment 2010
112. Several Opinions of the State Development Planning Commission concerning the Promotion and Guidance of Private Investment 2001
113. Temporary Provisions of the Ministry of Construction on Utilizing Foreign Capital in Municipality Public Utilities was issued in 2000
114. The Administrative Procedure Law of the People's Republic of China 1990
115. The Administrative Reconsideration Law of the People's Republic of China 2009
116. The Anti-Unfair Competition Law of the People's Republic of China 1993
117. The Arbitration Law of the People's Republic of China 1994
118. The Beijing Urban Infrastructure Concession Regulation 2005
119. The Bidding Law of the People's Republic of China 1999
120. The Civil Procedure Law of the People's Republic of China 2012
121. The Company Law of the People's Republic of China 2006
122. The Constitution of the People's Republic of China 2004
123. The Consumer protection Law of the People's Republic of China 1993
124. The Contract Law of the People's Republic of China 1999
125. The Criminal Law of the People's Republic of China 1997
126. The Government Procurement Law of the People's Republic of China 2002
127. The Guarantee Law of the People's Republic of China 1995
128. The Highway Law of the People's Republic of China 2004
129. The Land Administration Law of the People's Republic of China (2004 Amendment)
130. The website of China Western Development, <http://www.chinawest.org.cn/news/show-4328.html> accessed on 9th March 2020
131. The notice of encourage and guide the healthy development of private investment management issues relating to foreign exchange 2012
132. The notice of encourage private capital to participate in the construction of low-rent housing projects 2012
133. The notice of the Ministry of Finance, the Ministry of Housing and Urban-Rural Development, the Ministry of Agriculture, and the Ministry of Environmental Protection on Comprehensive Implementation of Public-Private Partnership in Sewage and Waste Treatment Projects Participated in by the Government 2017
134. The notice on the technology policy and technical guidelines on the environmental infrastructure in small town of Chinese western 2008
135. The Oil and Natural Gas Pipeline Protection Law of the People's Republic of China 2010
136. The opinion on encourage and guide private capital investment in railway 2012
137. The opinions on encourage and guide the healthy development of private investment 2010

138. The People's Republic of China on Economic Contract Involving Foreign Interest 1985, expired in 1999
139. The Property Law of the People's Republic of China 2007
140. The Regulation of the People's Republic of China on Foreign Exchange Administration (2008 Revision)
141. The Regulations of the People's Republic of China Concerning Diplomatic Privileges and Immunities 1986
142. The Shenzhen Urban Public Utilities Concession Regulation 2004
143. The Urban Infrastructure Concession Regulation (Beijing) 2005
144. The Xinjiang Public Utilities Concession Regulation of China 2005

UK

145. Contract and Third Party Act 1999
146. Counsil Regulation (EC) No 44/2001 on jurisdiction and the recognition and enforcement of judgments in civil and commercial matters
147. EC Directive 96/92 concerning common rules for the internal market in electricity [1997] O.J. L27/20
148. Planning Act 2008 (c. 29) Introductory Text
149. Public Contracts Regulations 2006/5 2
150. The Diplomatic Privileges Act 1964
151. The State Immunity Act 1978

UN

152. UNCITRAL, *Legislative Guide on Privately Financed Infrastructure Project* (2001) (A/CN.9/SER.B/4)
153. UNCITRAL, *Model Legislative Provisions on Privately Financed Infrastructure Projects* (2004) (A/58/17)
154. UNCITRAL, *Model Law on Public Procurement* (2011)
155. UNCITRAL, *The UNCITRAL Guide: Basic Facts about the United Nations Commission on International Trade Law* (United Nations Vienna, 2007)
156. UNDSD, *Agenda 21* (1992) 2.37 (d) A/CONF.151/26/REV.1 (VOL.I)
157. UNIDO, *Guidelines for Infrastructure Development through Build-Operate-Transfer (BOT) Projects* (1996)

Others

158. New York Arbitration Convention
159. Washington Convention
160. WTO Government Procurement Agreement (GPA)

News

161. *Economy Improving in China's West Region.* China daily Newspaper (22nd July, 2013)
162. *ESCAP is Looking for the Solution to the Asia-Pacific Region Lack the Infrastructure.* UN news (19th March, 2007)
163. *'Question and Answer Equivalent project relief'* published in Construction Newsletter (2006)
164. *Western Development Strategy.* China daily Newspaper (22nd December, 2009)
165. BBC news on 23 November 2012, *Road Built Around House as Chinese Couple Refuse to Move*
166. Huang, Qianwei, *China February Increases Holding of US Treasury Securities*, Newspaper *Nanfang Daily* (Guangdong, 18th, April 2013) A17
167. Southern Weekly Newspaper, *BOT Failure: HuangQiao Case.* South weekly (GuangDong Province, China, 29th January, 2003)
168 Tian Jun-rong, *Whose Foreign Exchange Reserves?* (Newspaper People's Daily, 17th October, 2011) 017
169. Zheng Yong Nian, *Land Ownership Reform.* News of the communist party of China Website

Report: China

170. National Bureau of Statistics of China, *Basic Industries and Infrastructure Building Have Brilliant Achievements.* published on 15th September, 2009
171. The People's bank of China, *China's Western Development Finance Reform Survey* (19th December, 2005)
172. The Supreme People's Procuratorate of the People's Republic of China, *Report on 20 Typical Corruption Cases on Infrastructure Projects* (18th May, 2011)

UK

173. HM Treasure, *Standardisation of PF2 Contracts* (December 2012)
174. HM Treasury and Infrastructure UK, *Strategy for National Infrastructure* (March, 2010)
175. HM Treasury, *National Infrastructure Plan 2010* (25 October 2010)
176. HM Treasury, *Standardization of PFI Contracts (SoPC) Version 4 (March 2007)*
177. House of Common Treasury Committee, *Private Finance Initiative: Government, OBR and NAO Responses to the Seventeenth Report from the Committee.* 25th Report of session 2012-12 (House of Commons, 19th December 2011)
178. House of Common Treasury Committee, *Private Finance Initiative.* 17th Report of session 2010–12 (House of Commons, 18th July 2011)
179. Infrastructure UK, *PF2: A User Guide* (December 2012)
180. Office for National Statistics, *Government Deficit and Debt Under the Maastricht Treaty,* Calendar Year 2012

UN

181. Official Records of the General Assembly, 21st Session, Resolution 2205 (XXI), A/RES/2205(XXI), 17 December 1966
182. UNCITRAL, *Concept Note Prepared for French Business Association (MEDEF) And World Bank Group Meeting March 2013*
183. UNCITRAL, 26th Session, A/CN.9/378-*Possible future work: proposals for possible future work made at the UNCITRAL Congress: note / by the Secretariat*
184. UNCITRAL, 27th Session, A/CN.9/399-*Build-operate-transfer projects*
185. UNCITRAL, 28th Session, A/CN.9/414-*Possible future work: Build-Operate-Transfer projects*
186. UNCITRAL, 29th session, A/51/17-*Report of the United Nations Commission on International Trade Law on its twenty-ninth session*
187. UNCITRAL, 29th session, A/CN.9/424-*Possible Future Work: Build-Operate-Transfer projects*
188. UNCITRAL, 30th session, A/52/17-*Report of the United Nations Commission on International Trade Law on its thirty session*
189. UNCITRAL, 30th Session, A/CN.9/438-*Privately-Financed Infrastructure Projects: Draft Chapters of a legislative guide on privately-financed infrastructure projects*
190. UNCITRAL, 31st session, A/53/17- *Report of UNCITRAL on the work of its thirty-first session*
191. UNCITRAL, 31st session, A/CN.9/444/Add.2-*Privately Financed Infrastructure Projects - Draft chapters of a legislative guide on privately financed infrastructure projects - Chapter I. General Legislative Considerations*
192. UNCITRAL, 31st Session, A/CN.9/444-*Privately Financed Infrastructure Projects - Draft chapters of a legislative guide on privately financed infrastructure projects*
193. UNCITRAL, 32nd Session, A/54/17-*Report of UNCITRAL on the work of its thirty-second session*
194. UNCITRAL, 32nd session, A/CN.9/458/add.2—*Privately Financed Infrastructure Projects: Draft Chapters of a legislative guide on privately financed infrastructure projects - Chapter I. General Legislative Considerations*
195. UNCITRAL, 33rd session, A/55/17-*Report of UNCITRAL on the work of its thirty-third session*
196. UNCITRAL, 33rd session, A/CN.9/471-*Privately financed infrastructure projects: draft chapters of a legislative guide on privately financed infrastructure projects*
197. UNCITRAL, 34th Session, A/56/17-*Report of the United Nations Commission on International Trade Law on its thirty-forth session*
198 UNCITRAL, 34th session, A/CN.9/488-*Possible work on privately financed infrastructure projects*
199. UNCITRAL, 34th session, A/CN.9/488-*Possible work on privately financed infrastructure projects*
200. UNCITRAL, 35st session, A/57/17-*Report of UNCITRAL on the work of its thirty-fifth session*
201. UNCITRAL, 35th session, A/CN.9/505-*Report of the Working Group on Privately Financed Infrastructure Projects at its fourth session*
202. UNCITRAL, 36th Session, A/58/17-*Report of the United Nations Commission on International Trade Law on its thirty-sixth session*
203. UNCITRAL, 36th session, A/CN.9/521-*Report of the Working Group on Privately Financed Infrastructure Projects on the work of its fifth session*
204. UNCITRAL, 46th session, A/CN.9/779-*Possible future work in the area of public-private partnerships (PPPs): Report of the UNCITRAL colloquium on PPPs* (Vienna, 2–3 May 2013)
205. UNCITRAL, 46th session, A/CN.9/782-*International Colloquium on Public-Private Partnerships (PPPs): Discussion paper*
206. UNCITRAL, UNCITRAL Executive Report: International Colloquium- *Privately Financed Infrastructure: Legal Framework and Technical Assistance*
207. UNCTAD, *Total number of Bilateral Investment Treaties Concluded, 1 June 2011*
208. UNCTAD, *World Investment Report 2011: non-equity modes of international production and development*

Others

209. Asian Development Bank, *Some Important Issues and Recommendations on Marketization (PPP) of China Urban Water Industry*, under Policy Reform Support project-4095
210. European Bank for Reconstruction and Development, *Funding public Infrastructure: Challenges and Horizons* (Law in transition online, October 2012)
211. European Bank for Reconstruction and Development, *Public Private Partnerships*
212. French MEP Marielle de Sarnez report to Committee on International Trade of European Parliament, *EU and China: Unbalanced Trade?* (2010/2301(INI))
213. Ibid. The data are shown in a bar chart in the website of World Bank and I reform them into a pie chart which is clearer
214. International Bank for Reconstruction and Development, *Procurement Under IBRD and IDA Loans* (Washington, D.C., 1996) para. 3.13 (a)
215. World Bank (2009), *Country Snapshots: China. Private Participation in Infrastructure Database* <http://ppi.worldbank.org/en/snapshots/country/china> accessed on 6th March 2020. The data are shown in a table in the website of World Bank and I reform them into a bar chart which is clearer
216. World Bank, *Doing Business 2011: Making a Difference for Entrepreneurs* (November 4, 2010)
217. World Trade Organization Website, *Agreement on Trade Related Aspects of Investment Measures*

The manufacturer's authorised representative in the EU is Springer Nature Customer Service Centre GmbH, Europaplatz 3, 69115 Heidelberg, Germany. If you have any concerns regarding our products, please contact ProductSafety@springernature.com

Printed and bound by CPI Group (UK) Ltd, Croydon, CR0 4YY
30/09/2026
02225559-0006